Tara Ebert

Trust as the Key to Loyalty in Business-to-Consumer Exchanges

GABLER EDITION WISSENSCHAFT

Tara Ebert

Trust as the Key to Loyalty in Business-to-Consumer Exchanges

Trust Building Measures in the Banking Industry

With a foreword by Prof. Dr. Dres. h. c. Arnold Picot

GABLER EDITION WISSENSCHAFT

Bibliographic information published by the Deutsche Nationalbibliothek
The Deutsche Nationalbibliothek lists this publication in the Deutsche Nationalbibliografie; detailed bibliographic data are available in the Internet at http://dnb.d-nb.de.

Dissertation Ludwig-Maximilians-Universität München, 2009

D 19

1st Edition 2009

Editorial Office: Claudia Jeske / Anita Wilke

Gabler is part of the specialist publishing group Springer Science+Business Media.
www.gabler.de

Cover design: Regine Zimmer, Dipl.-Designerin, Frankfurt/Main
Printed on acid-free paper
Printed in Germany

ISBN 978-3-8349-1622-8

Foreword

Trust, as a key factor in business relationship, cannot be bought or ordered. Also, trust cannot be replaced through control mechanisms. Rather, it is a fragile psychological construct which develops through mainly intransparent reasons. Trust research is, therefore, vital for an analysis of business to consumer relations.

The present work is connected with the comprehensive and long continuing scientific examination of trust in and between organizations as well as between organizations and customers. The banking industry serves a field of research in which trust plays a key role. The question is to find out how banks can strengthen customers' trust. The work especially focuses on the question whether customers trust their bank due to performance and service quality or reputation (reputation being defined as the result of experienced and approved performance quality). On the other hand, the work also deals with the possibility that trust depends on entirely different reasons like the trust propensity of each individual. Thus, organizations can only partially influence their customers' trust by their own measures. Based on these aspects, the author formulates the central research question of her work: Which trust building measures should the appropriate policy of a bank consist of? This is a very challenging question as it includes existing long-range trends and traditions as well as experience, publicly communicated values as well as concrete transaction and service experiences of customers including their personal historical backgrounds. The author seeks a comprehensive empirical approach and successfully applies this method to her research question.

This work contributes new data to trust research. The author successfully integrates theoretical knowledge into a comprehensive empirical analysis. Trust is defined by three dimensions: an emotional, a rational, and an activity component. Her systematic analysis of a large number of high-ranking published trust articles leads to a complex trust model with 18 constructs and is complemented with additional empirical investigation.

Beside the possibilities of what banks can do to strengthen the three trust dimensions, the moderating role of the personality of the bank's customers is empirically analyzed. Reputation and perceived security of the bank are pinpointed as the two key factors in trust building. The satisfaction of the bank customers plays a major role in deciding whether a bank and its staff are perceived as trustworthy or not. Only such banks will have a competitive advantage which take care of their customers. This publication contributes to trust research and spurs the discussion of practical measures for the retail banking industry to rebuild customers' trust.

Prof. Dr. Dres. h.c. Arnold Picot

Preface

The search for factors which contribute to a company's success increasingly takes place in intangible areas. Consumer trust is one of the unobservable and intangible assets that are of special interest to business. Theory and practical experience have identified trust as a critical factor for outcomes such as loyalty and cooperation in business-to-consumer relationships. Trust seems to be needed in every interaction to minimize costs through control or in cases of perceived risk. Often, trust is perceived as a kind of essence or "je ne sais quoi." The comparative advantages found in a business can be considered as this special essence – highly valued but also very elusive. Each whit of suspicion of misuse leads to the breach of trust. The consequences of trust abuse can sometimes be reparable, but are mostly irreparable.

Banks manage one of our most important goods – money. We need to trust our banks. The German banking industry is one in which there are strong control and hedging mechanisms which have been developed even further over the last years. Does this mean that there is no residual risk? No one, especially no individual bank customer, knows exactly which investment strategies their banks pursue. Consumer trust in our banking industry was obviously shaken by the subprime and stock exchange crash in 2007/2008. Which levers do banks have to engender customer trust?

The measurement of these unobservable variables, here called constructs, aids the deduction of useful implications for marketers. Empirical marketing research sheds new light on relationships that consumers form unconsciously. They are difficult to inquire about and to identify while observing consumers. Structural equation modeling is, however, the preferred method to analyze the relationships between constructs. This approach enables the consideration of formative and reflective specified constructs. The former is gradually being adapted, while the latter has already been accepted in research. This formative measurement approach helps to identify relevant levers that cannot be empirically measured through a reflective specification of the construct. Marketers can use these levers to optimize their marketing strategies.

During the last few years, I have been fascinated by the question whether trust as a psychological manner can be given a manifest character through mathematics. This publication provides an answer to this ostensibly simple question through empirical surveys and a meta-analysis. Theoretically and empirically, it tries to answer the research question: What are trust building measures? To some extent, the work closes a research gap concerning this question. The first results of the meta-analysis were published as a preliminary work (Ebert 2007). The enhancement of this meta-analysis and its refinement through feedback from the conference "Relationship Marketing Summit" in Buenos Aires in December 2007 was accepted for publication in the Special Issue of the Journal of Business Market Management at the end of 2008. Aspects of the results of this interdisciplinarily positioned meta-analysis were deduced and adapted to the business-to-consumer trust relationship in the banking industry. The conceptualizations of consumer trust were thereafter deduced from recent consumer theories which enabled a critical and best possible way of analyzing trust building levers for marketers in the banking industry. The concretion of the conceptualizations and, thus, the measurement of trust and other required constructs were developed from recent and ongoing research discussions on the "right" measurement of constructs. It will deduce hypotheses regarding the positive impacts of reputation and security on consumer trust and, thus, loyalty. Trust building levers will be deduced in a second step through reputation and security. Furthermore, the approach employed in the current work recognizes the moderating impact of personal characteristics on consumer trust. The work will not only use structural equation modeling to identify trust building measures, but also to gain knowledge of the possible strength and direction of their impact on consumer trust.

This work was undertaken during my time as a research and teaching assistant at the Institute of Market-Based Management (IMM) at the Ludwig-Maximilians-University of Munich. Financial support was provided by the LMU Mentoring Program and the Interdisciplinary Laboratory that emanated from the LMU excellence program which is led by the Faculty of Economics.

In the first place, I want to thank my doctoral supervisor Prof. Dr. Manfred Schwaiger. He advised me to work on the very interesting, but also complex theme of trust, as it is relevant to marketing. He made it possible for me to discuss the challenges associated with this work with him at any time. Many thanks are also extended to Prof. Dr. Dres. h.c. Arnold Picot for assuming the role of the second appraisor, the interest he exhibited in my work, as well as for his feedback. Furthermore, I want to thank my colleagues at IMM for the good teamwork and their constructive feedback. Special thanks are also extended to Mrs. Gabriela Latinjak for her support through the long period that led to this publication. I am also thankful to all the back staff at IMM, especially Dariya Yerusalymtseva.

Many thanks to Johannes Patzelt, Sonja Ferber, Simone Schüer, Nadine Hadder, Nico Grove, and my MBR group. I thank my parents, Jorinde and Rolf Ebert, and my brother Anselm for their understanding and support. This work is dedicated to my parents.

Dr. Tara A. E. Patzelt (née Ebert)

Table of Contents

List of Figures

List of Tables

List of Abbreviations

AMOS	Analysis of moment structures
ACSI	American customer satisfaction index
AGB	Allgemeine Geschäftsbedingungen
AVE	Average variance extracted
BaFin	Bundesanstalt für Finanzdienstleistungsaufsicht
BNT	Bank of no trust
BT	Bank of trust
B2B	Business-to-business
B2C	Business-to-consumer
CATI	Computer-Assisted Telephone Interviewing
CI	Citation index
C-OAR	Construct definition by object, attribute and rater entity
cp.	Compare
DiBa	Direktbank
DZ BANK	Deutsche Zentral-Genossenschaftsbank
EAEG	Einlagensicherungs- und Anlegerentschädigungsgesetz
e.g.	Exempli gratia (for example)
et al.	Et alia (and further)
etc.	Et cetera (and so on)
F & A	Finance & Accounting
GFI	Goodness of Fit Index
GwG	Geldwäschegesetz
HRM	Human Resource Management
i.e.	Id est (that is)
IR	Industrial Relations
KfW	Kreditanstalt für Wiederaufbau
KWG	Kreditwesengesetz
KM	Knowledge Management
LBS	Landesbausparkasse
LISREL	Linear Structural Relationships
MIS	Management Information System
MS	Management Science
n/a	Not applicable
O2O	Inter-organizational relationships
OR	Operation Research
OS/OB	Organizational Behavior/Studies
PDA	Personal Digital Assistant

POM	Production & Operations Management
P2P	Inter-personal interactions
P2O	Interactions between persons and organizations
PSD Bank	Post-Spar- und Darlehensverein
PSM	Public Sector Management
RechKredV	Kreditinstituts-Rechnungslegungsverordnung
SCHUFA	Schutzgemeinschaft für allgemeine Kreditsicherung
SEM	Structural equation models
smartPLS	Smart Partial Least Squares
VAF	Variance accounted for
VHB	Verband der Hochschullehrer für Betriebswirtschaft
VIF	Variance inflation factors
WGZ-Bank	Westdeutsche Genossenschafts-Zentralbank

List of Symbols

η	Latent dependent variables
Δ	Residual
r_{ij}	Correlation coefficients
β_j	Latent independent variables
ε_i	Error term for dependent indicator variables
λ, γ	Path coefficients
δ_i	Error term for independent indicator variables χ_i
x_i , y_i	Indicators
R^2	Coefficient of determination
f^2	Effect size of the exogenous construct on the endogenous construct
Λ_x	Weighting vector of indicators
X	Vector of indicators
ζ_k	Error term for latent dependent variables
Q^2	Stone-Geisser test

1 Introduction

The growing importance of increasing business performance through intangible assets has been recognized in theory and practical experience. **Trust** as one of them is a natural and essential component of relationships (SHEPPARD/SHERMAN 1998, p. 422). Trust facilitates both consumer loyalty and customer retention, but also compensates for information asymmetries, reduces transaction costs, and lowers perceived risk (PICOT ET AL. 2003; RIPPERGER 1998). Marginal changes in loyalty (e.g., 5%) disproportionately affect changes in profitability (25% - 100%; see REICHHELD ET AL. 2000). Consequently, trust has an immense impact on organizational performance.

The **banking industry** is one of the representative branches with an intransparent portfolio of products and services (GABRIEL/SCHALLER 2008). How do consumers know which banks best fit their personality, interests, and needs? The multifarious differentiation found in banking organizations and the consequent complexity of a choice of the right company, requires consumers to have "trust in the organization." In a representative survey undertaken for this work in 2007[1], 39.7% of Germans stated in December 2007 that "Sparkasse" is the bank that they trust most, while 24.4% state that they trust "Volksbank und Raiffeisenbank" most. Consequently, 64.1% of Germans – the majority – trusts banks that are regulated by public law. In the last months, the banking industry has been especially badly affected by the subprime and stock exchange crash. The damage of trust in the banking industry has led to a strong drop off of stock exchange values, thus, the stock exchange crisis is also called the "crisis of trust" (HÖFLING/ZSCHÄPITZ 2008). Another recent survey, undertaken before and after the crash, has revealed that there has been a significant impact on consumer trust in banks (RAITHEL/EBERT 2008). Consumer trust in banks has plummeted.

This leads to the important research questions: **How should banks engender trust in consumers?** Do customers trust an organization because of its services or because of its reputation? Or is trust rather the consequence of something completely different? How much of customers trust is caused by other factors, for example, the trust propensity of a consumer, besides the measures taken by banking organizations? What if organizations can only influence a part of consumer trust? Most studies have focused mainly on business relevant consequences of trust (GARBARINO/JOHNSON 1999; TAX ET AL. 1998). Therefore, although sufficient evidence exists to suggest that trust matters for business success, fundamental gaps remain in the understanding of trust building measures or mechanisms that might explain the process of trust enhancement.

---

[1] Results were obtained from the main study (see section 4.2) completed in November and December 2007.

The **goal** of this work is to shed new light on a very topical but also psychological question: What should trust building measures in the banking industry comprise? Trust is one of the most discussed and analyzed phenomena in literature. A critical conceptualization of consumer trust is deduced from the specific view that **consumer theory** takes. When compared to recent conceptualizations, the resultant new and more analytical insights can be employed to deduce better targeted marketing implications for consumer trust building by banks. Its intangible character results in a complex model established by means of an extensive trust research analysis, which will be empirically analyzed. The noteworthiness of this publication is that it is a **comprehensive empirical approach** towards deducing implications for banks regarding what trust building measures should comprise that are based on hard facts. The hypotheses were postulated in the light of consumer theories, a theoretical meta-analysis, expert interviews, and verified through two empirical surveys.

In **Chapter 2**, the research frame is clarified through the differentiation, definition, and conceptualization of the term trust. Consumer trust is distinguished into general and specific trust, the latter being the focus of this work. In the light of recent consumer theories, specific trust is conceptualized as an attitude. This leads to the possibility that all the effects of trust building measures and influencing variables that lead to a change in attitude (trust) can be analyzed. The distinctiveness of loyalty as a consequence of consumer trust is discussed briefly.

Chapter 3 reviews and discusses recent trust models for trust building measures. A meta-analysis bridges the existing research gap by identifying all the relevant trust antecedents and consequences that have not all been empirically researched, aggregated, and empirically proven in a single model. Clustering means the logical aggregation of variables to one topic (e.g. reputation). These antecedents and consequences are clustered in order to highlight the relevant constructs for the trust model. The analyzed and defined clusters have two advantages. They can be used to minimize the measurement approach of a construct by using the high-level variables which are on top of the hierarchic level and thus, represent the other low-level variables. The clusters can also be used to develop new construct conceptualizations by trying to consider all key variables belonging to the cluster. The clusters are later matched with trust interaction types. This leads to a first raw consumer trust framework, which includes and emphasizes relevant clusters for different trust interactions, like that of business-to-consumer. The relevant clusters for business-to-consumer trust interaction essential for the banking industry are aggregated in one single model. With this approach the development of a new conceptualization of security is done. A further differentiation of the chosen clusters leads to the identification of moderating variables (e.g. satisfaction). Furthermore, Chapter 3 discusses the measurements of each construct, as well as recent measurement discussions regarding formative, reflective, and single-item measurement and, misspecifications by previous researchers are corrected. The chapter describes how the chosen formative specifications of some constructs lead to the analysis of trust building measures and how single-item measurement helps to reduce and avoid content overlapping inside - or even between constructs - to gain better model results. For the enhancement of the goodness of model criteria and optimization of the questionnaire qualitative and quantitative surveys are done. In turn, the consideration of all these aspects lead to an extensive theoretical model that enhances previous trust building models.

Chapter 4 provides a description of interviews held with experts, thus verifying and enhancing the trust model, as well as refining the measurement of the constructs. The online pre-study, which produced 74 complete questionnaires whose data were employed to test and improve the theoretical model, is also explained. The main study was a representative CATI survey from which 400 complete interviews were gained, thus forming the basis of the empirical testing of the deduced hypotheses. Through this procedure, the most efficient levers for building trust and thus boosting loyalty can be identified and concrete implications can be deduced for marketers in the banking industry. Chapter 4 illustrates the results of trust building measures for the banking industry representative for Germany. The bank of trust and bank of least trust are identified. The results of the evaluation of Germans about their house bank in 57 questions are shown. Trust building measures are analyzed empirically through the formative reputation measurement approach by SCHWAIGER (2004) and theoretically through the new security measurement approach. The influence of consumer characteristics which moderate organizational measures is identified.

Chapter 5 summarizes and discusses the results and implications of this work, describes limitations of the surveys, and provides a future outlook.

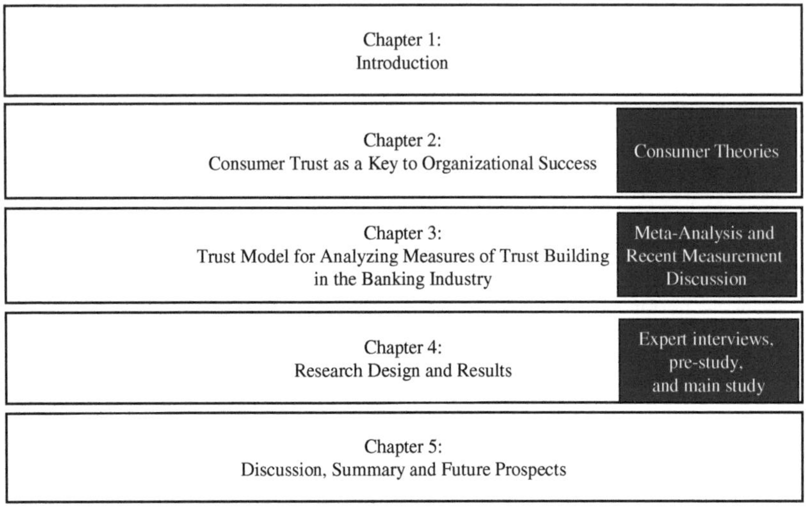

Figure 1: Structure of the publication

2 Consumer Trust as a Key to Organizational Success

In 1966, researchers began publishing articles on trust in highly rated journals. Until 1993, however, trust was rarely the focus of research. But, there has been a growing number of trust articles over the last few years, reaching a peak in 2003 (109 publications)[2].

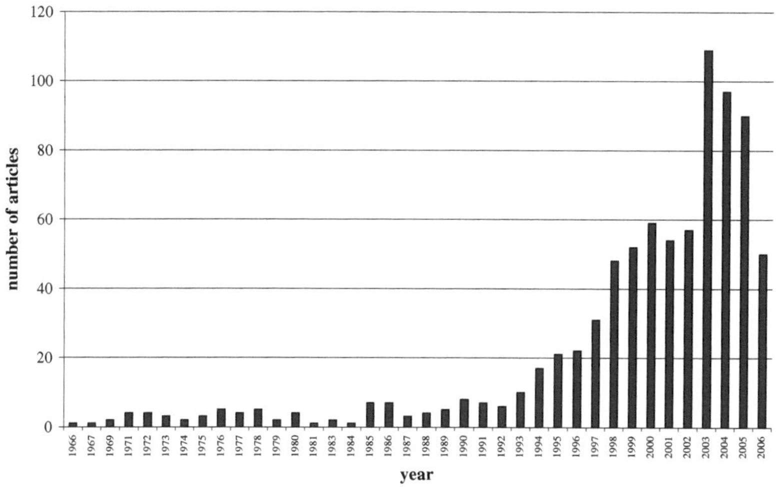

Figure 2: Development of the number of trust articles over time

This growth in publications probably developed due to the continuously increasing international stress emanating from competition over the last 15 years (RUGMAN/COLLINSON 2006, p. 33). Competition stress has led to a stronger focus on trust research, since trust as an intangible asset can be a strong comparative advantage in business (SEEMANN ET AL. 2000). Looking at the stock exchange market during the stock exchange crash in 2007 and 2008 the strong connection between trust and stock exchange value becomes clear. This effect on the stock exchange values can be described through the connection of trust with reputation. An organization with high reputation gains the trust of the people (see section 3.8). Reputation as an important intangible asset is highly correlated to the financial performance of a company (SABATE/PUENTE 2003). A damage of reputation leads to mistrust and to a lower exchange value. Furthermore, trust helps to gain sales from a regular clientele (CROSBY ET AL. 1990), to reduce control mechanisms and enhance conflict solving in cooperations (MORGAN/HUNT 1994). In addition, e-commerce has increased the likelihood of customers switching

---

2 This information is gained by the meta-analysis see section 3.3.

companies due to the easier access to price and service information (BECKETT ET AL. 2000). Trust coveys loyalty behavior which lowers consumers' willingness to seek variety. It is therefore undoubted that trust is an important intangible asset to research. However, another explanation for the growth in the number of articles might be the increased emphasis on publications generally. Summarized, trust research has developed into an important research field since 1993.

Consumer trust as an important intangible asset for organizations has an unobservable character. It is therefore described by means of many words and by different concepts in all kinds of research areas. The analysis of approximately 800 articles gained by a meta-analysis (see section 3.3) is an indication that the range of the research areas extends beyond the following fields.

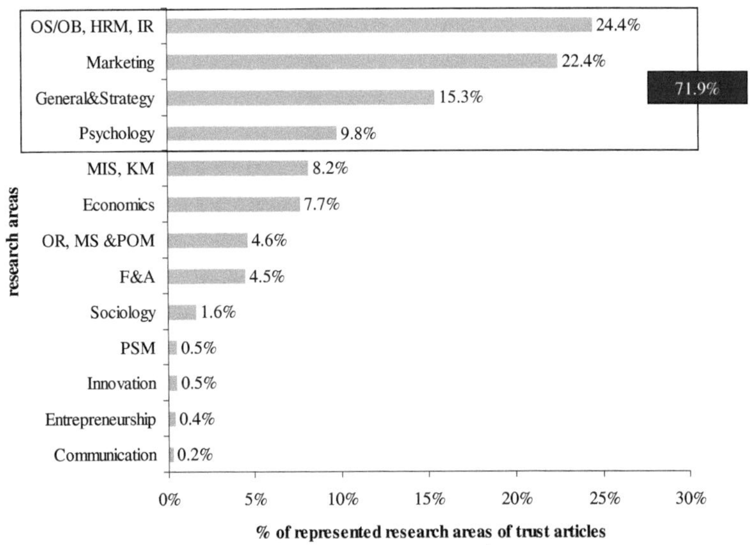

OS/OB, HRM, IR: Organization Behavior/Studies, Human Resource Management, Industrial Relations; MIS, KM: Management Information Systems, Knowledge Management Economics; OR, MS & POM: Operations Research, Management Science, Production & Operations Management; F&A: Finance & Accounting; PSM: Public Sector Management

Figure 3: Frequency of research areas of trust articles in % (EBERT *2009, p.73)*

72% of the examined trust articles were published in journals on human resource management, marketing, strategy, and psychology. There are several reasons for trust being predominantly researched in the fields. The augmented numbers of joint ventures and firm co-operations not only imply trust problems between organizational cultures and organization employees, but also the importance of trust mechanisms – as a complement to control – for contractual business-to-business relationships to achieve efficient work. Questions on relationship trust and programs on customer loyalty have specifically arisen in strategy and marketing departments. Psychology, as the fourth area of trust research, mirrors the psychological character of trust. Thus, these four fields can be described as the scientific trust community.

All these efforts endeavor to make trust a little more concrete, thus providing a possibility of measuring and identifying the mechanisms that might explain the process of trust building.

To have a clear research frame, it is necessary to differentiate trust as a term. Trust is very closely linked to the terms confidence and reliance. Distinguishing between the various words clarifies the differences and limits the relevant research literature, before the detailed definition of consumer trust follows. A conceptualization of trust is consequently developed from consumer theories. This step will lead to a special three-dimensional conceptualization of trust. To engender an attitude change (here, trust building) any or all of the three trust dimensions could be points of contacts used by trust building measures. This three-dimensional approach forms the core of the theoretical trust model and the deduced hypotheses. It will result in more in-depth implications for banks and the analysis of different impacts of trust and loyalty.

2.1. Trust, Confidence, and Reliance – Distinguishing between the Terms

When selecting relevant articles for a literature review on trust, it is necessary to consider the words used in research that ostensibly seem similar in content. This leads to the question: What is the difference between the terms "trust," "confidence," and "reliance"? Even though discussions do not generally distinguish between these words, some analysts have begun to recognize a distinction between these terms (see SMITH 2005, p. 307).

The terms "trust," "confidence," and "reliance" underlie global trade and have been explored by DESPORTES (2006). As a linguist, he states that "trust" is related to the words "tree," "truth," "true," "triggwa" (pact, alliance), "trêow" (faith, loyalty, truth), "tray," and "trog" (wooden vessel). The semantic relationship lies in the "wood" concept, which represents firmness and solidity. Trust therefore suggests the depth and certainty of feeling that is often based on inconclusive evidence, which, in turn, suggests morality. "Confidence", which implies less emotional intensity, frequently provides stronger cognitive grounds for certainty and the content of experience, thus performance. "Reliance" connotes a trustful and confident commitment to another (DESPORTES 2006).

Those authors who deal with the distinction between "trust" and "confidence" agree that they have differing meanings (LYONS/METHA 1997; FUKUYAMA 1995; TONKISS/PASSEY 1999). This linguistic differentiation has been empirically proven by EARLE/SIEGRIST (2006), who find that trust is based on judgments of value similarity, which is derived from morality-relevant information. Confidence is, however, based on heuristic judgments of past performance and derived from performance-relevant information. Value similarity is the judged similarity between the observer's currently active values and the values attributed to the Other (EARLE/SIEGRIST 2006, p. 388). In this context, SIEGRIST ET AL. (2005, p. 145) define general trust as a belief that other people can be relied on. Trust is based on social relations, group memberships, and shared values. Trust involves risk and vulnerability, and is especially important when there is a lack of familiarity. Conversely, general confidence is the conviction that everything is under control, familiarity is high, and uncertainty is low.

In addition to the content differences between "trust" and "confidence," there are also differences in trust objects. Per definition, objects of trust are persons or person-like entities, while objects of confidence can be anything (SIEGRIST ET AL. 2005, p. 147). Consequently, trust can be measured, for example, between managers and employees (trust objects are persons), while a consumer's confidence in an acquired product (which is not a person-like entity) can be determined.

The definition of the communication channel as a medium in trust research is given and a detailed overview of the different trust interactions - gained through the meta-analysis (see section 3.3).

Communication channels are not only defined as the conventional types of media, like TV, radio, journals, poster, advertisement in buses, stations or airports, and sponsoring, but also the Internet. In this article, the term "Internet" is broadened by the word "virtual reality"[3], according to COFFET/BURDEA (2003, p. 3), in order to include terms like e-commerce, e-vendor, or virtual communities. Thus, virtual reality is a sub-category of the communication channel.
The communication channel is in fact a medium through which an organization appears and interacts (cp. SAINI/JOHNSON 2005, p. 362). The direct interaction takes part between the person or organization and the communication channel. However, the person or organization also indirectly interacts with another person or organization. Thus, the communication channel makes interaction possible. When, e.g. a consumer has trust in an online provider, the consumer will interact with the website of the service provider, so the website is the virtual illustration of the interacting partner. Consequently, the communication channel or virtual reality (e-commerce) is defined as a medium which enables interactions between persons and

3 Virtual reality can be described as unifying realistic (or veridical) realities with artificial reality. It is a high-end user-computer interface that involves real-time simulations and interaction through multiple sensorial channels (Coffet/Burdea 2003, p. 3).

organizations. To summarize, there are three types of trust interactions (see below). A brief description of the three types of trust interactions follows.
In **inter-personal interactions (P2P)** only 2% of the 808 trust articles include the medium "communication channel". However, in 45% of all the articles, inter-personal relationships play a very important role in trust research. Inter-personal trust research can be structured in two interactive categories differentiating between:

1. Private interaction, which implies a relationship between persons outside an organization, for example, partners (the wife and husband), children, and neighbors; and
2. Business interaction, which implies a relationship between persons who belong to an organization, for example, (new) employees, the manager, and supervisor, etc.

27% of all the trust articles focus on **inter-organizational relationships (O2O)**. Approximately 1% of these consider the communication channel. The following analyzed interactions can be divided into relationships between:

1. Internal interactions (joint organizations), for example, partner firms (alliance partner), parent firms, affiliates, and network firms; and
2. External interactions (independent and separate organizations), for example, buyers, suppliers, and manufacturers, etc. The main interactions between organizations develop as a result of cooperations, supply chain businesses, or joint ventures.

The remaining 26% of the articles analyze **interactions between persons and organizations (P2O)**. Nearly 50% of these articles include the communication channel. The meta-analysis shows that interactions between persons and organization can be divided into the following two categories:

1. Internal interaction, in which the person is part of the organization. This kind of category is also called organizational trust (CALDWELL/CLAPHAM 2003), for example, the employee's trust in his or her organization, and
2. External interactions (the person is not part of the organization), for example, the consumer's trust in a service-provider.

The following figure presents the results.

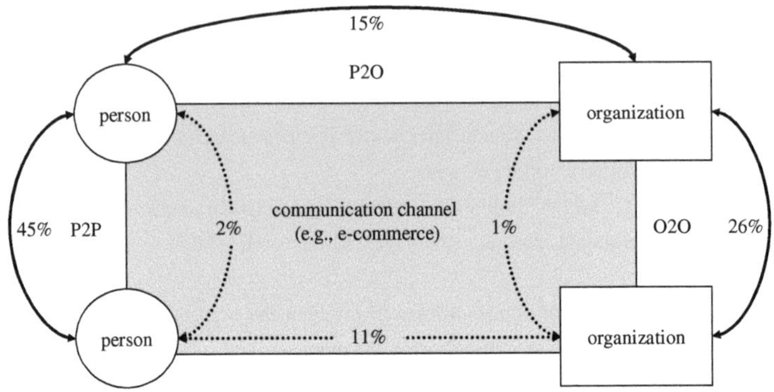

Figure 4: Categories and frequencies of listed trust interactions in % (**EBERT** ***2009, p.75)***

Summarized, trust suggests a stronger emotional feeling based on inconclusive evidence in relationships between persons or person-like entities (like organizations), which emphasizes its intangible character. Having distinguished between the terms in respect to their content and objects, this procedure guarantees a clear trust research frame needed for the meta-analysis in section 3.3. From another perspective, which will not be elaborated in this work, it might be interesting to include the terms "confidence" and "reliance" to obtain further indications for trust research. However, a definition of trust and differentiation between its various meanings is not precise enough for the analysis of trust building measures in business-to-consumer relationships. The following section thus focuses on and describes only consumer trust and its steering possibilities in detail.

2.2. Definition, Conceptualization, and Possibilities of Steering Consumer Trust

Consumer trust can be distinguished into general trust and consumer-specific trust (MAYER ET AL. 1995). The main focus of this work is on consumer-specific trust, which can be more easily influenced by organizations in contrast to general trust. In the light of consumer behavior theories, the conceptualization of consumer specific trust and its steering are explained by means of attitude change theories.

2.2.1. Consumer General Trust as an Antecedent of Consumer-Specific Trust

In general, trust predominantly develops in the first years of childhood and is an important facet of one's personality (KENNEDY ET AL. 2001, p. 74). According to BROWNE/HOWARTH (1977, p. 339), general trust is one of the personality's twenty factors. Trust is also defined as a general **personality trait** or a psychological state (MAYER ET AL. 1995). According to WEBSTER/MARTOCCHIO (1992), personality traits are relatively stable and invariant with regard to the intrinsic characteristics of situational stimuli. These characteristics are formed by extraneous developmental and social factors. Thus, personality-based trust is generally recognized and, consequently, **independent of a specific situation or an object**. In trust research, general trust is also termed "trust propensity" (HAMPTON-SOSA/KOUFARIS 2005; PAVLOU/GEFEN 2004; STEWART 2003), "disposition to trust" (ANDALEEP/ANWAR 1996; BALASUBRAMANIAN ET AL. 2003; EVERARD/GALLETTA 2005; GEFEN 2000; MCKNIGHT ET AL. 2002), as well as "general tendency to trust" (KENNEDY ET AL. 2001).

The common definition of general trust originates from ROTTER (1967, p. 651), who defines it as: "A generalized expectancy held by an individual that the word of another ... can be relied on". This form of trust is therefore based on a belief that others are usually reliable and well-meaning. Such a belief is nothing more than a trust credit offered to others before experience can provide a more rational interpretation (GEFEN ET AL. 2003, p. 62). It refers to the tendency to believe, or not believe, in others and to trust them (e.g., FARRIS ET AL. 1973; MAYER ET AL. 1995; MCKNIGHT ET AL. 1998).

As mentioned, trust propensity is a personality trait, and thus a stable factor. Therefore, an organization can largely not influence it. Nevertheless, this trust disposition is highly important in the initial stage of any relationship (MAYER ET AL. 1995; MCKNIGHT ET AL. 1998). However, due to their increased interactions, both parties gain more experience and these initial trusting beliefs become less important (ZAND 1972). Owing to its **significant impact on specific trust** (e.g., ANDALEEB/ANWAR 1996, p. 47; GEFEN 2000, p. 732), it is necessary to include trust propensity in the theoretical model.

2.2.2. Consumer-Specific Trust as an Attitude Construct

In contrast to general trust, **specific trust depends on the perception of a specific situation and a specific object**, which includes organizations and persons (MAYER ET AL. 1995, p. 712). Thus, specific trust is not a personality trait and can be more easily influenced by organizations such as banks. It is of vital importance to have a detailed concept of specific trust in order to arrive at a detailed answer to the research question regarding how trust should be engendered in consumers. The most suitable approach is a multi-dimensional construct, which enables trust building measures to build consumer trust on several contact points (each trust dimension).

There are different **theories** that relate to trust. RIPPERGER (1998, p. 268) describes specific trust as found in new institutional economics research as a rational decision process based on a cost and benefit calculation related to individual preferences and risk propensity. Trust is a mechanism used to stabilize uncertain expectations regarding interacting partners. This mechanism leads to decreased behavior complexity and reduces control actions against opportunistic behavior. In addition, the decision process related to consumer behavior theories adds an emotional component to the rational decision process.

Specific trust as a perception of a specific situation or object has **various definitions** in the literature. Some authors define consumer trust as a belief in the motives or intentions of another party (SALAM ET AL. 2005, p. 75), or positive expectations that allow a "leap of faith" towards trust (MÖLLERING 2006, p. 191). Others define specific trust as a motivation, outcome, or value (ROTH 1994, p. 127). Some authors point out fundamental conditions, like the likelihood of the partner to abuse trust or disappoint the expectations of the customer, which suggests that trusting involves future contingencies during which the trusted partner is likely to disappoint the expectations of the trusting party (e.g., LUHMANN 1979, p. 42). MÖLLERING (2006, p. 191) goes a step further in asserting that trust is the suspension of vulnerability and uncertainty. Further definitions of specific trust are used, which include: Benevolence, honesty, faith, dependability, predictability, fairness, confidence, hope, openness, integrity, promise, fulfillment, and consideration (BHATTACHERJEE 2002, p. 213).

On examining these definitions and characteristics of specific trust and integrating these aspects in consumer theories, **trust can be defined as an attitude**[4]. This is also reflected in topical studies in which authors discuss trust as an attitudinal construct (e.g., SERVA ET AL. 2005; SALAM ET AL. 2005, p. 75; GÄCHTER ET AL. 2004; AMBLER 1997, p. 287). "Attitudes are mental states used by individuals to structure the way they perceive their environment and guide the way they respond to it. There is a general acceptance that there are three related components that form an attitude: A cognitive or knowledge component, a liking or affective component, and an intention or action component. Each component provides a different insight into a person's attitude" (AAKER ET AL. 2007, p. 286). Therefore, in this work, specific trust is defined as an attitude, which leads to a three-dimensional (cognitive, affective and intention trust component) measurement approach.

4 An attitude is defined as a relatively global and enduring evaluation of an object, issue, person, or action (Hoyer/MacInnis 2001, p. 131). Attitudes can be described in terms of five main characteristics: Favorability, attitude accessibility, attitude confidence, persistence, and resistance. Favorability describes how much an attitude object is liked or disliked; an accessible attitude can be easily and readily retrieved from memory; attitude confidence refers to the strength of a person's attitudes; persistence or endurance signifies the time that an attitude lasts; resistance explains the receptiveness of an attitude change to subsequent change (Hoyer/MacInnis 2001, p. 131). Transferring these attitude characteristics to trust further supports the statement that trust is an attitude. Trusting an interaction partner demonstrates preference for the organization. Consumers can easily retrieve a trust attitude from their memory, which will not change within a brief time. A long-term relationship will not grow until the partners trust each other and will not be destroyed until one of the partners has abused the trust.

The development of a three-dimensional trust measurement approach is quite advanced and has started in 2002 (McKnight et al. 2002; Bhattacherjee 2002). It has been improved over the last years. A short overview of the historical development of trust measurement from one dimension up to even four dimensions will be given. The different labeling of the dimensions are shown in the Table 1. This step is done to explain how researchers tried to integrate the different aspects of trust (benevolence, integrity etc.) and in a further step adjust the multi-dimensional measurement concerning consumer theories. Therefore, dimensions were defined as affective (instead of e.g. benevolence), cognitive (instead of e.g. competence), and behavioral trust aspects (e.g. willingness to provide personal information).

An example of a **one-dimensional consumer trust conceptualization** is provided by Agustin/Singh (2005, p. 97), who define trust "as a consumer's confident belief that he or she can rely on the sellers to deliver promised services." A one-dimensional conceptualization of trust does not analyze the emotional and cognitive components of consumer trust separately by considering consumer behavior theories. Therefore, Ganesan (1994, p. 2) argues that a multidimensional approach provides greater diagnostic accuracy as more dimensions provide a better definition of the word trust with respect to the effect of trust on long and short-term orientation. Furthermore, Bhattacherjee (2002, p. 213) maintains that multidimensional measurement is the only way to capture the breadth and complexity of this construct.

However, a **two-dimensional approach** is applicable, taking the precondition that information processing in the consumer's mind should be considered due to the evaluation of the situation or object into consideration. The evaluation of cognitive and affective information is defined as information processing (Kroeber-Riel/Weinberg 2003, p. 51). Activating processes are associated with internal uproars and tensions (e.g., emotions). In contrast, cognitive processes are associated with information processing (e.g., a salesman's perceived competence or expertise) and refer to the beliefs that a consumer harbors about an attitude object (e.g., Solomon et al. 2006, p. 140; Lewis/Weigert 1985, p. 970). In research, this affective or emotional component of trust is, for example, called faith (Rempel et al. 1985, p. 97) or benevolence (Larzelere/Huston 1980, p. 596), whereas the cognitive dimension of trust is labeled reliability (Johnson-George/Swap 1982, p. 1308), predictability (Rempel et al. 1985, p. 96), honesty (Larzelere/Huston 1980, p. 596), competence, or responsibility (Butler 1991). Ganesan´s (1994) work has made the two-dimensional consumer trust measurement popular. This measurement measures trust two-dimensionally, using "benevolence and credibility" as a trust definition. The two-dimensional measurement was later modified and became "benevolence and competence" or "benevolence and expertise" (see Table 1). Doney/Cannon (1997) adopt these two dimensions and describe trust on the background of consumer theories as an affective (e.g., benevolent) and a cognitive (e.g., competent, expertise) dimension. Thus, a two-dimensional approach to the measurement of consumer trust is required to understand consumer behavior more precisely. It describes trust as a motivation, which is defined as a combination of affective and cognitive processes, but without behavioral intention (KROEBER-RIEL/WEINBERG 2003, p. 141).

However, the best conceptualization of trust based on consumer research has not as yet been completed. A third dimension can still be added to the two-dimensional measurement (affective and cognitive trust). A two or three-dimensional approach to consumer trust is closely connected to the question of trust as an attitude (consisting of three trust dimensions) or trust as a motivation (two dimensions). Some researchers maintain that trust should be defined by means of the three dimensions cognitive, affective, and behavioral aspects of trust (GANESAN 1994; LEWIS/WEIGERT 1985; MCALLISTER 1995; SWAN ET AL. 1999; WILLIAMSON 1993). In these studies the behavioral (conative) trust dimension functions as an implicit dimension affected by affective and cognitive trust. Conative trust implies trusting behavior (intentions)[5], with the trustors taking the risk of being hurt or constricted in their freedom, for example, their willingness to provide personal information, their problems, or needs. Conative trust also implies a suspension of behavior (intentions), which is a mirror signal of distrust, for example, not controlling the partner, no extended gathering of information on the other party, searching for alternatives, or soliciting a compromise.

Research into **three-dimensional trust conceptualizations in previous studies** identified four different concepts, which were used in seven publications (see Table 1). Contrary to the preferred approach, six of the seven publications did not cover the conative dimension. The six publications mentioned three measurement dimensions, which can be allocated to the affective and cognitive trust dimensions. For example, BHATTACHERJEE's (2002) "benevolence" dimension can be allocated under the "affective trust" dimension, while the dimension "ability" fits into the cognitive trust dimension. As the third dimension, "integrity" seems to be more likely a driver of affective and cognitive trust and not a further third dimension. A further three-dimensional approach by LIANG ET AL. (2005) only recognizes cognitive elements (calculus-based trust, knowledge based-trust, and institution-based trust) (see Table 1). Emotional trust aspects are not recognized at all in their measurement. Their approach is therefore rated as unsuitable for measuring consumer trust in the banking industry. These conceptualizations regarding an affective, cognitive and conative trust dimension reveals that the conative dimension is not even covered implicitly through the affective and cognitive trust dimensions. This measurement approach is in general accepted in research, as long as each dimension does not have the same content or covers another dimension. Therefore, the goal is to find the best measurement approach with a clear content

5 The third dimension mainly covers behavior intentions in trust research, as behavior intention is easily determined, while consumer behavior is more difficult to ascertain.

separation. This is provided by the attitude approach. Incorporating the idea of trust as an attitude reveals that the conative trust dimension plays an important role and has to be included in the conceptualization of consumer trust. Only AIKEN/BOUSH's (2006, p. 312) recent study measures the effects of different signals simultaneously on the three components (affective, cognitive, and conative) of online trust.

A trust measurement approach through **four dimensions** (see Table 1) can also be found in literature (GEFEN/STRAUB 2004; VAN DEN BERG/VAN LIESHOUT 2001). In the theoretical measurement approach of VAN DEN BERG/VAN LIESHOUT (2001) no emotional trust component is recognized, which would leave out important aspects of consumer behavior. The four-dimensional trust measurement approach by GEFEN/STRAUB (2004) seems to be more likely a two-dimensional trust measurement, where the dimension integrity should be defined as driver of benevolence and ability, while the dimension predictability should be defined as a consequence of benevolence and ability. If a person seems to be integer, this might lead to the perception of benevolence and ability. And this will again lead to a more predictable behavior of a person. Both four-dimensional approaches seem to be less suitable, than the three-dimensional attitude trust approach.

Table 1 provides a summary of the **complete list of trust conceptualizations** in person-to-organization contexts, encompassing between one and four dimensions.

Author(s)	Labeled trust dimensions			
	1. dimension	2. dimension	3. dimension	4. dimension
SHEMWELL ET AL. (1994, p. 57); GARBARINO/JOHNSON (1999, p. 84); CHIOU ET AL. (2002, p. 114); BALASUBRAMANIAN ET AL. (2003, p. 879); ANDERSON/SRINIVASAN (2003, p. 129); ARYEE/CHEN (2004, p. 324); BART ET AL. (2005, p. 150)	trust			
GANESAN (1994, p. 3)	benevolence	credibility		
SINGH/SIRDESHMUKH (2000, p. 156); GARBARINO/LEE (2003, p. 500)	benevolence	competence		
WHITE (2005, p. 142)	benevolence	expertise		
ANDALEEB/ANWAR (1996, p. 37)	conative trust	cognitive trust		
DONEY/CANNON (1997, p. 36); JOHNSON/GRAYSON (2005, p. 501)	affective trust	cognitive trust		
MARTIN/CAMARERO (2005, p. 84)	intentions/ value	capability/ competence		
BHATTACHERJEE (2002, p. 211); YOUSAFZAI ET AL. (2005, p. 184); SCHLOSSER ET AL. (2006, p. 135)	benevolence	integrity	ability	
MCKNIGHT ET AL. (2002, p. 338); WANG/BENBASAT (2005, p. 87)	benevolence	integrity	competence	
LIANG ET AL. (2005, p. 53)	calculus-based trust	knowledge-based trust	institution-based trust	
AIKEN/BOUSH (2006, p. 312)	affective trust	cognitive trust	conative trust	
GEFEN/STRAUB (2004, p. 413)	benevolence	integrity	ability	predictability
VAN DEN BERG/VAN LIESHOUT (2001, p. 516)	calculus-based trust	knowledge-based trust	reference-based trust	identification-based trust

Table 1: Complete list of consumer-specific trust conceptualizations** (*EBERT ***2009, p.68)

Table 1 indicates that trust **researchers differ on these conceptualizations**. No common and consistent approach has hitherto been widely accepted. Thus, the number of dimensions and the names of each trust dimension vary. If a measurement of trust is the focus of one of the studies examined, more dimensions are applied, which are predominantly the result of different concepts and definitions of trust. Consumer trust dimensions are an example of construct measurement that has increased over the last 15 years. Furthermore, when trust is measured, the degree of trust measurement accuracy depends on the research question.

As trust is in the main focus in this work a multi-dimensional approach is preferred. Consequently, **specific trust is defined** here as an attitude with the three dimensions:

1. Affective beliefs about the organization (affective trust - "gut instinct" or comparable to the trust dimension benevolence see Table 1);

2. Customer's cognitive belief related to the trustworthiness of the organization (cognitive trust – "rational estimation" or comparable to the trust dimension competence, credibility, expertise, or ability see Table 1); and,
3. Willingness to provide personal information (i.e. provide address or telephone number) or to refrain from actions (i.e. controlling the partner - conative trust).

The three-dimensional approach to consumer-specific trust conceptualization is accepted in trust theory and thought to reflect consumer attitude behavior best.

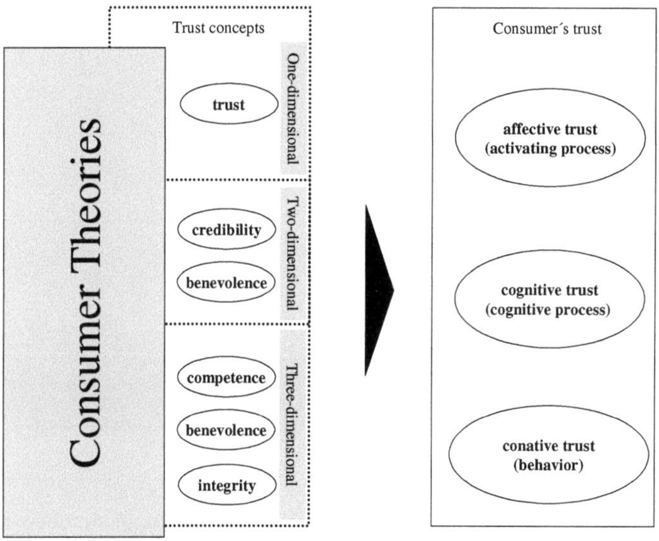

Figure 5: Conceptualization of consumer trust as an attitude

The **great value** of the three-dimensional approach is that it provides more possibilities to steer trust.

2.2.3. Steering of Consumer Trust

The traditional view of steering consumer behavior through affective and cognitive processes is explained by KROEBER-RIEL/WEINBERG (2003, p. 50). The traditional understanding is that **affective and cognitive processes interact with each other** and lead to a consumer behavior in a second step. Consequently, a feeling of hunger (affective process) will lead to an increasing information process (cognitive process) to obtain food (behavior). However, the advertising of a film (cognitive process) also leads to a motivation (affective process) to visit the cinema (behavior). Translating the classical model (KROEBER-RIEL/WEINBERG 2003, p. 50) to the trust concepts would correlate affective and cognitive trust dimensions and lead as a consequence to trust behavior (see Figure 6).

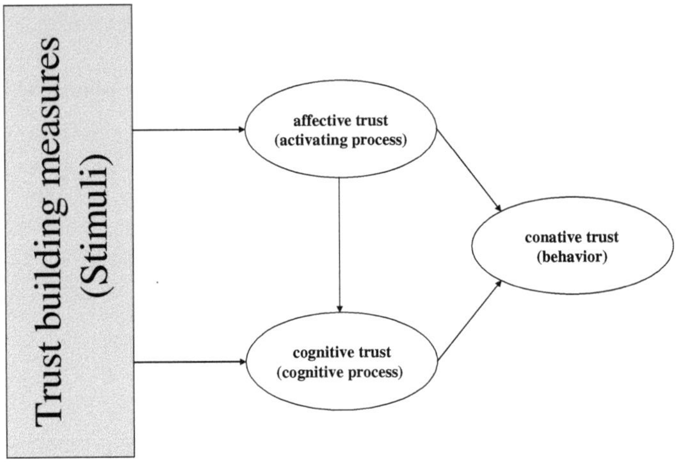

Figure 6: Traditional understanding of consumer affective, cognitive and conative trust processes influenced by trust building measures

While the traditional model implies that in a second step these two dimensions influence consumer behavior, newer models already state that stimuli can simultaneously affect all three dimensions (HAWKINS ET AL. 2004, p. 388). A change in one attitude component tends to produce related changes in the other components (HAWKINS ET AL. 2004, p. 391). This effect is due to the **cognitive consistency principle**. According to this principle, people value harmony between trust thoughts, trust feelings, and trust behavior. Recognizing all three dimensions and their distinctive interaction leads to the ABC model (SOLOMON ET AL. 2006, p. 141), in which there are three kinds of attitudes that have specific, unidirectional interactions between the three attitude (trust) dimensions. Each kind of attitude depends mainly on the type of information processing or consumption, which leads to a trisection of attitudes: Attitude based on cognitive information processing, attitude based on behavioral learning processes, and attitude based on hedonic consumption. In extension to the traditional model by KROEBER-RIEL/WEINBERG (2003, p. 50) the defined behavior (conative) dimension is no longer an implicit second step which follows through affective and cognitive trust. Thus, **trust behavior can also be directly influenced by trust building measures** (see Figure 7).

Consequently, a bank's trust building measures can focus on just one, two or three of the three trust dimension to pursue an efficient marketing strategy.

Trust research has not yet analyzed most possible **interactions between the three trust dimensions**. JOHNSON/GRAYSON (2005, p. 505) find that cognitive trust has a significant effect on affective trust. Even if researchers working on "attitude" are aware of the bidirectional relationship between cognition and affect in attitude formation (e.g., MCALLISTER 1995) no research has been done on the reverse causation from affective on cognitive trust, which makes more sense for the present research question.

Why observe the **impact of affective on cognitive trust** and not the other way around? In the banking industry, affective trust seems to have a positive impact on cognitive trust. There is no real possibility for bank customers to control and check bank transactions as a whole (e.g., investment strategies). Consequently, customers may rely on trust feelings gained through affective signals from the financial service provider. These are generated by a level of concern and care the service provider demonstrates (JOHNSON-GEORGE/SWAP 1982). The trust feelings function as an indicator of the knowledge-driven cognitive trust. The validation of the right cognitive trust appraisal of the service provider mainly develops through experience over time. But even long experience will not lead to a complete certainty regarding the financial service providers´ future actions (JOHNSON/GRAYSON 2005, p. 501). A "leap of faith" will remain as a permanent feature in business-to-consumer trust relationships, which leads to the following hypothesis:

H1: ***Affective consumer trust is positively related to customers' cognitive trust in an organization.***

The direction, from **affective to conative trust** follows the traditional understanding of information processing where the behavioral (conative) trust aspect functions as a consequence of affective trust (KROEBER-RIEL/WEINBERG 2003). In contrast, the assumption that conative trust (trust behavior) leads to higher trust feelings (affective trust) might be true for attitudes based on learning processes (SOLOMON ET AL. 2006, p. 141). But, as already mentioned, in financial services there will always be a remaining uncertainty, whereby trust feelings will be the leading reason for trust behavior and not the other way round. Consequently, it has been chosen due to the assumption that if bank customers have a positive trust feeling, they are more likely to provide further personal information besides the bank's required standard information (e.g. lifestyle information). Consequently, the following hypothesis is deduced.

H2: ***Affective consumer trust is positively related to consumer trust behavior (or intention) (conative trust).***

Why analyze the **impact of cognitive on conative trust** and not vice versa? In attitude research the behavioral trust dimension is treated implicitly as a consequence of affective and cognitive trust (JOHNSON/GRAYSON 2005, p. 501). Positive customer experience over time and thus, cognitive trust with the financial adviser leads to the assumption that bank customers provide more and more personal information. In contrast, the effect of conative trust on cognitive trust can be found in attitudes based on hedonic consumption (SOLOMON ET AL. 2006, p. 141). Even if sometimes customers have to provide personal information, for example contact address (conative trust) before they exactly know what happens to their given information, it is assumed that bank customers first try to gain cognitive trust over experience and provide extended private information in a second step. Consequently, the following hypothesis is deduced.

H3: ***Consumer trust beliefs (cognitive trust) are positively related to trust behavior (conative trust).***

The following figure summarizes the first hypotheses about the interaction between the trust dimensions and the presumption of the contact points of trust building measures.

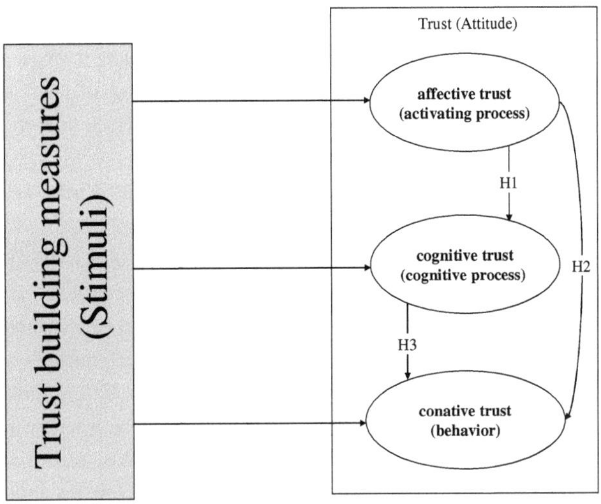

Figure 7: Enhanced understanding of consumer affective, cognitive and conative trust processes influenced by trust building measures

What are the main business advantages in the banking industry of trust steering or trust building?

2.3. Relationship of Loyalty and Consumer Trust in Business

Loyalty as a critical factor for firm's long-term survival, innovativeness, and bottom-line returns, is one of the important and meaningful consequences of consumer trust (AGUSTIN/SINGH 2005, p. 96). The researchers HART/JOHNSON (1999, p. 10) even state, that "a total trust strategy ... is the ultimate test of consumer loyalty."

The uniqueness of loyalty in business lies in eliciting desired consumer behavior, which includes a stable business relationship over time and recommendation behavior (AGUSTIN/SINGH 2005; SIRDESHMUKH ET AL. 2002). Trust has been observed as a "cornerstone" of long-term relationships (SPEKMAN 1988, p. 79). A stable business relationship (one facet of loyalty) is expressed through greater customer commitment, a greater share of the customer's wallet and repeat buying (AGUSTIN/SINGH 2005, p. 97). Furthermore, customers' willingness to seek variety and their switching behavior are lower (LOHMANN 1997, p. 160; BECKETT ET AL. 2000). The need of a stable and longtime relationship in the banking industry is given through a study by REICHHELD/SASSER (1991). It shows that customer must at least be bonded for two years to achieve the break-even. In the first year of bank customer life time cycle losses are made, which turn into growing profits in the following years. These growing profits in the banking industry are gained through lower administrative costs, higher likeability of choosing a service or product from this bank, through mark-on, and recommendation behavior. Consumers' recommendation behavior (other facet of loyalty) in respect of their friends has a strong effect on obtaining new customers. REICHHELD ET AL. (2000) even state that recommendation behavior is one of the most meaningful behaviors and should be recognized and analyzed by marketers. At least, bonded and loyal customers are a kind of entry barrier for other companies (SCHWAIGER 2000, p. 176). Consequently, these stable and active customer relationships, gained through loyalty, form the basis of profit security and market share in the banking business (MEIDAN 1996).

A recent study by LEWIS/SOURELI (2006) analyzes the effects of consumer trust (measured two-dimensionally) on consumer **loyalty in retail banking.** Their research findings stress that cognitive rather affective trust enhances bank loyalty. Their results indicate that banks have to find ways to encourage the development of trust between customers and their contact employees to enhance loyalty. This again emphasizes the need for trust building measures. In their study, LEWIS/SOURELI do not distinguish between three trust dimensions. It is possible to improve upon their measurement of the trust construct, which leads to the next hypothesis.

H4: ***Consumer a) affective, b) cognitive, and c) conative trust is positively related to consumer loyalty.***

Ultimately, the degree to which each dimension of trust impacts loyalty will be analyzed. The following figure summarizes the first propositions in Chapter 2.

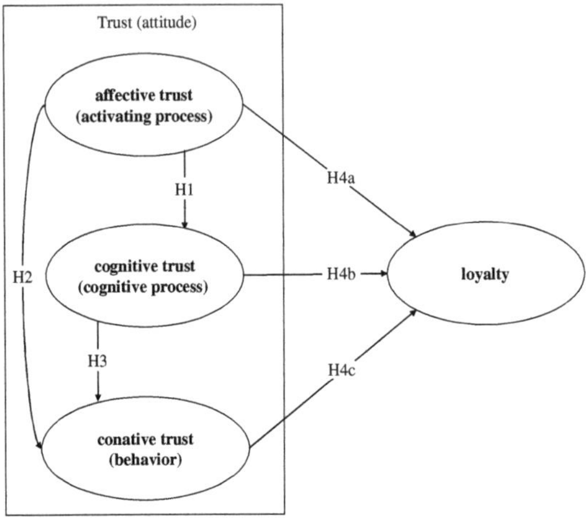

Figure 8: Dimensions of consumer trust and the hypothesized impact on loyalty

Summary of Chapter 2:

The increased interest in trust leads to a high development of trust articles in the last 60 years. The intangible character of trust makes trust a multidisciplinary research issue, which mainly appears in human resource management, marketing, strategy, and psychology. A distinction was made between trust, confidence, and reliance. In contrast to the other terms, trust suggest especially emotional feelings based on inconclusive evidence. Thereafter, a more detailed description of consumer trust was provided of a one-dimensional general trust conceptualization in respect of consumer behavior, as well as of the three dimensions of consumer-specific trust. General trust as a personal trait can hardly be influenced by organization. In contrast, specific trust depends on the perception of a specific situation or a specific object (for example a bank), which leads to three contact points of trust building measures by organizations. The importance of analyzing loyalty, which is as a result of consumer trust, was emphasized. It forms the basis of profit security especially in the banking industry through the need of longtime customer relationships. Despite the well-recognized significance of trust building in business-to-consumer relationships, few studies have analyzed business behaviors that build or deplete consumers trust (SIRDESHMUKH ET AL. 2002, p. 15). The relevant research question is: How can organizations, and especially banks, engender consumer trust?

3 Trust Model for Analyzing Measures of Trust Building in the Banking Industry

The German banking industry[6] is one of the largest in the world. In January 2007, there were a total of 2,038 banking institutes in Germany with a total asset of 7,230,671 million euro. Bank customers can be divided into private customers, business clients, countries, and other banks. There are three types of banks, namely credit unions, banks regulated by public law, and private credit banks. In contrast to banks regulated by public law and credit unions, the goal of private banks is profit maximization. The main providers of private banks are the five major banks, also called the Cash Group, which run the Deutsche Bank, Commerzbank, HypoVereinsbank, Postbank, and Dresdner Bank. These banks mainly service large industry concerns and well-off customers, as well as other private banks, foreign banks, private real credit institutes, and private building societies. Banks regulated by public law comprise: Eleven state banks, the federal institute (KfW), approximately 500 "Sparkassen," the federal building society (LBS), and mortgage banks. The "Sparkassen" are the main financers of medium-sized businesses in Germany. They also sell service products that originate from state banks, which are the principle banks of each county and supervise major clients. Credit unions include central institutes ("DZ Bank", "WGZ-Bank"), approximately 1,250 other German banks (e.g., "Volks- und Raiffeisenbank", "Sparda Bank," and "PSD Bank"), and special banking institutes (e.g., "Union Investment," "Beamtenbank").

The German federal financial supervisory agency (BaFin) supervises theses credit and financial institutions, specifically authorizing bank transactions through the German Banking Act (KWG). Thus, the banking industry is characterized by high-quality services, which makes differentiation based on products or service quality difficult. The standard of security is quite high through the regulation by the BaFin, which naturally leads to a general high trust in the banking industry[7]. Nevertheless, there are still grey zones in the regulations, which will presumably not be fully avoided, because of the permanent changes in the banking industry for example through new developed products, for example special kinds of credits, loans of money or portfolios. Thus, there will always be a kind of risk left, and trust will be a permanent issue in financial transactions (KNIGHTS ET AL. 2001).

The **goal** of Chapter 3 is to develop a theoretical model of specific trust building measures that German banks can apply. It is important for the banking industry to know two matters: Which measures are important in gaining a customer's trust and the extent to which

---

6 This information was mainly gained from the German Central Bank (www.bundesbank.de).

7 This higher general trust in banks in contrast to general trust in organization could be empirically tested in the pre-study (see section 4.1.2).

organizations can influence consumer trust. Do consistent trust propensity and personality factors play an important role? What are the major actions that affect consumer trust that an organization such as banks can influence? The use of smartPLS (Partial Least Squares) as the method to analyze structural equation models is given. The conceptualization and operationalization of each construct needed for the structural equation model (SEM) for trust building measures are discussed. Evident misspecifications and operationalizations of constructs in highly ranked articles will be disclosed and explained, with the correction, based on the recent literature, deduced to avoid potential sources of errors in the empirical study.

3.1. Highlights of and Unclear Causalities in Trust Research

Highly **cited[8] articles** gained through the following meta-analysis in section 3.3 which contain important highlights shaped the research field of trust. To guarantee the best content for the **theoretical model of consumer trust building measures**, it will be developed taking the research results of the ten most cited articles in trust literature into account. A short mention of the main seven highlights gained through the ten articles is given below:

1) Transition of the one-dimensional to a multi-dimensional trust measurement approach:

GANESAN 1994 (Citation index, short CI[9]: 189) suggests that long-term orientation in a buyer-seller relationship is a function of two main factors: Mutual dependence and the extent to which both partners trust one another. Dependence and trust are related to environmental uncertainty, transaction-specific investments, reputation, and satisfaction in a buyer-seller relationship. He also defines trust as two-dimensional; being credibility the first and benevolence the second dimension (see section 2.2.2).

2) Five cognitive processes for trust building:

DONEY/CANNON 1997 (CI: 169) examine five cognitive processes - calculation, prediction, capability, intentionality, and transference - through which industrial buyers can secure the trust of a suppliers firm and its salesperson. Antecedents of the buying firm's trust in the supplier firm and its salesperson were characteristics of the supplier firm (reputation, size) and the salesperson (expertise and power) as well as the characteristics of the relationship to the supplier firm (willingness to customize, confidential in-formation sharing, and length of relationship) and certain traits of the salesperson (likeability, similarity, frequent business contact, frequent social contact, length of relationship). In the developed theoretical model the content of cognitive trust processes as analyzed by DONEY/CANNON (1997) merges with emotional trust and the consideration of trust antecedents (see section 2.2.2 and 3.8).

---

8 "Highly" means more than 150 citations in the EBSCO database in November 2006.
9 A citation index (CI) of 189 equals 189 times citied in other published articles.

3) Relationship of customer's characteristics (e.g., satisfaction) and organizational consequences:

CROSBY ET AL. 1990 (CI: 242) analyze the quality of the relationship between salespersons and the customer that determines the probability of continued interchange between those parties in the future. Future sales opportunities are mostly dependent upon relationship quality (i.e., trust and satisfaction).

ANDERSON/NARUS 1990 (CI: 407) present a trust model of working partnerships of a distribution firm and a manufacturer firm. Communication and cooperation were antecedents which promoted less conflict and higher satisfaction as consequences of trust. Especially the respecification of cooperation as an antecedent rather than a consequence of trust is found.

MOHR/SPEKMAN 1994 (CI: 158) examine primary characteristics of partnership success (satisfaction and sales volume). These characteristics are partnership attributes like commitment, coordination, trust, communication quality, participation, and the conflict resolution technique of joint problem solving.

GARBARINO/JOHNSON 1999 (CI: 173) classify the customer base of an organization into low and high relational groups to assess how evaluations vary for these groups. The authors analyze the relationships of satisfaction, trust, and commitment to future intentions. For high relational customers (consistent subscribers of theatre against occasional subscriber), trust and commitment are analyzed as mediators.

Summarized, the articles by CROSBY ET AL. (1990), ANDERSON/NARUS (1990), MOHR/SPEKMAN (1994) and GARBARINO/JOHNSON (1999) were especially important for a more detailed analysis of trust relationships between customer's personality (e.g. trust propen-sity, see section 3.10) and organizational consequences (see sections 2.3).

4) Customer's personality as a moderator:

MAYER ET AL. 1995 (CI: 344) present a definition and propose a model of antecedents and outcomes of trust including characteristics of the trustor, the trustee, and the role of risk. Factors of perceived trustworthiness which influence trust are ability, benevolence, and integrity. Their model includes primarily the identification of general trust (or trust propensity) as a moderator (see section 3.10.3)

5) Important trust antecedents:

LARSON 1992 (CI: 164) examines social control in network organizational forms through an inductive field study in high-growth entrepreneurial firms. A process model of network formation that highlights the importance of reputation, trust reciprocity, and mutual interdependence is presented. The study offers important trust antecedents (see section 3.8).

6) Enhancement of trust antecedents:

MOORMAN ET AL. 1993 (CI: 160) show that interpersonal factors are most predictive for trust. Variables most strongly associated with trust were: Integrity, willingness to reduce uncertainty, confidentiality, expertise, tactfulness, sincerity, congeniality, and timeliness. Further variables, which also affected trust, were: Formalization of the user's organization, culture of organization, organizational power, and customization. The identified trust antecedents are an enhancement of LARSON´s (1992) trust antecedents (see section 3.9).

7) Trust building in the banking industry:

MORGAN/HUNT 1994 (CI: 522) study B2B relationship marketing and examine commitment and trust as key mediating variables of successful relationship marketing. Shared values, communication, and less opportunistic behavior influence trust. Consequences of trust are cooperation, functional conflict, and less uncertainty. Their study gives important insights of some of the identified trust building measures for the banking industry (see section 3.2).

All ten articles are different in their research question and used methods. Each researcher tries to solve his or her specific research question from their point of view dependent on the situational context (specific industry, business-to-business relationship versus social network etc.). However, they all work on trust relationships and added important factors to the developed trust model. Some of them have contrary research results, for example, the two most-cited articles – ANDERSON/NARUS (1990) and MORGAN/HUNT (1994). ANDERSON/ NARUS (1990) maintain that cooperation is an antecedent of trust and specifically found in a B2B relationship. In contrast, MORGAN/HUNT (1994) demonstrate that the consequences of trust is cooperation in a B2B relationship. This leads to the realization that the causality of some consequences and antecedents of trust is unclear. What engenders trust initially? Does good cooperation lead to increased trust, or is it the other way round? Good cooperation could lead to a higher trust, but trusting a business partner could also lead to better cooperation. Thus, some consequences or antecedents of trust seem to have a positive feedback loop. There are, however, other antecedents, like risk or satisfaction that have an **unclear causality** in research. This duality is vital in trust research as it is an indication of the **complexity of this topic**. Researchers on trust have to cope with these unclear causalities. Variables with an unclear causality, which are especially relevant in B2C relationships, will be discussed at a later stage (see section 3.10.1).

3.2. Models for Analyzing Trust Building

In a further step four important studies are shortly explained which form the basis for the developing of a new trust building model. These four studies focus on different, but relevant aspects of trust models, which should be recognized in the trust model. In a second step three theoretical works about trust in the banking industry and in a third step two empirical trust studies in the banking industries are given to include special focal points of the banking industry.

To date, the most **recent and suitable models for analyzing trust building measures** were developed by AIKEN/BOUSH (2006, p. 312), CHO (2006, p. 27), MAYER ET AL. (1995), and JOHNSON/GRAYSON (2005, p. 502).
The empirical study by AIKEN/BOUSH (2006) analyzes online trust and the nature of internet signals. Internet signals in the study are trustmarks, ratings and implied investments in marketing. The purpose of the study is to provide results of the effectiveness of internet marketer´s various attempts to engender consumer trust through web signals. Consumer trust is defined through three trust dimensions such as affective, cognitive, and conative trust. In their experiment eight web sites, each with different signals, were rated by 1252 participants. Each participant was given one of the eight possible websites, and consequently every participant had to answer the same survey questions after exposure. The result of the study is that the trustmark had the greatest effect on perceived trustworthiness, influencing respondents´ beliefs about security and privacy (affective trust), general beliefs about the firm trustworthiness (cognitive trust), and the willingness to provide personal information (conative trust). The relationship between Internet experience and trust was in the form of an inverted U. In early stages of the relationship (low experience), behavioral trust increases. At higher levels of experience, trust declines, because customers know what problems may occur and to what extend their privacy and security is unprotected. Their study offers the most advanced measurement of consumer trust regarding consumer theories through its three-dimensional trust approach.

The empirical study by Cho (2006) examines the mechanism of trust and distrust formation and their relational outcomes in two online purchasing contexts, books and clothing. Security, core offering, site design, tangible reward, communication, prefential treatment, competence, benevolence are analyzed as influencing factors of global online trust and distrust. Consumers´ self-disclosure and willingness to commit are outcomes of consumer trust and distrust. 881 online responses were used for the analysis. Their results support the proposition that trust and distrust are shaped by different dimensions of trustworthiness, and trust affects behavior intentions differently from distrust. The study offers an important theoretical aspect by distinguishing between consumer (dis-)trust as well as company's perceived trustworthiness (e.g. competence) in the context of business-to-consumer Internet exchange relationships.

The theoretical study by MAYER ET AL. (1995), one of the top ten cited articles[10], considers especially the characteristics of the trustor and the trustee as well as the role of risk in their integrative model of organizational trust. Their theoretical model of trust introduces - besides the differentiation of perceived trustworthiness and trust - trustor's propensity as a moderator for the first time (the definition of moderators will follow in section 3.4.2) and not as an antecedent of consumer trust.

In the model by JOHNSON/GRAYSON (2005) the interaction between the two trust dimensions (affective and cognitive trust) is analyzed in the context of the finance industry in the United Kingdom. Furthermore, it includes important trust building variables such as service provider expertise, product performance, firm reputation, satisfaction with previous interaction, and similarity. Therefore, their model is quite advanced. The results were gained through 349 banking customers who answered a survey mailing. The authors empirically identify a significant positive relation from customer's cognitive to affective trust as well as part wise positive effects of the given antecedents on the both trust dimensions.

In addition to these four studies, further articles - theoretical (see KNIGHTS ET AL. 2001; SEAL 1998; WHITLEY 1991) as well as empirical (see ADAMSON ET AL. 2003; MUKHERJEE/NATH 2003) - are described to get to the **banking industry's specific focal point**.

The theoretical work of WHITLEY (1991) concentrates on business systems of financial institutions in Asian countries like Japan, Korea and China. The different business systems reflect historical patterns of authority, trust and loyalty. Differences between the business systems developed because of differences in their institutional environments (especially the political and financial systems). Nevertheless, the author state that similar processes exist in western societies.

SEAL (1998) states that trust may derive from a person-to-person interaction and/or from an impersonal, symbolic presentation base. Especially intra- as well as interfirm policies through organizational routines and trainings are important for developing trust and assessing trustworthiness in the banking industry.

The theoretical paper by KNIGHTS ET AL. (2001) focuses on trust in the newest distribution channels like internet financial services and smart cards. The authors argue that technologies

[10] This information is gained by the meta-analysis in section 3.3.

of control, and their associated rituals of distrust, such as fingerprint, paradoxically, will contribute to manufacturing an atmosphere of trust in financial dealings.

The empirical study by ADAMSON ET AL. (2003) examines that the banks´ marketing strategy and long-term orientation is positively correlated with consumer trust in the Hong Kong's corporate banking sector. The authors recommend that banks must develop parallel communication channels with their customers and show flexibility in their dealings.

The study by MUKHERJEE/NATH (2003) analyzes - besides communication - significant effects of shared values and opportunistic behavior on consumer trust in online banking. Their study transfers main results - from one of the top ten cited articles by MORGAN/HUNT (1994) (see section 3.1) - to the banking industry.

In this publication a new model will be developed on the basis of the described one. The different focal points and results of the four general trust studies will be aggregated **into one single trust model**. These articles mentioned above provide a three-dimensional trust measurement (affective, cognitive, and conative trust) (see section 2.2.2), the differentiation between trust (consumer specific trust) and trustworthiness (perception of the organization) (see section 3.4.2), trustee propensity identified as a moderator (see section 3.10.1), and relevant trust antecedents for example reputation, which are considered in the developed model (see section 3.11). The theoretical and empirical works on trust in the banking industry complement identified trust antecedents like communication, opportunistic behavior, security technologies and innovations of banks. Communication will be considered indirectly in the trust model through the perception of trustworthiness of the house bank by the consumer. Perceived opportunistic behavior and security technologies (later named protection) complement the developed model (see section 3.11).

Some of the studies focus on internet banking, thus a transfer to general banking transactions is needed. The three dimensional (affective, cognitive, conative) measurement of online-trust is transferred to the three dimensional consumer trust in a service provider. Further, the interaction of each trust dimension (affective, cognitive, and conative) is taken into account and placed in the model. The measurement dimensions of perceived trustworthiness are improved. Effects, like reputation and security, on three trust dimensions (instead of two) are analysed. Previous model will be expanded by adding more trust antecedents which influence consumer's trust. The use of moderators is considered in more detail than in previous trust models. Summarized, the new developed trust model will contain previous research findings, but it will still add further trust antecedents, moderators, relationships between trust dimensions and it will test the effects for the German banking industry.

To take a very objective approach to improve previous trust models a meta-analysis and expert interviews were used in a first step. The meta-analysis will help to identify the relevant trust building measures out of a huge amount of different influencing variables (see section 3.3.2).

3.3. Meta-Analysis to Build a Trust Framework

The objective is to identify all kinds of trust articles covering different research areas and focal points, from theoretic articles to empirical studies. It is not enough to simply refer to the most recent models if one wishes to capture consumer trust research in its entirety; prior work should also be analyzed and summarized if one does not wish to neglect important trust antecedents. This section contains a **meta-analysis** of the trust literature between 1966 and 2006.
The comprehensive trust meta-analysis[11] undertaken to help answering the research question comprised 800 highly ranked trust articles. This is the largest meta-analysis that has been undertaken in this research field to date. Furthermore, this meta-analysis is a structured tool. Recent trust models will be improved and developed into a more sophisticated trust model.

The **contribution** of this analysis is that it empirically clarifies the aspects: The topicality of trust (see chapter 2), scientific trust community (see chapter 2), objects and interactions of trust (see section 2.1), highlights in trust research (see section 3.1), and the netting of trust (see sections 3.3.2).

3.3.1. Method of Analyzing Articles

The basis of the meta-analysis comprises a total of 290 A+, A, and B-ranked[12] journals from the "Journal Quality List[13]" to guarantee that only the highest quality articles of the last 60 years were used in the analysis. The meta-analysis was undertaken during June and July 2006. In the first step, all of these journals were scanned for articles containing the word "trust"[14]. Approximately 3,200 articles were found. In the next step, non-relevant articles were excluded[15]. The meta-analysis ultimately comprised the remaining 808 relevant articles.

---

11 The participants in the Relationship Marketing Summit in Buenos Aires in 2007 are thanked for their comments in this regard.

12 The VHB03 ranking system was chosen for this meta-analysis. This ranking was developed on behalf of the Association of University Professors of Management in German-speaking countries (*Verband der Hochschullehrer für Betriebswirtschaft* – VHB). A+ implies an index ≥ 9, A ≥ 8, B ≥ 7. Henning-Thurau is the initiator and main author of the first VHB ranking (HENNING-THURAU ET AL., 2004).

13 The "Journal Quality List" is compiled and edited by Anne-Wil Harzing, with the primary goal of assisting academics to target papers that appear in journals of an appropriate standard.

14 The analysis was done with the help of the research database EBSCO. This is an electronic research database of articles from 10,000 academic journals and other sources published since 1922.

15 These included articles (and book reviews) in which the use of "trust" is negligible, or in which the term "trust" has a completely different meaning as in the treated context.

How can a massive portfolio of 808 theoretical and empirical studies be **analyzed**? Traditional meta-analyses are based on empirical surveys, which cannot integrate theoretical or conceptual papers (EISEND 2004, p. 5). Structuring or combining variables like means, correlation coefficients, and resiliencies can, however, be done with mathematical algorithms or formulas. Nevertheless, the use of mathematical algorithms alone would not help to solve this problem. These algorithms would be unsuitable in this case because:

1. All the articles use different types of analyzing methods (e.g., regression, structural equation modeling, and case studies), which means that the results are not comparable;
2. Each article analyzes other key variables (e.g., trust and risk or trust and commitment);
3. Each article has a different number of survey variables (e.g., some just analyze trust and risk, others analyze trust, risk satisfaction, and cooperation);
4. Some articles focus on antecedents, others on consequences of trust, while still others include both antecedents and consequences, and, in some surveys, trust is just a small part of the model; and
5. Some papers are theoretical and not empirical. Thus, a mathematical comparison of all the results is not possible in this case and does not lead to the desired results.

Consequently, a different way of analyzing theses trust articles was chosen.

Basic and easy accessible information on the 808 articles, for example, year, research area, and citation index, was used to answer the question concerning the development of trust articles and its scientific community. The question requiring the analysis of trust interaction types could be answered by examining the abstract or the entire content of articles. The abstracts of all the trust articles were analyzed to answer the question on other variables (called key variables) analyzed or discussed in connection with trust. The defined key variables should not be confused with the key words provided by the journal or with different trust concepts. The last question regarding the finding of the main clusters in trust research could be answered by aggregating the key variables after a logical procedure.

3.3.2. Clusters and Key Variables in Trust Research

The goal of this section is the explorative analysis of all other variables – in relationship with trust – that have been surveyed as well as their **clustering**. A traditional mathematical approach of clustering variables according to a special scheme does not seem to be correct in this case, because – besides the reasons mentioned above – there is no sense in clustering variables that are often analyzed together in a survey. This would just lead to a confusion of the antecedents and consequences of trust. Therefore, key variables that belong together or are very closely connected are grouped into one cluster. Clustering in this work implies the logical aggregation of variables (e.g. competence) to a special content (e.g. reputation).

The following step was a **descriptive analysis** of the data, leading to important input for the later analyses. The output – the frequency of key variables – made a valuable contribution to finding indicators for the next approach and a more in-depth analysis. Even if the frequency of a key variable is not comparable to its impact strength, it is still indicative of its importance in trust research. The gained results were used to develop a theoretical trust model.

Only the key variables that appeared in at least 2% of the 808 articles are used for the further clustering, which guarantees these variables' relevance in research. Some key variables have very similar contents but different terms, e.g. (re-)purchase (3.59%) versus purchase size (0.25%) or (in-)dependence (5.82%) versus autonomy (0.37%) or risk (7.43%) versus fear (0.37%). Thus, through this procedure the term which was more often used was taken into account. Some other key variables for example praise (0.12%) do have a correlation to trust, but seem to be more likely not a causal correlation of trust. That means that other key variables, e.g. sympathy are the reason for the trust building instead of praise.

The following figure lists the key variables found in the 808 articles and their frequencies in percentage, which will be clustered in a further step in the ensuing figure.

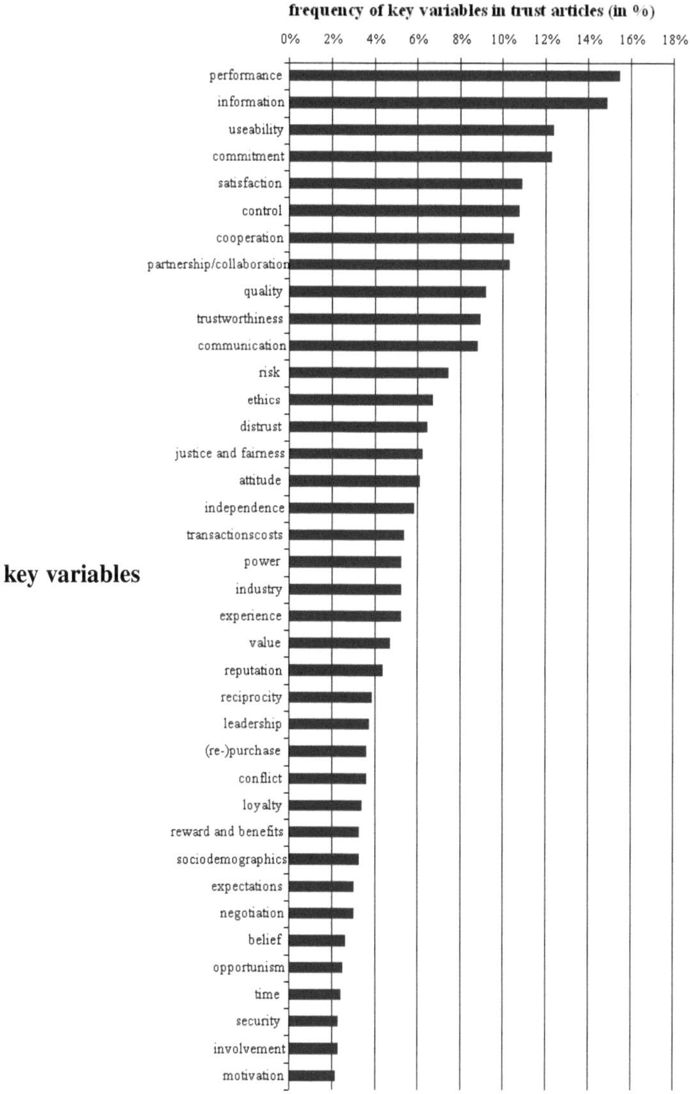

Figure 9: Frequencies of listed key variables in the 808 trust articles (EBERT ***2009, p.76)***

Performance and information are the most frequently mentioned key variables beside trust. However, such a **list of key variables** does not really help to gain a deeper understanding of trust literature. Thus, to reduce the nearly 40 key variables found in trust literature, clustering of the variables seemed a suitable way to gain more insight.

This meta-analysis's unique approach follows the clustering of variables as done with a **logical systematic** approach. Figure 10 illustrates the clusters of key variables. Two main aspects should be taken into account when examining Figure 10: The font size of each variable in the figure is an indication of the frequency of its listing. Variables in a larger font are listed in 8-16% of the articles, variables in a medium-sized font are listed in 6-7%, while variables in a small font are listed in 2-5% of the articles and second, only variables that were closely related to one another were clustered.

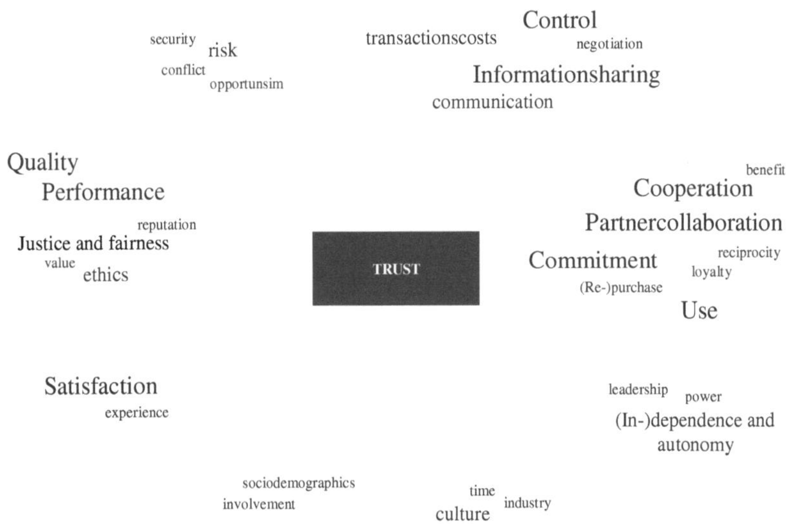

Figure 10: Clusters of key variables from 808 trust articles (EBERT ***2009, p.77)***

All clusters had to be independent of one another as far as possible. Eight main clusters were identified and labeled. The labeling follows a hierarchical structure, so that the clusters name covers the highest aggregation level of all key variables inside one cluster (gained from theory or empirical research). Some of the cluster names can also be identical to key variables, if one of the key variables covers all the other key variables in the cluster (e.g., reputation). The clusters are: Dependency, environment, future intention, person, reputation, satisfaction, security/risk, and transaction costs (see Figure 11).

The cluster labeled **dependency** covers the variables (in-)dependence, autonomy, leadership, and power. There are different kinds of interactions. Some include, for example, hierarchies comparable to interactions between a leader and its team, which leads to dependencies and power positions (cp. Principle Agent Theory). The cluster labeled **environment** covers the variables time, industry, and culture. The logical clustering is based on the works by SCHEIN (1985) and HOFSTEDE (2001), who combine culture with trust. The cluster labeled **future intention** covers the variables cooperation, benefit, collaboration, commitment, reciprocity, loyalty, (re-)purchase, and use of product/service. These are all actions that express future intentions of trust. The cluster labeled **person** covers the variables sociodemographics and involvement, while the cluster labeled **reputation** covers the variables reputation, quality, performance, justice, fairness value, and ethics. The basis for this logical clustering is supported by the Signaling Theory and the Game Theory (cp. HOLLER/ILLING 2003), which explain trust building through trust signals (e.g., reputation). Reputation is the hierarchical upper variables, as it mirrors the other hierarchical lower variables in the cluster. If, for example, the quality of a company's products/services and performance is high, and it still acts socially responsible, it has a high reputation (cp. SCHWAIGER 2004). The cluster labeled **satisfaction** covers the variables satisfaction and experience since satisfaction is the result of the perception of experience with a product or service, or an interaction with a trust partner (e.g., Customer Satisfaction Theory, TAYLOR 1996; HOM 2002). Consequently, satisfaction (with prior experience) seems to be the right label for the cluster. The cluster labeled **security/risk** covers the variables security, risk, conflict, and opportunism. If, for example, a partner behaves opportunistically, conflicts will occur, and the perceived risk will be high (cp. Game Theory). Thus, as a complement of perceived risk, perceived security will be low. **Transaction cost** covers variables that can be separated in ex ante and ex post transactions costs according to the Transaction Cost Theory (COASE 1937; PICOT ET AL. 2003; WILLIAMSON 1975). Ex ante transaction costs develop through variables like communication, information (sharing), and negotiation, while ex post transaction costs result from the control mechanisms used. The more an interaction partner has to be controlled, the greater the costs that arise. The final cluster **trust** in the middle of Figure 11 is that of different characterizations of trust, which include the terms belief, trustworthiness, attitude, motivation, and confidence. Since the different characterizations of trust (also see the definition of trust in this work) do not include the influences or consequences of trust, this is strictly speaking not a cluster and is therefore not taken into consideration.

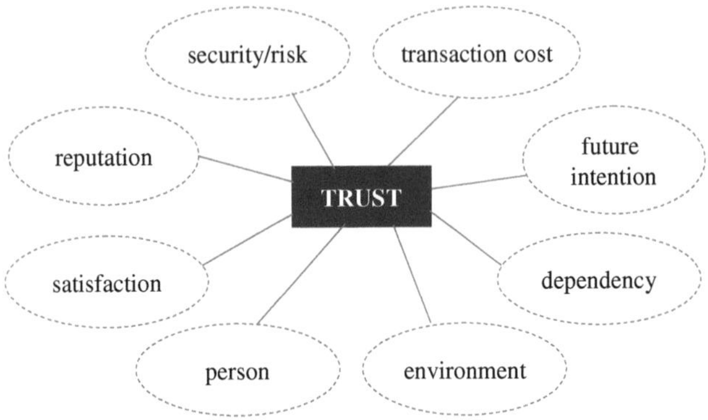

Figure 11: Labeling the clusters (EBERT ***2009, p.78)***

The possible hierarchical structuring of the key variables within each cluster will be described in the conceptualization sections (see sections 3.6 - 3.10). The clustering can be used in two ways: 1) For the optimization of measurements by identifying the most important (hierarchical upper) key variables: Thus, less important key (hierarchical lower) variables, which have already been covered by the description of the most important variables, will be omitted in the model analysis, and 2) For the development of more diagnostic conceptualizations of constructs: The cluster provide an advice for new measurement conceptualizations, which could lead for example to second-order constructs (like the new developed security construct in section 3.9).

3.3.3. The Relevant Clusters in Each Trust Interaction (P2P, P2O, and O2O)

In a following step, each cluster was filtered in respect of a specific trust interaction (interpersonal: P2P, interaction between person and organization: P2O, and inter-organizational: O2O see chapter 2) to retain the relevant clusters and find the research focus of every trust interaction and possible research gaps. The initial thought that filtering would reduce the number of clusters, turned out to be wrong. Consequently, each cluster is relevant in every trust interaction, although some are more important than others. The following figure presents the clustered key variables and trust interactions. Each closed line is one trust interaction type (P2O, P2P, and O2O). The percentage is the mean of the frequency of all the key variables in each cluster. The cluster "reputation," for example, covers the variables performance (7.7% in P2O), quality (14.5%), justice and fairness (4.8%), value (6.8%), ethics (9.2%), and reputation (8.2%). Consequently, the mean of these six values is 8.5% (see Table 2). This value is shown for the P2O trust interaction in Figure 12. By following the P2O line clockwise to the next cluster, satisfaction is reached. The cluster "satisfaction," covers the variables experience and satisfaction. Experience was listed in 9% of the P2O articles and satisfaction in 17%. Consequently, the mean (see Table 2) of these two values is 13%.

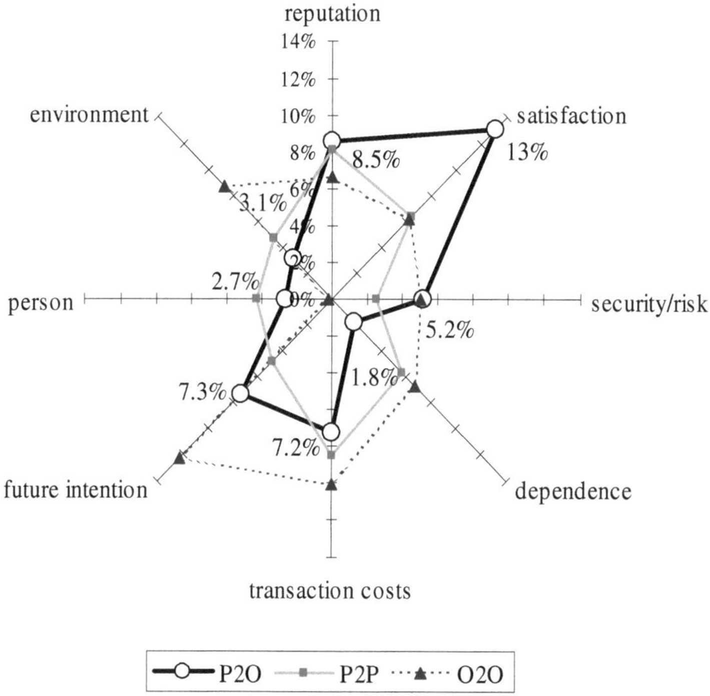

Figure 12: Clustered key variables matched with each trust interaction type (P2P, P2O, O2O) (EBERT ***2009, p.79)***

The next table shows the percentage of the mean of the frequency of all key variables in each cluster for each trust interaction type.

	reputation	satisfaction	security/risk	dependence	transaction costs	future intention	person	environment
P2O	8.5%	13.0%	5.2%	1.8%	7.2%	7.3%	2.7%	3.1%
P2P	8.1%	6.4%	2.5%	5.7%	8.5%	4.8%	4.2%	4.7%
O2O	6.6%	6.2%	5.0%	6.7%	10.0%	12.2%	0.2%	8.7%

Table 2: Percentage of the mean of the frequency of all key variables in each cluster for every trust interaction type (P2O, P2P, and O2O) (EBERT ***2009, p.80)***

The information gained about relevant clusters in trust interactions can be used to improve previous trust models (see Figure 13). They can be enhanced by including clusters as latent variables called constructs (marked with dotted line). The trust model by JOHNSON/GRAYSON (2005) (see Figure 13 a), which analyzes the relationships between the variables cognitive and affective trust, antecedents of trust and consequences of trust, can, for example, be enhanced (see Figure 13 b)). On examining the meta-analysis closely, it is apparent that performance and expertise is one of the key variables of the cluster reputation (see Figure 10). The first step is to aggregate performance and expertise under the cluster reputation, which will include performance and expertise, but also other key variables. SCHWAIGER´s (2004) reputation measurement approach provides a very detailed analysis (where the similarity construct could possibly covered through the reputation item "of all companies, my house bank is a company with which I can best identify"), but also other reputation models could be used to measure the cluster reputation. Sales effectiveness is aggregated under the cluster future intention. The second step is to include the four remaining clusters (dependency, security/risk, person, environment, and transaction costs) to cover all eight clusters found in the meta-analysis. This model promises better model results by reflecting the most important clusters in trust research.

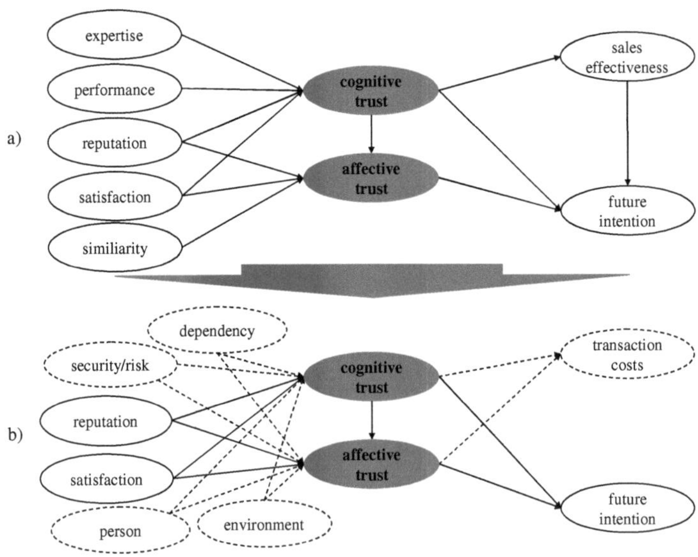

Figure 13: An example of an enhanced B2C trust model

This method can generate a detailed understanding of the factors or specific measures that build or deplete trust. It might also explain the mechanisms and processes of trust enhancement.

3.3.4. Key Contributions of the Meta-Analysis

The meta-analysis helps to define the scientific trust community. Trust research can be structured into three interaction types P2P, O2O, and P2O. The communication channel (e.g., e-commerce) can be defined as a medium in trust research. Eight main clusters have been identified in trust research. Every formed cluster participates in each interaction type (P2P, P2O, O2O). Special focal points have been identified in respect to each interaction. The focal points are, for example, "satisfaction," which has been the focus of research on P2O interactions, "future intention" and "transaction costs" found in O2O research, and the cluster "person," which has been most researched in the P2P interaction type. The results suggest that the overlap of the projection areas (see Figure 12) from the three trust interactions makes a transfer of the results from one projected area to another possible. The key contribution could be the transfer of results from, for example, P2O (e.g., B2C) to O2O (e.g., B2B). In other words, if new empirical studies identify new trust building measures in a business-to-consumer relationship, it could be possible, that these measures are the same for a business-to-business relationship even if the strengths of effect could be different. Existing trust models can be enhanced by including further important clusters (constructs), which lead to improved results regarding trust building antecedents or consequences (see Figure 12). The results of this meta-analysis will be used as a framework for the development of a trust model and the conceptualization of the constructs.

3.4. Relevance and Conceptualization of Clusters for B2C Trust Interactions

The focus of this work lies in person-to-organization (P2O)[16] trust interactions and especially in business-to-consumer trust (B2C). Therefore, P2P and O2O, and minimal relevant clusters for P2O trust interactions will be excluded from further research.

3.4.1. Relevant Clusters in B2C Trust Interactions

It is now important to reduce P2O interactions further by focusing on B2C, which will exclude "organizational trust" from P2O. "Organizational trust" is an organizational member's trust in its own organization (a sub-category of P2O). The cluster (see Figure 12) "dependency" (1.8%) is mainly connected to "organizational trust" or important in an B2B relationship as Ganesan (1994) states. In B2C relationships in the banking industry, German consumers tend to have more than one bank (see results of the main empirical study in section 4.2). Dependency seems to be a minor issue for answering the research question and will thus be excluded from the theoretical model. Consequently, the cluster "dependency" will not be considered in the further analysis.

---

16 P2O can also be defined as O2P, because interactions can go both ways. For this work, P2O has been selected, as the consumer is the main focus. Thus, B2C is a sub-category of P2O (=O2P).

The seven clusters (see Figure 12) satisfaction (mean of 13%), reputation (8.5%), future intention (7.3%), transaction costs (7.2%), security/risk (5.2%), environment (3.1%), and person (2.7%) play a particularly important role in **B2C trust interaction**.

To address the research question what organizations can do to build up trust, a further structuring of the clusters is needed. The **remaining seven clusters** have to be grouped into four characteristics: Organization, customer, environment, and the relationship itself. **Organizational characteristics** are represented by the clusters "reputation" and "security/risk." They are the two clusters where trust building measures can be deduced. **Customer characteristics** are mirrored by the cluster "person" and "satisfaction." They are regarded as measuring the influence of each customer's personality. Satisfaction, one of the most important clusters, has an ambiguous character, which will be discussed in section 3.10.1. A highly satisfied customer is a result of high quality services or products, thus satisfaction might be considered a lever for trust building measures. However, satisfaction also depends on customer expectations. Customers who have low expectations are easier satisfied with the services that an organization - such as a bank - offers than customers who have high expectations will be with the same services. Thus, satisfaction is strongly dependent on the person and will therefore be considered as a personal characteristic.

The **relationship characteristics** are defined by the clusters "transaction costs" and "future intention." Each trust interaction in B2C leads to ex ante or ex post costs for both the organization (e.g., advertisement) and the customer (switching costs). Theory states that high trust decreases transactions costs (PICOT ET AL. 2003). Since the focus of this work is on trust building measures and not on costs, the interesting question of how much costs can be saved, and thus, the cluster "transaction costs" will not be analyzed in this trust model. Loyalty will be included in the model as a suitable variable for future intentions (see section 2.3).

Environmental characteristics, the final characteristic, is only mirrored by the cluster "environment." Contrary to all the other characteristics, environment is given fixed values in the analysis. Therefore, the specification "environment" is defined by the key variables industry (banking business), culture (Germany), and time (long-term relationship, which is what bank customers are generally interested in).

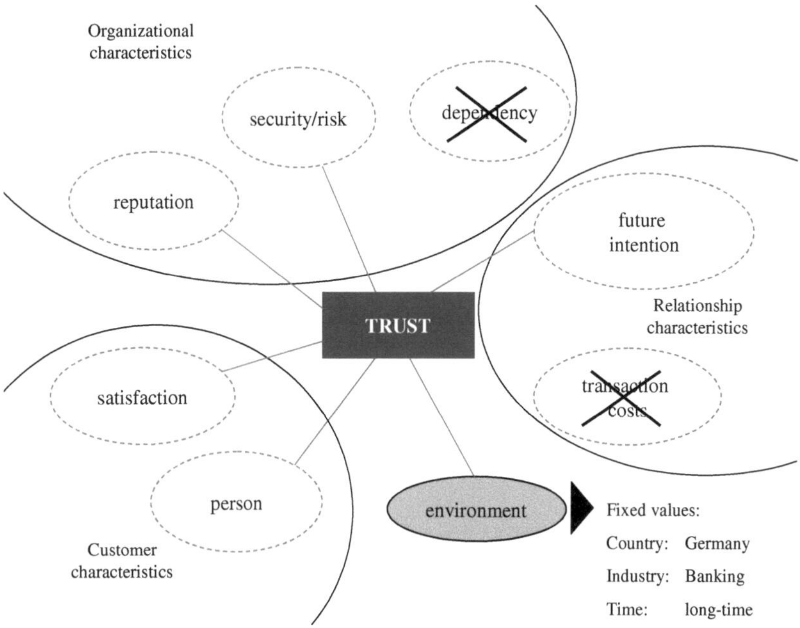

Figure 14: Six remaining clusters for the B2C trust model

The **conceptualization** of trust antecedents includes the concrete definition, as well as the characterization of clusters as an antecedent, mediator or moderator. This need to characterize constructs is the result for building a structural equation model.

Structural equation models (SEM) are suitable for measuring relationships between unobservable variables (ROSSITER 2002), i.e., perceived reputation and consumer trust. Using structural equation modeling in research leads to two main problems (EGGERT ET AL. 2005): First, in many structural equation models, mediating effects are implicitly tested, but not explicitly; second, moderating effects in structural equation models are often not considered in research, even if the literature stresses the importance of recognizing moderators to understand complex relationships. If these two facts are not considered, there is a lack of model validity and relevance. Consequently, it is essential that moderators and mediators are considered and structural equation modeling is the relevant method in this work.

Within the area of **recent trust research**, **moderators and mediators** have not as yet been sufficiently considered. Thus, these types of variables are of special interest to this work and will be taken into consideration in the analysis.

3.4.2. Moderators and Mediators in Structural Equation Modeling in Consumer Trust Research

Today, the term **moderator** is understood as someone who manages an interaction of several individuals. It is derived from the Latin word *moderare* and means "to steer" or "to direct." In general, a moderator variable affects the direction and/or strength of a relationship between an independent[17] and a dependent[18] variable. The moderator is a third variable that affects the zero-order correlation[19] between two other variables and can be either a qualitative or quantitative variable. The moderator variable should not be correlated with the independent and dependent variables to provide a clear interpretation of the interaction term. On the same level, independent variables and moderators have similar natures and, as causal variables, are similarly exogenous or antecedent to certain criterion effects. Consequently, moderator variables always act as independent variables (BARON/KENNY 1986, p. 1174).

The following figure demonstrates the relationship between the variables.

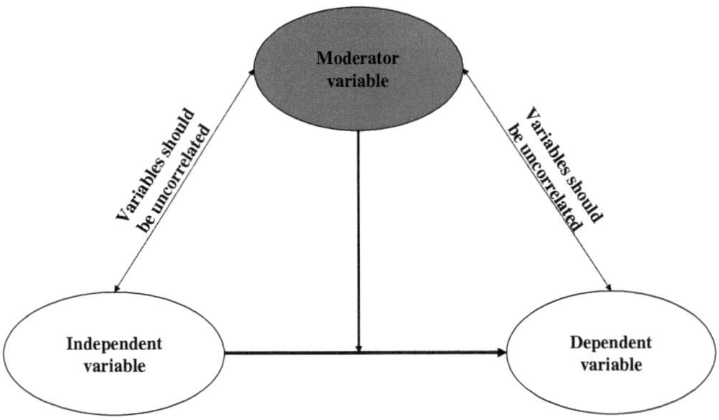

Figure 15: Moderator relationship between a dependent and an independent variable (according to BARON/KENNY 1986, p. 1174)

Conversely, **mediators** explain how or why such effects occur. Different mediator variables, like transformation and information processes, are internal to the organism and are connected to the stimuli and behavior (BARON/KENNY 1986, p. 1176).

17 Often also called a predictor and exogenous variable (BACKHAUS ET AL. 2006, p. 50).

18 Often also called a criterion and endogenous variable (BACKHAUS ET AL. 2006, p. 50).

19 The zero-order correlation is the relationship between two variables, which ignores the impact of other variables in a prediction (BARON/KENNY 1986, p. 1174).

In order to obtain a way of mathematically calculating path coefficients, "A," "B," and "C" are introduced. The **relationship between the independent and the mediator variable** is called "A," the relationship between the dependent and the mediator variable is called "B," and the relationship between the independent and dependent variable is called "C." The result of the paths A x B should be significantly higher than path C in respect of a mediating effect (BARON/KENNY 1986, p. 1176). The following figure demonstrates the relationship between these variables.

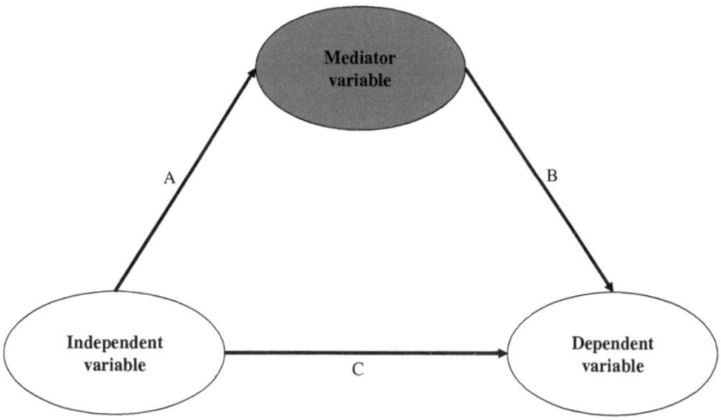

Figure 16: Mediator relationship between a dependent and an independent variable (according to BARON/KENNY 1986, p. 1176)

To explain the **moderator and mediator** relationship, an example is provided, which is based on the Signaling Theory. Signaling is not only mentioned in the game theory (e.g., HOLLER/ILLING 2003, p. 124), but is also covered by another, separate theory called the Signaling Theory. This theory, which is already recognized in trust research, is strongly influenced by Game Theory thinking (MÖLLERING 2006, p. 41). Signals support the identification of an interacting partner as either trustworthy or untrustworthy during the relationship, while deciding which strategy is most efficient to achieve equilibrium. Assessing a partner before a contract is concluded can reinforce the feeling that the partner is trustworthy and will not act opportunistically (the assessment of the likelihood is a subjective assessment by means of "gut instinct"). The contrary is to evaluate the partner during the relationship by calculating the assessment by means of the interacting partner's observable signals (i.e., guarantee promises).

Bank customers try to find meaningful signals and information about a banking organization to decide whether or not the organization is trustworthy. These signals are the trust **antecedents** that can be built by means of trust building measures. On the basis of perceived trustworthiness, the consumer calculates the costs (risk/loss) and values (gains) (**mediating effect**) of trusting an organization.

Personal characteristics (e.g., those of the consumer) **moderate** signals given by organizations (e.g., banks). These personal characteristics cannot or can hardly be influenced by organizations. This means that the strength of the impact of organizational measures is influenced by personal characteristics, like trust propensity. Depending on what a person's characteristics (e.g., trust propensity) are, organizational characteristics (likeability, competence, and security) could have a stronger or less strong impact on consumer trust. This result will lead to a conclusion regarding the extent to which an organization can influence consumer trust, if at all, and how much of this trust originates from the consumer himself. In other words, if, for example, the consumer has a low trust propensity, even a high reputation and security will not have a strong impact on this consumer's trust. Conversely, if the consumer has a high trust propensity, reputation and security will have a strong impact on the consumer's trust. The described effects are indicated in the following figure.

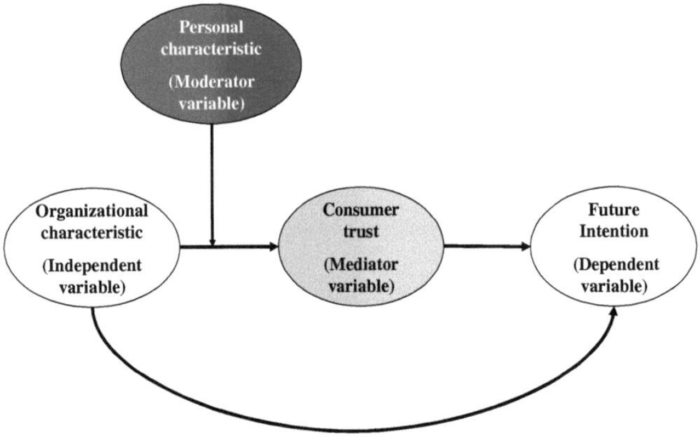

Figure 17: Example of mediating and moderating effects

Having introduced the characteristics of moderators and mediators in general, the **clusters** defined in the meta-analysis will be classified as antecedents, moderators, or mediators.

In this study, the organizational signals and, thus, trust antecedents are "reputation" and "security." Moderator variables are defined by "person" and "satisfaction." The mediating variables are trust dimensions, as they entail the internal information evaluation process of organizational signals ("reputation" and "security") by the consumer. Trust lies between organizational signals ("reputation" and "security") and future intention ("loyalty") and thus mediates this relationship (see Figure 17).

3.5. PLS as the Preferred Approach to Structural Equation Modeling

The clear advantage of structural equation models (SEM) is the analysis of relationships between several constructs. SEM became an accepted standard method in research (BAUMGARTNER/HOMBURG 1996; HILDEBRANDT 2004; HILDEBRANDT/HOMBURG 1998; HOMBURG/BAUMGARTNER 1995). There are two main methods for analyzing SEM – LISREL (Linear Structural Relations) and PLS (Partial Least Squares). LISREL is the covariance-based analysis of SEM developed by JÖRESKOG (1967; JÖRESKOG/SÖRBOM 2001) and PLS the variance-based analysis of SEM (WOLD 1966). In recent years, PLS – whose structural equation modeling **mathematical basis** was designed by BETZIN/HENSELER (2005, p. 49) – has become increasingly established in research (BLIEMEL ET AL. 2005, p. 22). Various authors have discussed the advantages, disadvantages, and the differences between the various methods, as well as providing concrete recommendations in respect of the specific method that should be used under specific circumstances (SCHOLDERER/BALDERJAHN 2005, p. 87; HERRMANN ET AL. 2006).

LISREL can only be used for very large surveys and a manageable number of variables with well-defined measuring structures, as it provides error-corrected estimates and statistical evaluations of models with co-variance structures. In contrast, PLS is appropriate for small sample sizes, as it enables robust forecasting of fuzzy defined criterion variables through fuzzy defined predictor variables, and a high number of observable variables.

The following table shows the differences between PLS and LISREL in detail.

Criterion	PLS	LISREL
Goal	forecasting orientated	parameter orientated
Method approach	variance-based analysis	covariance-based analysis
Assumptions	specification of predictor	multi normality and independent observations
Parameter estimator	consistent if the sample size and number of indicators are large (largely consistent)	consistent
Latent variable	explicitly estimated values	values not determined
Measurement model	reflective and/or formative	reflective
Specification of theory	Flexible	High
Complexity of model	analysis of highly complex models is possible	limited
Sample size	also appropriate for small samples	large (200 plus)
Implications	optimal for forecasting accuracy	optimal for parameter accuracy

Table 3: Comparison of the PLS and LISREL method (BLIEMEL ET AL. 2005, p. 11)

Four main criteria selected from Table 3 will explain why **PLS is the more suitable** method to provide answers to the research question: "How can banks engender trust in consumers?" Firstly, due to the goal of predicting the main construct trust through the drivers as possible. Secondly, PLS offers the possibility to analyze formative constructs used in the theoretical model. The research question implies that a formative specification should be used to analyze possible adjusting levers. PLS is able to analyze models with formatively and reflectively specified constructs, whereas LISREL was designed to analyze models with reflectively specified constructs. Thirdly, PLS can deal with high complexity (18 constructs). Even mediator and moderator variables can be identified and quantified by means of PLS (EGGERT ET AL. 2005, p. 101) and are important sources for further research implications. Fourth, fewer[20] data sets suffice to evaluate the SEM. Consequently, all the arguments underline this work's preference for PLS.

3.5.1. Types of Measurement Models in SEM

There are two **types of specification** of constructs – the reflective and the formative specifications. The specification chosen depends mainly on the research objectives as each specification type leads to different research implications. The following mathematical equations for reflective and formative constructs are used by smartPLS, but also provide an evaluation of construct validity. Since the present empirical study needs both reflectively and formatively specified constructs, both types are described in the next paragraphs.

The **reflective specification** provides answers on construct consequences. Observable consequences are indicators that are reflective (FORNELL/BOOKSTEIN 1982, p. 441) or effects (BOLLEN/LENNOX 1991, p. 305). The occurrences of observable variables (consequences) are caused by unobservable variables. The typical function of a reflective model is defined (EDWARDS/BAGOZZI 2000, p. 161) as:

$$\mathrm{X} = \Lambda_x \eta + \Delta$$

The symbol X is the vector of the indicators $(x_1, x_2, ..., x_n)$, Λ_x represents the weighting vector $(\lambda_1, \lambda_2, \lambda_3, ..., \lambda_n)$ of the indicators, Δ is the vector of the residual values $(\delta_1, \delta_2, ..., \delta_n)$, and r_{ij} (i=1,...q; j=1,...,q) are the correlation coefficients. In a reflective measurement model, changes in the construct η lead to a change in all the observable variables $(x_1, x_2, ..., x_n)$. If the indicators measure the construct without any errors, the correlation coefficients r_{ij} between the indicators would be +/-1 (see Figure 18).

[20] The extent of the survey should be ten times the number of indicators of the most complex formative construct and the highest number of the exogenous constructs, which affect an endogenous construct (CHIN 1998).

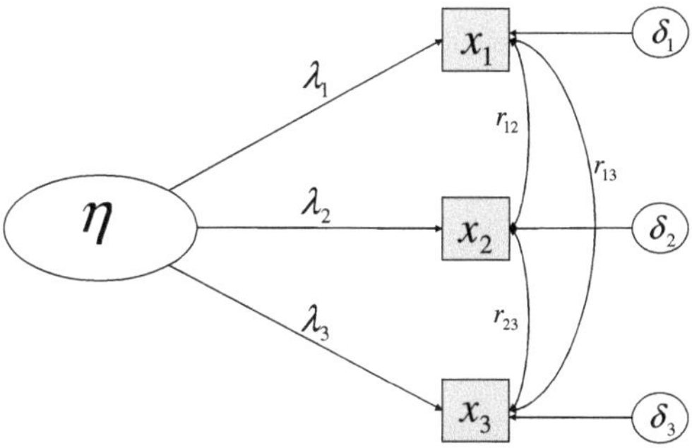

Figure 18: Reflective measurement model with three indicators according to BOLLEN/LENNOX (1991, p. 306)

In a reflective measurement model, all indicators should be highly correlated, which leads to high correlation coefficients r_{ij}. A typical example of a reflectively specified construct is the measurement of human traits like parsimony, which can be observed through special types of behavior (buy cheapest products, save money), defined as indicators (ROSSITER 2002, p. 316). If a human trait were to change from parsimonious to generosity, all the indicators that define parsimony would change as well (buy expensive product, spend money).

In contrast, by examining **formative specification,** the drivers or operating levers of certain constructs can be analyzed instead of the consequences. The observable drivers here are indicators, which are called "formative" (FORNELL/BOOKSTEIN 1982, p. 441; BAGOZZI 1994, p. 332; EDWARDS/BAGOZZI 2000, p. 162) or "causes" (BLALOCK 1964, p. 163; BOLLEN/LENNOX 1991, p. 306). The typical function of formative specification is defined (BOLLEN/LENNOX 1991, p. 306) as:

$$\eta = \lambda_1 x_1 + \lambda_2 x_2 + ... + \lambda_q x_q + \zeta$$

The coefficients $\lambda_1, \lambda_2, \lambda_3, ..., \lambda_n$ define the loadings of the indicators to their construct η. The term for error is symbolized by ζ (see Figure 19).

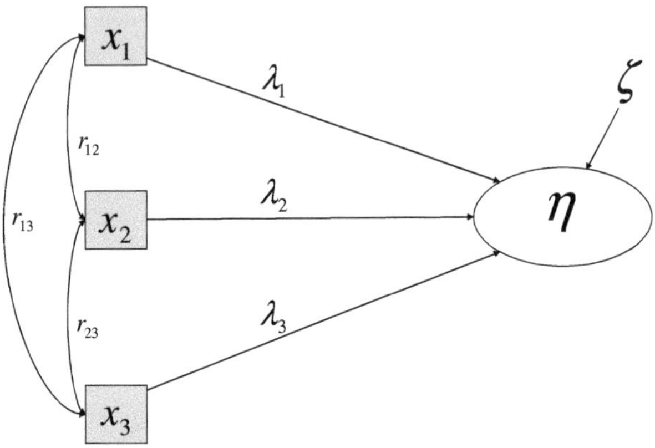

Figure 19: Formative measurement model with three indicators according to BOLLEN/LENNOX (1991, p. 306)

In a formative measurement model, the observable variables $x_1, x_2, ..., x_n$ cause the construct. Thus, changes in the indicators lead to a change in the construct. In contrast to the reflective measurement, a change in the construct does not automatically imply a change in all the indicators (JARVIS ET AL. 2003, p. 201). Furthermore, these indicators are not compatible and cannot be exchanged with others as is possible with the reflective measurement. All indicators that cause the construct have to be considered in the measurement to guarantee a comprehensive examination of that construct. An example of a formative measurement model is the construct "status" of a person, which is caused by the indicators education, income, and prestige of the job (HAUSER 1973, p. 268).

The following figure illustrates the two types of measurement models in a SEM with its independent and dependent latent variables (constructs).

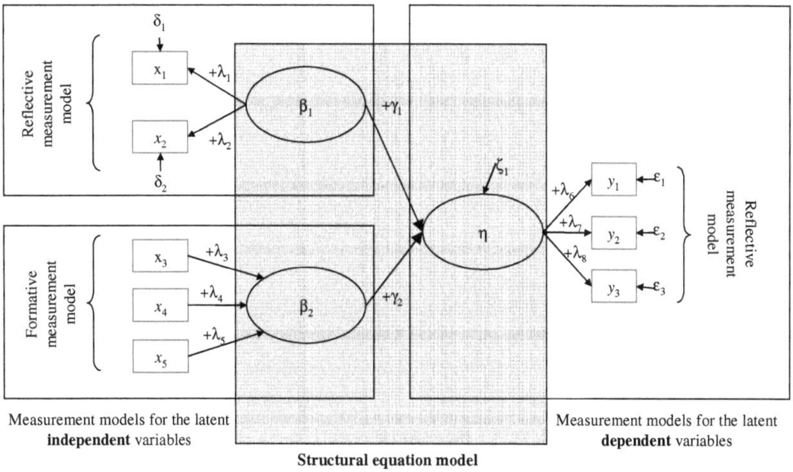

x_i, y_i = indicators
β_j = latent independent variables
ζ_k = error term for latent dependent variables
δ_i = error term for independent indicator variables x_i
η = latent dependent variables
ε_i = error term for dependent indicator variables y_i
λ, γ = weighting coefficients (+/- shows hypothetical direction)

Figure 20: Reflective and formative measurement models in a SEM

The evaluation of the two types of measurement models and the structural equation model's validity is discussed in the subsequent section.

3.5.2. Decision Rules for and Validity of Reflective and Formative Measurement Models

Choosing a formative measurement approach opens the possibility to analyze empirically trust building measures, which is the converse of the reflective specification, and would result in drivers of trust were trust building measures have to be deduced theoretically in a second step. However, only identifying **formatively specified** constructs from the trust literature is not as easy as it seems. Although the formative model approach can be traced back to CURTIS/JACKSON (1962, p. 199), the peak of the discussion on the formative and/or reflective specification of constructs has largely occurred during the last two decades (DIAMANTOPOULOS ET AL. 2008; BOLLEN/LENNOX 1991; EWARDS/BAGOZZI 2000; JARVIS ET AL. 2003; and EBERL 2006). Meta-analyses indicate that 96% of all constructs in marketing journals are operationalized reflectively (JARVIS ET AL. 2003; FASSOTT 2006). Furthermore, MACKENZIE ET AL. (2005) found that one third of reflective constructs have been misspecified. Consequently, all operationalizations of constructs taken from literature published before

2005 and/or not specifically discussed concerning their specification should be carefully discussed and modified if necessary.

The goal to answer – what trust building measures are – and to analyze them in an empirical and quantitatively way is only possible over a formative specification of the trust drivers. Therefore, it is important to discuss the specification type of found trust drivers in the literature. Reflective constructs can also be used to deduce trust building measures by theory. In both cases, misspecification of constructs must be corrected to a clear reflective or formative specification of the trust driver. Otherwise determinants and consequences of constructs are mix up and lead to wrong path coefficients and model results. Furthermore, trust building measures (in form of indicators) gained through the expert interviews are added to some of the operationalizations. Some of the indicators of constructs are adjusted a little bit to fit better in the context of banking services. In these cases it is necessary to decide if these indicators belong to a formative or reflective approach.

The answer to whether observable variables (indicators) are caused by a construct (=reflective) or cause the construct (=formative) themselves can be ascertained through experiments (EDWARDS/BAGOZZI 2000, p. 159), the TETRAD test (BOLLEN/TING 2000), or by answering a list of questions that various authors have developed (FORNELL/BOOKSTEIN 1982; BAGOZZI 1984; BOLLEN 1989; DIAMANTOPOULOS/WINKLHOFER 2001; FORNELL 1989; MACCALLUM/BROWNE 1993; LAW/WONG 1999; ROSSITER 2002; CHIN 1998; JARVIS ET AL. 2003). This latter list of questions (decision rules), which was developed by JARVIS ET AL. (2003, p. 203), is often used to help identify indicators gained from theory and interviews (see Chapter 3) on a reflective or formative measurement. The questions even uncover misspecifications of constructs in theory. Consequently, this work applies these **decision rules** (see Table 4) to ascertain whether observable variables belong to a reflective or formative measurement of the construct used in the trust model.

Direction of causality from the construct to the measure implied by the conceptual definition
1. Do the indicators define the characteristics (formative model) or manifestations (reflective model) of the construct?
2. Would changes in the indicators cause changes in the construct (formative model) or not (reflective model)?
3. Would changes in the construct cause changes in the indicators (reflective model) or not (formative model)?
Interchangeability of indicators
4. Should the indicators have the same or similar content? Do they share a common theme? (Yes: Reflective model; usually not: Formative model)
5. Would omitting one of the indicators alter the conceptual domain of the construct? (No: Reflective model; possibly: Formative model)
Covariation between the indicators
6. Could a change in one of the indicators be associated with changes in the other indicators? (Yes: Reflective model; not necessarily: Formative model)
Nomological net of the construct indicators
7. Are the indicators expected to have the same antecedents and consequences? (Yes: Reflective model; not required: Formative model)

Table 4: Decision rules for determining whether a construct is formative or reflective according to JARVIS ET AL. (2003, p. 203)

After the decision whether the indicator fits in a reflective or formative approach, all measurements or operationalizations of the constructs must be analyzed for **validity and reliability** (BORSBOOM ET AL. 2004; PETER/CHURCHILL 1986). A measurement's validity is given if the composite structure (construct consisting of many indicators) measures what it is supposed to measure. It is the extent to which a measurement represents characteristics found in the phenomenon under investigation (MALHOTRA/BIRKS 2007, p. 358). Systematic errors between a construct's observed score and a theoretically modeled score will determine whether a measure is valid. There is a high reliability when random errors are minimized as analyzed by means of repeated or equivalent measures of the same persons or objects.

The achievement of high validity and high reliability, as well as the evaluation of the specification type of each construct in the trust literature and the enhanced scale development (selection and number of indicators) is possible against the background of two main types of Operationalization processes in the literature (CHURCHILL 1979; ROSSITER 2002).
CHURCHILL (1979, pp. 66) proposes a step-wise procedure to develop measures for reflectively specified constructs. First, all relevant indicators, which are important to define

the constructs, should be analyzed through a literature review and/or interviews. A "universe" of items belonging to one content construct should be analyzed. This procedure is called the domain specification of the construct and domain sampling (NUNNALLY 1967, p. 175, NUNNALLY/BERNSTEIN 1994, p. 216). The required quality criterions have to be calculated to purify the scale (to reduce the "universe" and, thus, the number of items and to select suitable ones) in order to obtain high validity and high reliability in respect of the reflective measurements.

The **reliability of a reflective measurement model** can be tested by means of the software smartPLS, for example, by the quality criteria that are loaded/weighted through "Cronbach´s alpha" and "composite reliability".

In a reflective measurement model, the loadings/weighting are equivalent to the correlations of one construct's indicators. High values in respect of **Cronbach´s alpha** [21] (above 0.7, see PETERSON 1994; CRONBACH/MEEHL 1955) mirror high correlations between indicators, which are preferable for the measurement and are arrived at by eliminating "wrong" items (items with a low item-to-item correlation). If there are 2 or 3 indicators, the values in respect of Cronbach´s alpha should be above 0.4 (PETER 1997, p. 180). Consequently, the scale becomes more reliable, smaller, and thus manageable. A high item-to-item correlation (values 0.7 – 1.0) result in all observable variables (indicators) changing simultaneously in the same direction if the underlying reflectively specified construct changes. Furthermore, through smartPLS's bootstrapping procedure, it is possible to test every indicator's level of significance.

Composite reliability (construct reliability) analyzes the strength of all indicators' correlations with their construct. The bootstrapping procedure calculates the composite reliability and should be above 0.6 (BAGOZZI/YI 1988).

SmartPLS can test a **reflective measurement model's validity**. The bootstrapping procedure of smartPLS is able to analyze the discriminate validity through the **average variance extracted (AVE)** by using the standardized estimation values of the indicators and constructs. Discriminant validity belongs to construct validity, which is one of the three validity types researchers can assess: Content validity, criterion validity, and construct validity. Content validity is a subjective but systematic evaluation of how well the content of a scale represents the construct, which is important for the formative measurements that will be discussed later. Scale indicators should adequately cover the entire domain of the construct (see CHURCHILL 1979). Criterion validity examines whether the measurement scale performs as expected in relation to other selected variables' meaningful criteria (MALHOTRA/BIRKS 2007, p. 358). The main validity is the construct validity, which includes convergent, nomological, and

[21] Cronbach´s alpha is the average of all possible split-half coefficients resulting from different ways of splitting the scale indicators (MALHOTRA/BIRKS 2007, p. 358).

discriminant validity. Convergent validity is the extent to which the scale correlates positively with other measurements of the same construct. Nomological validity is the degree to which a construct behaves as it should within a system of related constructs. Discriminant validity is the extent to which a measure does not correlate with other distinct constructs concepts (BAGOZZI/PHILLIPS 1982, p. 469). Discriminant validity analyzes whether the construct has more variance with the own indicators than with others. The AVE of the constructs should be higher than the squared correlations between the constructs (FORNELL/LARCKER 1981, p. 46), while the AVE value should be above 0.5 (HOMBURG/BAUMGARTNER 1995, p. 361).

The following table summarizes the quality criteria for reflective constructs as calculated by smartPLS.

Quality criterions (Output smartPLS)	Limit	Source
Cronbach's Alpha	≥ 0.7	PETERSON 1994
in the case of 2 to 3 indicators	≥ 0.4	PETER 1997
Composite (construct) reliability	≥ 0.6	BAGOZZI/YI 1988
Average variance extracted (AVE)	≥ 0.5	HOMBURG/BAUMGARTNER 1995

Table 5: Quality criteria for the evaluation of reflectively specified constructs by smartPLS

As mentioned before, the trust model includes reflective as well as formative measurement models. Formative measurements are much more difficult to develop than reflective measurements, because there is a lack of scale evaluation measures (reliability and validity). In **formative measurement approaches**, the overlap between complementary indicators should be minimized, but the regression's R square (R^2) should be maximized (CHIN 1998). R^2 is called the coefficient of determination and compares the explained variance (variance of the model's predictions) with the total variance (of the data). Trying to minimize the overlap between indicators leads to the problem, that a reduction in the scale produces different effects than those that reflective measurement produces. Omitting an indicator in the formative measurement would lead to a part of the construct being omitted. The relevant influencing factors that result in the construct would therefore be left out (BERGVIST/ROSSITER 2007, p. 176). Consequently, all relevant indicators that cause the construct must be considered and it is therefore impossible to calculate the measuring error (BOLLEN/LENNOX 1991, p. 306; EBERL 2004, p. 5; FORNELL/BOOKSTEIN 1982, p. 441).

As a result of considering all indicators, the correlation of the indicators must not approach -/+1, as the indicators can be uncorrelated. Thus, the evaluation of the quality of the scale (**reliability**) through, for example, Cronbach´s alpha as in the reflective measurement, is not possible. However, when high correlations occur, multicollinearity[22] problems arise (JARVIS

[22] A perfect multicollinearity is at hand if the correlation between two independent variables is equal to 1 or -1.

ET AL. 2003, p. 202; EBERL 2004, p. 9; EBERL/ZINNBAUER 2004, p. 5; CASSEL ET AL. 2000; BOLLEN/LENNOX 1991, p. 377). A high multicollinearity of the regression coefficients, indicated by a variance inflation factor (VIF)[23] above 10, is problematic in a formative measurement. It should be avoided, and a VIF below 4 is preferable (DIAMANTOPOULOS/ SIGUAW 2002, p. 270). The VIF can be calculated with a standard static program, e.g. SPSS. Multicollinearity can also be identified through the correlation matrix. **Bivariate correlations** between indicators which are near the value "1" are a sign for multicollinearity. To achieve a significant relationship (weight) between the indicator and construct, the **weights** measured by smartPLS should be at least above 0.1 (LOHMÖLLER 1989) or better above 0.2 (CHIN 1998, p. 324). The level of **significance of weights** can be calculated by the bootstrapping procedure (critical ratio).

In contrast to the discriminant validity used in reflective measurement, the **validity of formatively specified constructs** can only be evaluated regarding **content validity**. ROSSITER (2002) developed a new procedure and enhanced the four-step model by DIAMANTOPOULOS/ WINKELHOFER (2001, p. 271)[24] for developing measures, especially in terms of a construct's content plausibility and measurement validity, thus avoiding unnecessary indicators. This procedure is called C-OAR-SE. The main criticism of content validity is its subjectiveness, but EBERL (2006, p. 98) demonstrates how subjectiveness can be minimized through three main quality criteria: Content specification, indicator relevance, and external validity.

The following table summarizes the quality criteria for formatively constructs as calculated by smartPLS.

Quality criterions (Output smartPLS)	Limit	Source
Bivariate correlations	Not near the value „1“	BLIEMEL ET AL. (2005)
Weights (path coefficient from indicator to the formative construct)	> 0,1 > 0.2	LOHMÖLLER (1989) CHIN (1998)
Critical Ratio (t-value: Significance of path coefficients)	> z1-α/2 (~ N(0;1); e.g. 1.96 for α= 5%) through the bootstrapping procedure	BACKHAUS ET AL. (2006)

Table 6: Quality criteria for the evaluation of formatively specified constructs by smartPLS

Quality criteria are important for evaluating reflective and formative constructs with more than one indicator. There is an ongoing and new discussion on single (one indicator) vs. multi-item (more than one indicator) measurements of reflectively specified constructs.

23 The VIF is the reciprocal value of tolerance (= 1 – R^2).

24 The four steps were: Content design, indicator design, multicollinearity, and external validity (DIAMANTOPOULOS/ WINKELHOFER 2001, p. 271).

Single-item measurements reduce questionnaires to a minimum and make a survey more manageable, but less informative. Complex models with a rather large number of constructs – like the model for trust building measures – specifically need an optimized scale to reduce the data collection time (e.g., through interviews) (DROTLET/MORRISON 2001, p. 196; HOMBURG/RUDOLPH 1997, p. 46) and costs (KWON/TRAIL 2005, p. 72; WANOUS ET AL. 1997, p. 250; NAGY 2002, p. 77; SLOAN ET AL. 2002, p. 480; GORSUCH/MCFARLAND 1972, p. 53; BERGKVIST/ROSSITER 2007, p. 176). Taking this aspect into account will result in the trust model only making use of single items for a few constructs.
There are **two types of single-item measurements**: First, a common single-item measurement for observable variables such as age, gender, and education (KWON/TRAIL 2005; ROSSITER 2002); second, single-item measurement for unobservable variables like psychological constructs (CHURCHILL 1979; WANOUS ET AL. 1997; KWON/TRAIL 2005). In marketing science, the measurement of unobservable variables was first carried out by means of with a single indicator (DIAMANTOPOULOS/WINKELHOFER 2001; HOMBURG/GIERING 1998; BERGKVIST/ROSSITER 2007; JACOBY 1978). Since it is more difficult to ascertain unobservable variables directly, the multi-item measurement of complex constructs was only established at the end of the 1970s. The measurement of complex unobservable variables through a multi-item measurement mainly became common through the works of CHURCHILL (1979), PETER (1979), and JACOBY (1978).

Nevertheless, researchers do accept single-item measurements of simple constructs or single dimensions of constructs that are defined by one indicator (ROSSITER 2002; BERGKVIST/ROSSITER 2007; KWON/TRAIL 2005; NUNNALLY 1967). The present discussion on the usage of single-item measurement of constructs (unobservable variables) should be regarded as a further development of measurement approaches. However, many of these discussions are often only a critical analysis of when a single-item measurement is suitable and when a multi-item measurement is not appropriate. On the other hand, previous multi-item measurements tended to achieve high Cronbach's alpha (high internal consistency reliability) through the addition of highly correlated, but unnecessary and often conceptually inappropriate, indicators (ROSSITER 2002).

BERGKVIST/ROSSITER (2007) compare the **predictive validity of single-item** and multiple-item measures of attitude and conclude that constructs that consist of a concrete singular object (i.e. one object that is easily and uniformly imagined) and a concrete attribute i.e. easily and uniformly imagined) should be measured with a single item. Customer satisfaction is a suitable example. Initially, this was measured with one indicator (YI 1990, p. 71; DANAHER/HADDRELL 1996, p. 5); later, multi-item measurements were taken (BEARDEN/TEEL 1983; p. 23; CHURCHILL/SURPRENANT 1982, p. 495; OLIVER 1980, p. 463; RUST/ZAHORIK 1993, p. 201), but currently single-item measurements are again used to measure global customer satisfaction (KOOT 2005, p. 160; FESTGE 2006, p. 105). This change justifies single-item measurements of some constructs in the presented trust model.

3.5.3. Validation of Structural Equation Models

The evaluation of the structural equation model had to be done by taking fewer quality criterions into consideration (RINGLE 2004a, p. 9) than the covariance structural analysis did (LISREL/AMOS). WOLD (1980) recommends tests that accommodate the distribution without bias concerning estimations and assumptions. Partial least squares models cannot be evaluated by estimation criteria for the determination of goodness of covariance. It is necessary to use estimation-orientated goodness criteria, which are also non-parametric. Therefore, the criteria were analyzed by means of the Stone-Geisser test for the estimation of assimilation relevance (Q^2), the Fornell-Larcker criterion for the estimation of the average extracted variance, and bootstrapping as well as jackknifing approaches to diagnose the stability of the estimation.

The evaluation of **SEM validity** can be done through R^2, path coefficients, "effect size" (f^2), the Stone-Geisser test (Q^2), and "redundancy," as well as mediator and moderator effects, all of which are explained next.

The criterion R^2 is suitable for the evaluation of the structural equation model. It is gained through the regression analysis' statistical approach (CHIN/NEWSTED 1999, p. 316). In a multi-linear regression model, the latent exogene variables represent the independent variables, while the latent endogene variable presents the dependent variable. According to CHIN (1998), an R^2 above 0.67 is substantial; above 0.33 is average; above 0.19 is poor; and under 0.19 is not relevant. High R^2 is preferable, but not the primary goals when compared to studies in which main constructs in the study have to be explained as well as possible (HOMBURG/BAUMGARTNER 1995, p. 172).

Path coefficients can be interpreted as standardized beta-coefficients (GÖTZ/LIEHR-GOBBERS 2004) and describe the relationship between constructs. The path coefficients should be above 0.1 (SELLIN/KEEVES 1994), Significance is measured by the boostrapping procedure in smartPLS.

Effect size (f^2) is the degree of the exogenous construct's affect on the endogenous construct. It analyzes whether one independent latent variable has a substantial impact on the dependent latent variable (CHIN 1998, p. 316). According to COHEN (1988, pp. 412), f^2 values around 0.35 imply a strong impact on the dependent latent variable, values around 0.15 a medium impact, and values around 0.02 very little impact.

The evaluation of the estimation relevance (Q^2), which recognizes cross-validation approaches and the results of the Stone-Geisser test (GEISSER 1975; STONE 1974), can be done in smartPLS through the blindfolding procedure. When Q^2 is above "0," the model has estimation relevance. Values under "0" imply that the model lacks estimation relevance, which leads to a doubtful determination of the latent variable. The criterion "cross validated

redundancy," which evaluates the measurement models, can also be used to evaluate the entire structural equation model. The cross-validated redundancy coefficient is obtained if prediction is made by those latent variables that predict the block in question. Cross-validated redundancy measures the predictive relevance of a structural equation model, if the range lies between "0" and "1" (CHIN 1998, p. 318).
The significance of mediator and moderator variables can be analyzed by the bootstrapping procedure and the VAF in smartPLS.

The previous sections explained that the measuring of constructs must be accurate. Thus, the conceptualization and operationalization of constructs such as consumer trust, reputation, security, loyalty, trust propensity, satisfaction, and involvement, which are relevant for the trust model need to be discussed and carefully tested regarding their validity and reliability. To guarantee the highest level of results, the conceptualization and operationalization of each construct is discussed and summarized in each section.

3.6. Measurement of Consumer Trust

The goal of the present empirical study is the conceptualization of consumer trust as an attitude construct, which implies three dimensions – the **affective, cognitive and conative dimensions** (see Chapter 2). All three dimensions (trust constructs) will be specified reflectively in the empirical study.

Looking closely at trust research it becomes clear that the three terms affective, cognitive, and conative trust are often worded differently in their conceptualization and operationalization.
Affective trust (DONEY/CANNON 1997; JOHNSON/GRAYSON 2005; AIKEN/BOUSH 2006) is also called "benevolence" (GANESAN 1994; SINGH/SIRDESHMUKH 2000; GARBARINO/LEE 2003; WHITE 2005) or "integrity" (BHATTACHERJEE 2002; YOUSAFZAI ET AL. 2005; SCHLOSSER ET AL. 2006; MCKNIGHT ET AL. 2002; WANG/BENBASAT 2005; and GEFEN/STRAUB 2004). Therefore benevolence and integrity aspects have to be included if suitable indicators are to be obtained for affective trust.
Cognitive trust was operationalized through constructs called "cognitive trust" (ANDALEEB/ANWAR 1996; DONEY/CANNON 1997; JOHNSON/GRAYSON 2005; AIKEN/BOUSH 2006), "credibility" (GANESAN 1994), "competence", "capability" (SINGH/SIRDESHMUKH 2000; GARBARINO/LEE 2003; MARTIN/CAMARERO 2005), "expertise" (WHITE 2005), and "ability" (BHATTACHERJEE 2002; YOUSAFZAI ET AL. 2005; SCHLOSSER ET AL. 2006; GEFEN/STRAUB 2004).
Hitherto, **conative** trust has been only operationalized in a study by AIKEN/BOUSH (2006) through the construct "conative trust". In their study online trust and the nature of internet signals is analyzed. The purpose of their experiment with 1,252 participants is to provide results of the effectiveness of internet marketer's various attempts to engender consumer trust

through web signals. In their study the conative dimension implies the willingness to provide personal information.

There is no agreement between researchers regarding which of the operationalizations are the most suitable. Although the only available **operationalization of consumer trust as an attitude**, which was undertaken by AIKEN/BOUSH (2006), covers all three the required dimensions (affective, cognitive, conative), these authors' measurement cannot be used in this work's empirical study. The indicators that these authors chose for their affective and cognitive trust dimension cover aspects of security and privacy, which are in fact antecedents of consumer trust and not indicators of trust dimensions; they cannot therefore be used. Conversely, their indicators for conative trust can be used and will be supplemented in the empirical study. JOHNSON/GRAYSON (2005) present a more suitable measurement of affective and cognitive trust, as their measurement best mirrors the results of the qualitative interviews with experts on trust building measures in the banking industry.

JOHNSON/GRAYSON (2005) understand **affective trust** as "emotions and feelings about the interactions of benevolence by the trust partner or organization," which are, for example, a caring response and attitude to problems and an open communication combined with serious listening. All these indicators are consequences of affective consumer trust and are correctly specified as reflective (decision rules by JARVIS ET AL. 2003 in section 3.5.2). The Cronbach's alpha in the pre-study was 0.898.

The understanding of **cognitive trust** by JOHNSON/GRAYSON (2005) covers aspects of "the belief in competence abilities of the partner or organization" like trusting advice, not doubting competence, acceptance of advisors' opinions, relying on advisors' work. All these indicators are the result of cognitive consumer trust and are correctly specified as reflective. The Cronbach's alpha in the pre-study was 0.763.

The **conative trust** dimension was taken from AIKEN/BOUSH (2006), but adjusted and supplemented by two further items to improve the results and, thus, the marketing implications. The specialty of the enhanced operationalization is the integration of different aspects of personal information. Four aspects are chosen beginning from general asked information, going over more private information like life-style and finance situations, ending with deeply personal information (in general, only known by relatives). Consequently, the behavioral trust dimension covers aspects of providing personal information and thus, showing weak points of oneself, for example, a private address, lifestyle information, private information on earnings for asset planning, and information about illnesses for old-age plans. All indicators convey the consequences of trusting the partner and are specified reflectively. The Cronbach's alpha in the pre-study was 0.851.

Summarizing, the results lead to a three-dimensional (affective, cognitive and conative) trust measurement with reflectively specified constructs. Furthermore, all indicators of the three consumer trust dimensions gained from theory cover results from the qualitative expert interviews (marked with *).

Scales	**Item loading**	**Item weights**	**Coefficient alpha of main study (and pre study in parantheses)**	**Author**	**Specification**
Affective trust (1. I totally disagree - 7. I totally agree) 1. I can talk freely with my financial adviser about my problems at work and know that he or she will listen* 2. If I share my problems with my financial adviser, I feel he or she would respond caringly* 3. My financial adviser is warm and caring towards me	0.905 0.896 0.853	0.390 0.372 0.367	0.861 (0.898)	JOHNSON/GRAYSON (2005) (* indicator also named in expert interviews: see appendix)	reflective
Cognitive trust (1. I totally disagree - 7. I totally agree) 1. I have to be cautious about acting on the advice of my financial adviser because his or her opinions are questionable* (recoded) 2. I can not fully depend on my financial adviser since he or she may complicate my affairs with careless work* (recoded) 3. Given my financial adviser´s track record, I have good reasons to doubt his or her competence (recoded)	0.760 0.859 0.867	0.347 0.419 0.434	0.774 (0.763)	JOHNSON/GRAYSON (2005) (* indicator also named in expert interviews: see appendix)	reflective
Conative trust (1. I totally disagree - 7. I totally agree) 1. I would entrust my house bank with my private contact information (private telephone number, address, e-mail) 2. I would entrust my house bank with life-style information about my asset management 3. I would entrust my house bank with all information about my finances (income, retirement provision, life insurance) for asset planning 4. I would entrust my house bank with personal information (family diseases, addictive behavior) for the planning of my retirement provision	0.787 0.650 0.881 0.742	0.361 0.230 0.392 0.297	0.769 (0.851)	according to AIKEN/BOUSH (2006) according to AIKEN/BOUSH (2006) new new	reflective

Table 7: Operationalization results and specification of the three dimensional trust measurement

3.7. Measurement of Loyalty as a Consumer Trust Consequence

In previous trust studies, loyalty has been operationalized by between one and three dimensions (AGUSTIN/SINGH 2005; ANDERSON/SRINIVASAN 2003; CHIOU ET AL. 2002; SIRDESHMUKH ET AL. 2002; HARRIS/GOODE 2004). In all these studies, loyalty was specified reflectively.

The **measurement** of loyalty by AGUSTIN/SINGH (2005) focuses on product loyalty (i.e., "share a greater amount of wallet") and not on loyalty within organizations. ANDERSON/SRINIVASAN (2003) developed an operationalization of e-loyalty, but these indicators were not suitable for adapting or adjusting to this study. The measurement of loyalty by

HARRIS/GOODE (2004) recognizes consumer theories and loyalty in an organization, but since the authors use a three-dimensional approach, this would have been too detailed for the present study. A three-dimensional approach would have lengthened the questionnaire unnecessarily, as loyalty is not the primary focus of the current study. The operationalization of loyalty by SIRDESHMUKH ET AL. (2002) fits the context of the study – loyalty towards a company – best with the following originally indicators:

1. How likely are you to do most of your future activity with this company?
2. How likely are you to recommend this company to friends, neighbors, and relatives?
3. How likely are you to use this company's services and products the very next time?
4. How likely are you to take more than 50% of services or products from this company?

Beside the four given indicators, one question refers to the possibility of recommending the own bank, which is one of the most meaningful indicators of loyalty (REICHHELD ET AL. 2000). The forth indicator was deleted after the pre-study, because of the Cronbach's alpha. The first indicator was a little modified. Instead of asking if the customer would do future activities with the bank, it was asked if the customer is doing most of the activities with the house bank. As the bank relationships, in general, are long time relationships this modification was necessary. The third indicator was modified, because bank services are generally used quite often and regularly. Therefore, the indicator was changed to how likely a switching behavior can be expected (which is a meaningful indicator of loyalty, see ZINS 2001). Cronbach's alpha of the three indicators was 0.964 in the pre-study.

Scales	Item loading	Item weights	Coefficient alpha of main study (and pre study in parantheses)	Author	Specification
Loyalty (0. unlikely - 11. very likely)					
1. How likely are you to do most of your banking transactions with your house bank?	0.837	0.463			
2. How likely are you to recommend this bank to friends or/and relatives?	0.769	0.414	0.666 (0.964)	according to SIREDESHMUKH ET AL. (2002) and REICHHELD ET AL. (2000)	reflective
3. How likely are you to change your house bank in the near future? (recoded)	0.716	0.412			
Deleted item after pre study: - How likely are you to make more than 50% of your bank transactions with your house bank?					

Table 8: Operationalization and specification of the construct loyalty

3.8. Measurement of Reputation as a Consumer Trust Antecedent

Reputation is more and more recognized as one of important intangible assets of companies, as it leads to higher trust and higher financial performance (DONEY/CANNON 1997; SABATE/PUENTE 2003, p. 161). One suitable definition of reputation based on a meta-study by GOTSI/WILSON (2001) is: "A corporate reputation is a stakeholder´s overall evaluation of a company over time. This evaluation is based on the stakeholder´s direct experiences with the company, any form of communication and symbolism that provides information about the firm´s actions and/or comparison with the actions of other leading rivals" (GOTSI/WILSON 2001, p. 27). Ever though, there is no clear agreement about the definition of reputation (EBERL 2006, p. 9). Corporate reputation should not be mixed up with corporate image. Contrary to corporate image, reputation is regarded as public information about the trustworthiness of a player (PICOT ET AL. 2003, p. 126). Image is a rather more short-lived changeable reproduction of the organization, while reputation is the more "realistic" picture of the company, which is determined by direct experiences (EBERL 2006, p. 11). Therefore, reputation will be used in the study[25].

Its strong significant effect on trust has already been analyzed for business-to-business, business-to-consumer relationships and social networks. Results of the relationship between reputation and trust in business-to-business (B2B) relationships as also social networks is researched by the two top ten cited articles by DONEY/CANNON (1997) and LARSON (1992) (see section 3.1). The influence of reputation in business-to-consumer (B2C) relationships – which is the focus of this work - has been analyzed since 2002 by scientists (WANG/CHEN 2006; EINWILLER ET AL. 2005; SCHOENBACHLER/GORDON 2002; PAVLOU 2003; KIM ET AL. 2004; JOHNSON/GRAYSON 2005). Going a step further and focusing on the banking industry, ADAMSON ET AL. (2003, p. 355) analyze the effect of "negative reputation" on consumer trust, while LEWIS/SOURELI (2006) identify "corporate image" as a trust antecedent. Since reputation is a very important influence factor in **banking** (ZINNBAUER ET AL. 2004, p. 271), it will therefore be included in the trust model.

3.8.1. Conceptualization of Reputation

As a main trust antecedent, it deserves special focus to determine the best conceptualization of it for a theoretical model. Although researchers have considered reputation in the context of the banking industry to some extent, the influence of reputation on three trust dimensions has not yet been determined.

To date, trust research has mainly been carried out in respect of a one-dimensional reputation construct. However, in his research, SCHWAIGER (2004) has demonstrated that reputation can be conceptualized as a **two-dimensional** construct. According to this author, reputation is built by means of the dimensions "competence" and "likeability." SCHWAIGER (2004) thus splits corporate reputation into one cognitive and one affective component on the assumption that a company's reputation consists of the knowledge and emotions of individuals. The cognitive component,not only includes objective knowledge, but also subjective perceptions.

---

[25] GOTSI/WILSON (2001, p. 24) provide a detailed differentiation between "corporate image" and "corporate reputation."

SCHWAIGER calls the cognitive component of reputation "competence" and the affective one "likeability." Competence and likeability are explained by the antecedents: Attractiveness, quality, performance, and responsibility. The split into a cognitive and an affective component allows a much more differentiated analysis of reputation. Thus, the research question arises whether consumer trust is more influenced and built by the cognitive dimension "competence" or by the affective dimension "likeability."

Prior trust research has already demonstrated that the **cognitive and affective antecedents of consumer trust** are analyzed by means of a broad portfolio of constructs. Thus, the cognitive influence is analyzed by generic trust antecedents such as competence (KENNEDY ET AL. 2001; CHO 2006), while more situation specific cognitive trust antecedents are comfort (SPAKE ET AL. 2003) and/or web site usability (HAMPTON-SOSA/KOUFARIS 2005). The affective influence is analyzed by generic trust antecedents such as likeability (ANDALEEB/ANWAR 1996), familiarity (KENNEDY ET AL. 2001; GEFEN ET AL. 2003; GEFEN 2000; BHATTERACHERJEE 2002), and/or similarity (JOHNSON/GRAYSON 2005). There has not as yet been any trust research on the influence of both the "competence" and "likeability" dimensions in one single trust model.

Three-dimensional reputation approaches are only found in minor journals, none in high ranked ones. This might be due to the relative newness of reputation measurement. Nevertheless, three-dimensional reputation approaches have become accepted in business since 2007. INGENHOFF (2007) and EISENEGGER/IMHOF (2007) have developed such **three-dimensional reputation** approaches from a communication policy perspective. INGENHOFF's reputation approach contains a functional cognitive reputation, an affective-emotional reputation, and a social-cognitive reputation. The reputation approach of EISENEGGER/IMHOF has a very similar design, only differing in that what INGENHOFF calls an "affective-emotional" reputation dimension, EISENEGGER/IMHOF call an "expressive" dimension. "Functional reputation" is defined as the fulfillment of the functional performance expectations, "social reputation" as the fulfillment of social and moral expectations, and "expressive reputation" as ensuring an emotional attractive identity. The "affective-emotional" is defined as a company's likeability and fascination. Thus, the two dimensions "affective-emotional" and "expressive reputation" dimension mirror the same contents.

The expressive/emotional dimension cannot be considered a third dimension alongside the other two cognitive and social dimensions. As EISENEGGER/IMHOF and INGENHOFF consider consumer theories in their approach, however, as described in section 2.2.3, the presumption that only cognitive reputation has an impact on emotional reputation seems to be erroneous. In general, in respect of consumer theories, it should be kept in mind that the emotional and cognitive reputation dimensions are more likely to interact with each other.

A further aspect resulting from one-sided relationships is that the independence of the expressive dimension is not assured in respect of the other two dimensions. In EISENEGGER/IMHOF and INGENHOFF's approach, the existence of the expressive dimension is dependent on the emotionality of the functional and social reputation's evaluations (INGENHOFF 2007, p. 56; EISENEGGER/IMHOF 2007, p. 16).
Both approaches therefore maintain that there are two cognitive reputation dimensions. SCHWAIGER (2004) already aggregated cognitive elements that build reputation in one cognitive reputation dimension, which makes much more sense in the light of consumer theories. SCHWAIGER's stated functional and social dimensions are defined as up-stream reputation drivers. This approach has already distinguished the cognitive reputation drivers more diagnostically. SCHWAIGER considers four driver constructs (attractiveness, quality, performance and responsibility), which influence both the cognitive and emotional reputation. Furthermore, the third expressive dimension does not emanate from public information, which is a necessary condition for the definition of reputation in this work.
In conclusion, the reputation approach by INGENHOFF and EISENEGGER/IMHOF has a different approach through the communication policy perspective and will therefore not be used in this work.

SCHWAIGER's reputation model is the most suitable reputation approach for the empirical study. Its cognitive and emotional dimensions (competence and likeability) include the results of prior trust literature and entail an understanding of consumer theory. The dimensions are also independent of each other.
The great advantage and the main reason for the choice of this reputation model is the possibility to identify trust building measures through the formative specification of the four constructs (drivers): Attractiveness, quality, performance, and responsibility. In recent trust research, only reflective measurement has been done, which implies a focus on the results or consequences of constructs. Thus, no empirically and quantitative analyzed measures can be deduced by means of a reflective measurement. Consequently, the SCHWAIGER approach goes a step further in analyzing trust building measures by means of a formative specification beside the usual trust antecedents that have to date been gathered through reflective measurement.

As scientists have identified reputation as an important trust antecedent, using SCHWAIGER´s reputation model, the following hypotheses can be deduced:
H5: ***Bank likeability is positively related to a) affective, b) cognitive, and c) conative consumer trust.***
H6: ***Bank competence is positively related to a) affective, b) cognitive, and c) conative consumer trust.***

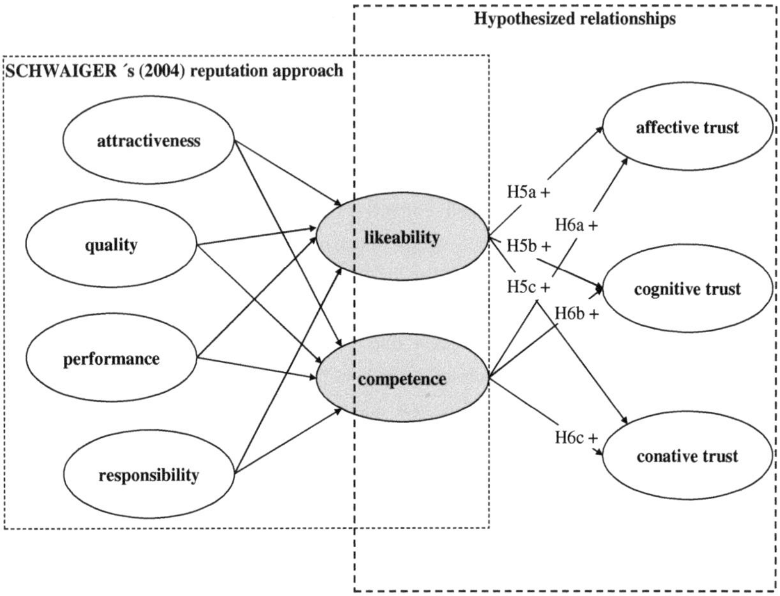

Figure 21: Hypothesized relationships of likeability and competence (= reputation) on the three trust dimensions

It is difficult for the banks to differentiate between their own and the competitors products and services. Each bank has equivalent products and services, for example online-banking, investment portfolios etc. (VON STEIN, 2000, p. 17). Thus, the customers perceive banks as almost similar competent. Consequently, the differentiation between banks might be more likely developed through their likeability. Assuming that the banking industry in Germany is considered equal competent, likeability might have a stronger impact on trust than competence. The following hypothesis is therefore deduced:

H7: ***Bank likeability has a stronger effect than competence on a) affective, b) cognitive, and c) conative consumer trust.***

3.8.2. Operationalization of Reputation

In the **trust literature**, the construct reputation was mainly operationalized as one reflective dimension (EASTLICK ET AL. 2006; JOHNSON/GRAYSON 2005; KIM ET AL. 2004; PAVLOU 2003; SCHOENBACHLER/GORDON 2002; WANG/CHEN 2006). The specialty of the SCHWAIGER (2004) approach is the division of reputation into two reflectively specified constructs: Competence and likeability. The four antecedents of these two reputation dimensions are "attractiveness," "quality," "performance," and "responsibility," which are specified formatively. SCHWAIGER (2004) already **operationalized** the construct reputation with the dimensions "competence" and "likeability" according to the C-OAR-SE process (section 3.5.2). In this publication, a few adjustments were made for the empirical study by deleting the two items "... is a trustworthy company" and "I have respect for all that which ... has achieved" from the 25 indicators, which does not basically change the approach. The deletion was necessary due to new research findings, as well as the past experience of reputation studies undertaken with industry and business partners. Furthermore, SCHWAIGER's approach covers the main results of the qualitative expert interviews concerning trust building measures.

Important trust building antecedents in research are also covered by SCHWAIGER's reputation approach. Additional insights can be gained through the reputation approach's formative specifications of the four constructs "attractiveness," "quality," "performance," and "responsibility." To emphasize the new indicators, the SCHWAIGER (2004) approach constructs that were used, were compared with already analyzed constructs in the trust literature. "**Competence**" was therefore reflectively analyzed as a trust antecedent (KENNEDY ET AL. 2001; CHO 2005; BALASUBRAMANIAN ET AL. 2003). The construct "competence" was thus operationalized reflectively with three indicators in the current work. The Cronbach's alpha in the pre-study was 0.828. The "**likeability**" dimension by SCHWAIGER covers aspects of sympathy, self-identification, and regret if the company no longer exists. These emotional contents were reflectively analyzed as a trust antecedent in prior trust literature, for example, likeability (ANDALEEB/ANWAR 1996); "similarity" (STEWART 2003; SARGEANT ET AL. 2005; JOHNSON/GRAYSON 2005), which is comparable to SCHWAIGER's indicator "self-identification;" empathy (KIM ET AL. 2004), and "familiarity" (KENNEDY ET AL. 2001; GEFEN ET AL. 2003; GEFEN 2000; BHATTACHERJEE 2002). The construct "likeability" was therefore operationalized reflectively with three indicators in this work. The Cronbach's alpha in the pre-study was 0.925. Consequently, the two reflectively specified constructs' affect on trust has more or less been analyzed, but not as yet the affect on the three trust dimensions.

Parts of the "**attractiveness**" dimension by SCHWAIGER can only be found in empirical e-commerce studies on trust that reflectively analyze, for example, the design of web pages (CHO 2005; BART ET AL. 2005; HAMPTON-SOSA/KOUFARIS 2005), investments in web sites (SCHLOSSER ET AL. 2006), and "no errors"/the quality of web pages (EVERARD/GALLETTA 2005). Although the "attractiveness" of salespersons has already been analyzed in trust research (SWAN ET AL. 1999), the "attractiveness" of an organization or even a bank in term of its physical appearance and its affect on trust has not as yet been analyzed. Furthermore, the indicators "imagine working at the bank" and "attraction for high quality employees" have not yet been considered in previous empirical studies.

"**Quality**," a further construct in the SCHWAIGER approach, was measured reflectively in prior trust research, but as a direct antecedent of trust and not indirectly through reputation in respect of, for example, the service quality level (KIM ET AL. 2004; KENNEDY ET AL. 2001; HARRIS/GOODE 2004); the quality of the system (KIM ET AL. 2004), information (KIM ET AL. 2004), product (KENNEDY ET AL. 2001), employees (CHIOU ET AL. 2002), company (CHIOU ET AL. 2002), and communication (SARGEANT ET AL. 2005; CHO 2005); the core offering (CHO 2006), and expertise (JOHNSON/GRAYSON 2005; ANDALEEB/ANWAR 1996). The new "structure" – quality was now defined as an antecedent of reputation and not as a direct antecedent of trust – and the formative operationalization of the construct, which covers more indicators than prior research ("the bank tends to be an innovator"), led to new results.

In SCHWAIGER's approach, "**performance**" as an antecedent of reputation had already been analyzed as a reflectively operationalized antecedent of consumer trust in prior literature (PEARCE/ZAHRA 1991; SARGEANT ET AL. 2005; PAVLOU/GEFEN 2004; JOHNSON/GRAYSON 2005). Again, the formative measurement of performance will lead to new insights, especially through the indicators "very well managed company" and "the risk for my bank is modest compared to that of its competitors."

In trust research, "**responsibility**," the last and fourth antecedent of SCHWAIGER's reputation approach, was also analyzed reflectively as a direct antecedent of consumer trust (SALMONES ET AL. 2005; SARGEANT ET AL. 2005). The formative operationalization will lead to further empirically proven levers of trust building measures through, for example, the indicator "the bank has a fair attitude towards competitors."

Consequently, this reputation approach mainly covers trust building measures gained through the expert interviews that contain important antecedents of trust building and analyze new trust building levers empirically and quantitatively through the formative specification of the four constructs "attractiveness," "quality," "performance," and "responsibility."

Summarizing, **trust building measures** can be analyzed through the formative operationalization of the four constructs "attractiveness" (three indicators), "quality" (seven indicators), "performance" (five indicators), and "responsibility" (four indicators).

Scales	Item loading	Item weights	Coefficient alpha of main study (and pre study in parantheses)	Author	Specification
Likeability (1. I totally disagree - 7. I totally agree)			0.853 (0.925)	SCHWAIGER (2004) (* indicator also named in expert interviews: see appendix)	reflective
1. Of all companies, I would regret missing my house bank most if it no longer existed	0.850	0.328			
2. Of all companies, my house bank is a company with which I can best identify	0.902	0.370			
3. I regard my house bank as a likeable company*	0.883	0.439			
Competence (1. I totally disagree - 7. I totally agree)			0.740 (0.828)	SCHWAIGER (2004) (* indicator also named in expert interviews: see appendix)	reflective
1. I believe that my housebank performs at a premium level*	0.798	0.493			
2. As far as I know my house bank is recognized*	0.803	0.357			
3. My house bank is a top competitor in its market*	0.824	0.388			
Attractiveness (1. I totally disagree - 7. I totally agree)			-	SCHWAIGER (2004) (* indicator also named in expert interviews: see appendix)	formative
1. I like the physical appearance of my house bank*	0.779	0.477			
2. I could see myself working at my house bank	0.488	0.146			
3. In my opinion, my house bank is successful in attracting high-quality employees*	0.884	0.631			
Quality (1. I totally disagree - 7. I totally agree)			-	SCHWAIGER (2004) (* indicator also named in expert interviews: see appendix)	formative
1. My house bank seems to be a reliable partner for customers	0.811	0.256			
2. My house bank holds customer concerns in high regard*	0.797	0.227			
3. The services my house bank offers are good*	0.672	0.240			
4. The product/services offered by my house bank are of high quality*	0.783	0.140			
5. I have the impression that my house bank is forthright in given information to the public (incident, growth)*	0.656	0.112			
6. I think that my house bank´s products/services offer good value for money	0.664	0.155			
7. In my opinion, my house bank tends to be an innovator, rather than an imitator with respect to banking	0.677	0.241			
Performance (1. I totally disagree - 7. I totally agree)			-	SCHWAIGER (2004) (* indicator also named in expert interviews: see appendix)	formative
1. My house bank is an economically stable company*	0.729	0.316			
2. I think that my house bank has growth potential	0.631	0.162			
3. My house bank has a clear vision of the future of the company	0.667	0.189			
4. My house bank is a very well managed company (e.g., strong growth of funds)*	0.834	0.499			
5. I assess the business risk of my house bank as modest compared to its competitors*	0.616	0.203			
Responsibility (1. I totally disagree - 7. I totally agree)			-	SCHWAIGER (2004) (* indicator also named in expert interviews: see appendix)	formative
1. My house bank is concerned about the preservation of the environment	0.645	0.294			
2. I have the feeling that my house bank is not only concerned with profit	0.650	0.246			
3. I have the impression that my house bank has a fair attitude towards competitors	0.764	0.357			
4. My house bank behaves in a socially conscious way*	0.847	0.446			

Table 9: Operationalization results and specification of the reputation approach

3.9. Measurement of Security as a Consumer Trust Antecedent

The **goal** of this section is to develop a new security approach, which contains physical and emotional aspects.

Previous studies on the relationship of **security on trust** only include physical security (BART ET. AL 2005). Physical security is, for example, the coding of online data (the transaction of data).

Emotional security emerges in situations where there is high expectation that one's counterparts have good intentions. Thus, when people cooperate with one another, security – here, the term for feeling safe and in good hands - plays an important role. A leap of faith is specifically necessary in the initial phase of any private or business relationship (MÖLLERING 2006), which therefore constitutes a risk. This risk has a direct relationship to feelings of security. Not until one of the partners takes a risk through a leap of faith, is cooperation possible. One of the most cited articles[26] by MOORMAN ET AL. (1993) demonstrates that interpersonal factors (e.g., willingness to reduce uncertainty) are most predictive of trust. Thus, the perceived security (or perceived uncertainty) of the interacting partner (who can be a person or an organization) influences the willingness to trust and thus affects the leap of faith.

The perceived security of banks and their services is a precondition or a "**hygiene factor**" for trust building. According to HERZBERG ET AL. (1959), hygiene factors are security and others such as company policies, administration, etc. By transferring his Motivation Hygiene Theory to the content trust (instead of, as originally, to satisfaction) hygiene factors become attributes that have little impact on global trust, but which are still important for bank customers. Distrust is primarily the result of hygiene factors. The presence of hygiene factors has little effect on long-term trust, but if they are absent or inadequate, customers do not trust the organization. Security in the banking industry includes secure online banking as well as the disclosure of private information through an active controlling or security standard (cognitive security), but also, for example, the perceived good intention (affective security). The circulation of personal data as in the Lichtenstein affair in 2008, for example, leads to a reduced feeling of security.

In Germany, the **banking industry has high security standards** as a result of the supervision of the German federal financial supervisory agency (BaFin). Whether bank customers recognize and know the regulations in detail and whether this knowledge adds to the feeling of security is unclear. The following are examples of the regulations securing bank transactions:

---

[26] Gained through the meta-analysis with a citation index of 160 (see section 3.3).

- The BaFin's determination of the designation "bank" (§ 32 KWG): The Bafin intervenes much stronger in the legal form than in other industries. Consequently, high standards are set regarding all banks' tasks and responsibilities.
- Demands regarding banks' equity and liquidity (§ 10 KWG, § 11 KWG): Banks have to have adequate equity and a special liquidity ratio when selling credits. These regulations have been revised since the bank crash in 2007. In no other industries are such regulations found.
- The reporting of large credits to the German Central Bank (§ 13 KWG, § 14 KWG, § 15 KWG): Operative bank business is tightly controlled by BaFin, which is not the case in other industries.
- Banks' deposit insurance (EAEG): Bearer liability is relevant in respect of Sparkassen and cooperative banking institutions.
- Information about security portfolios (§ 23 KWG): Banks have to inform their customers in an easily comprehensible way about security regulations.
- Banks are subject to special accounting regulations (RechKredV).
- BaFin's control of credit institutes (§ 6 KWG). The German Central Bank supports the BaFin in these tasks (§ 7 KWG).

Thus, the perceived feeling of security regarding bank transactions, which are controlled by laws and security technology standards, is generally very high. Still, there are **risks** in the banking industry, as demonstrated by the subprime and stock exchange crash in 2007, which neither laws nor technology could prevent. Banking crises happen when systemic problems occur, when all the bank capital in a system is exhausted, when borderline problems occur, through forced bank closures, government takeovers, etc. (HOGGARTH ET AL. 2002). Furthermore, the continuous development of new banking products can not always be covered by laws. Consequently, regulations will always lag behind. Thus, although high security standards help, there is still a risk. This is why security as a construct has to be included in the trust model. The following paragraphs explain the groups of security constructs that allow trust building measures to be put into place.

3.9.1. Conceptualization of Security

On examining the result of a meta-analysis in respect of security variables, it becomes clear that the key variables that have been identified (risk, conflict, and opportunism) do not mirror security in all its facets and, thus, do not offer a possibility of creating a suitable measurement approach. However, if one were to try to integrate all the security construct variables with a direct relationship to consumer trust, this would cause major difficulties such as content overlaps and individual trust antecedents no longer being independent of others.

However, an examination of the trust literature allows four constructs to be gained that may be defined as sub-constructs of security. These four main facets of security, which have a significant effect on trust, are:

- **Intention** (ANDALEEB/ANWAR 1996; DELGADO-BALLESTER ET AL. 2003; MARTIN/CAMARERO 2005; BEJOU ET AL. 1998; KENNEDY ET AL. 2001),
- **Opportunism** (ANDALEEB/ANWAR 1996; MARTIN/CAMARERO 2005),
- **Discretion** (WANG ET AL. 2004; EASTLICK ET AL. 2006; BART ET. AL 2005; SUH/HAN 2003), and
- **Protection** (CHO 2006; WANG ET AL. 2004; SUH/HAN 2003).

In the following, the mentioned literature is listed according to the date of publication and a short summary of each study is given.

1. A survey by ANDALEEB/ANWAR (1996) was done in a developing country (Bangladesh). High-involvement products like appliances, stereo systems, and automobiles were chosen and 226 interviews done. In these authors' study, **intention** is defined as the customer's perception of whether the salesperson has the customers' interest in mind or is opportunistically inclined (ANDALEEB/ANWAR 1996, p. 38). The authors maintain that **opportunism**, which is defined as self-interest-seeking behaviour with guile, is perhaps crucial as opportunistic salespeople are likely to distort information and shirk from obligations that can significantly affect the outcomes that the customer expects. The study indicates that salesperson attributes such as intention, expertise, and likeability influence customers' trust in salespeople.
2. In a study by BEJOU ET AL. (1998, p. 172), 568 telephone interviews were done with bank customers. The study identifies **ethics (=intention)**, sales orientation, customer orientation, and expertise as determinants of trust in financial services.
3. In a study by KENNEDY ET AL. (2001), 786 questionnaires filled in by buyers of automobiles were used for the analysis. The manufacturer's **ethical** concern **(=intention)** – beside salespersons competence, selling tactics, product quality, and service quality – is one of the influencing factors of trust.
4. In a survey by DELGADO-BALLESTER ET AL. (2003) 272 interviews were undertaken in respect of brands of products like shampoo and deodorant. This study develops a brand trust measurement through the two constructs reliability and **intention**.
5. A web survey by SUH/HAN (2003) collected 502 cases of Internet banking uses. The study analyzes customer perceptions of security control of e-commerce acceptance. Trust is examined as the mediating factor using Internet banking. This study concludes that perceptions of nonrepudiation, privacy **protection**, and data **integrity** **(=discretion)** have a significant impact on trust in e-commerce.

6. A study by WANG ET AL. (2004) identifies the signalling of small online retailers' trustworthiness through an experiment with a sample of 402 persons. The signalling effects that the authors identify are seals of approval, a return policy, awards from neutral sources, **security disclosures (=protection)**, and **privacy disclosures (=discretion)**. A privacy disclosure has a positive affect on willingness to provide personal information, while a security disclosure has a positive effect on trust. Security disclosures indicate how transaction data are encrypted during the transmission and what kind of technology is adopted to ensure the transaction security. The researchers maintain that providing privacy and security disclosures would help reduce the perceived privacy and security risks, and thus increase initial trust in the online retailer.
7. The study by MARTIN/CAMARERO (2005) analyzes consumer reactions to firm signals in asymmetric relationships in the automotive sector. It is an empirical test of the relation between firm signals and consumer trust in **intentions** and values. The company sends signals and customers develop trust in them, reducing their fear of the firm's **opportunism**. These authros' study shows how consumers react to the quality signals that the firm sends to the market.
8. A study by BART ET AL. (2005), undertaken with 6,831 participants, found privacy and order fulfilment to be the most influential determinants of trust in financial services' web sites. Privacy is defined as the protection of individually identifiable information on the Internet, involving the adoption and implementation of a privacy policy and disclosure of personal data **(=discretion)** of the Web site visitors. A web site's security is defined as the safety of the computer and credit card or financial information. In these authors' study, security had no affects on trust.
9. The study by EASTLICK ET AL. (2006) examines the roles of consumers; information **privacy** concerns **(=discretion)** and e-tailers' perceived reputation on the trust and purchase intention of consumers. The results show that the strongest relationships are found between trust and online purchase intention and between firm reputation and trust. Privacy concerns influenced purchase intent with strong negative effects, both directly and indirectly, through trust.
10. The study by CHO (2006) uses 881 online responses for the analysis of the mechanism of trust and distrust formation and their relational outcomes in two online purchasing contexts: Books and clothing. **Security** is defined as, for example, the company's infrastructure and privacy policy being reliable and secure **(=protection)**. Besides core offering, site design, tangible reward, communication, preferential treatment, competence, and benevolence, security is analyzed as an influencing factor of global online trust and distrust.

Next, each of these sub-constructs is described **in respect of the banking industry.**

"**Intention**" describes the counterpart's positive value system. The intentions of a bank with regard to its customer should entail ethical behaviour. Thus, the bank customer can rely on the good intentions of his or her bank. A bank's good intentions can be demonstrated through services which are not primarily profitable for the bank:

- Increasing the customer's money
- Improved access as a service to customers (subsidiaries in the country, a wide distribution of cash points, service personnel for consultancy in every subsidiary)
- Detailed guidance regarding bank products (especially complex bank products like certifications)
- Understandable general terms and conditions (AGBs)
- Offering competitive products besides the bank's own products

"**Opportunism**" describes the counterpart's negative value system and focuses on the likelihood of being ripped off by the counterpart (Game Theory). It is presumed that the counterpart has a self-seeking, profit-maximizing goal. Transferring this to the banking industry means that opportunism mirrors, for example, the bank's information behaviour in that it keeps relevant information to itself (e.g., by only mentioning funds that performed well in the last years). Ultimately, these banks only try to achieve profit maximization (PICOT ET AL. 2007, p. 15), which does not necessarily have negative consequences for the customer (as other banks' portfolios of competitive products achieve a similar performance). Opportunistic profit maximization can be achieved by:

- Offering only products, certificates and assurances from the own bank. Products from competitors are not mentioned or sold.
- Matching sales to the bank's predetermined sales goals. A financial adviser, for example, negotiates the sales of a special bank product, although the customer is well informed and feels that he has freedom of choice. Especially in the case of complex products (e.g., certificates) the price calculation can only be done if one has a strong mathematical background. In general, the customer has to trust the financial adviser. These information asymmetries do make opportunistic behaviour possible.
- Recommending share options that belong to the bank's portfolio. The bank can earn an option bonus if a share option of such a company is sold.

"**Discretion**" can be regarded as a kind of privacy protection by the counterpart. In other words, the counterpart will not actively provide private information to others who could abuse such information. Although the discretionary use of private customers' information is regulated by law (PICOT ET AL. 2007, p. 19), there are, nevertheless, areas in which, for example, customer information could be forwarded:

- Circulation of customer information to the finance office even though there is no reason to suspect this customer.

- Reporting of large credits to the German Central Bank (KWG).
- Reporting deposits over 15,000 Euros, or the exchange of securities, or the existence of safe deposit boxes if the financial adviser harbors suspicions (GwG).
- Circulation of customer data to the SCHUFA[27] after the customer has signed the "SCHUFA-Klausel"[28].
- Circulation of customer information to the customer's legal representative (e.g., parents) if the customer is underage or not sui juris.
- Circulation of customer data internally. According to law, customer information can not be given to "third parties". Nevertheless, customer information can be given to internal company divisions as long as they fall within the appropriations of provisions of the contract (e.g., §23 KWG). In a situation where a bank buys an assurance company (Dresdner Bank buys Allianz), the insurance company is legally no longer a "third party". A transfer of customer information would therefore be possible.
- Circulation of customer information by a financial adviser to, for example, friends despite legal prohibitions and high penalties.

"**Protection**" is a kind of shield that actively protects the customer against third parties. Safeguarding the customer of the bank is, for example, mirrored by actively securing ex ante and ex post private customer information against intruders:

- Allowing secure online transaction through security systems.
- Prohibiting external persons from entering internal service places by placing security gates.
- Screening computers so that outsiders can not see customer information.
- Limiting the financial adviser's access to customer information.
- Preventing financial advisers from installing computer programmes, as well as from freely surfing unsafe websites.
- Allowing e-mail to only enter through an installed firewall.
- Changing passwords at regular intervals.

The independence of these constructs has to be demonstrated unambiguously in order to prove the relevance all four determents of security. If two constructs correlate strongly, one of them can be omitted. Independence is given when one construct changes without consequences for the other three constructs. The independence of all four constructs is exemplified in the following relationship: Banks are likely to have neutral intentions in

---

27 The SCHUFA Holding AG (in German "Schutzgemeinschaft für allgemeine Kreditsicherung") is a credit bureau of Germany. It is a company that collects information from various sources and provides consumer credit information on individual consumers for a variety of uses.

28 The "SCHUFA-Klausel" contains the agreement that the lender may send personal data (credit amount, duration etc.) to the SCHUFA organization.

respect of customers, but do not necessarily have good intentions (intention). Even if a bank wants to maximize its profit by providing the customer with special information about its products (opportunism), the financial adviser will still actively try to protect the customer's personal information against intruders (protection). Nevertheless, the financial adviser would still have to disclose private information to SCHUFA (no discretion). Consequently, the four sub-constructs determine security and are independent of one another.

Since the four sub-constructs of security all influence trust as shown above, it can be asserted that security (physical and emotional) influences trust. This new security approach leads to the following hypotheses (see next figure):

H8: ***Bank security is positively related to a) affective, b) cognitive, and c) conative consumer trust.***

H9: ***Bank intention is positively related to security.***

H10: ***Bank opportunism is negatively related to security.***

H11: ***Bank discretion is positively related to security.***

H12: ***Bank protection is positively related to security.***

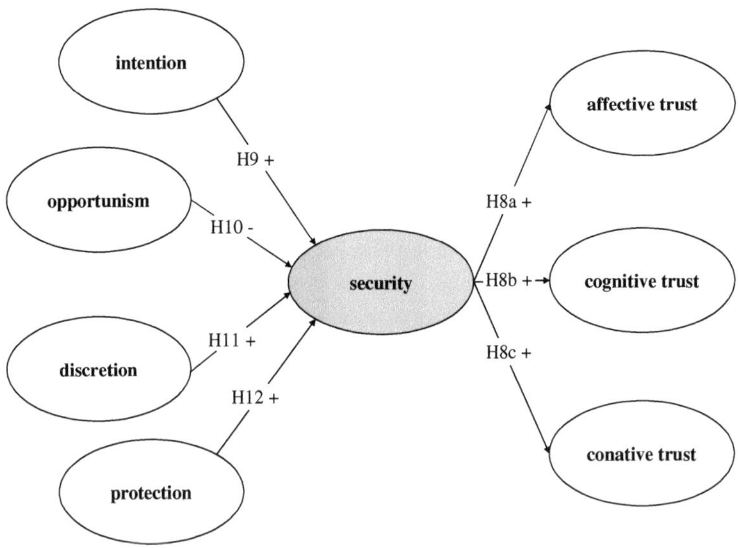

Figure 22: New conceptualization of security and its hypothesized influence on consumer trust dimensions

As mentioned above, security in the banking industry is a hygiene factor. Security seems to have a stronger impact on consumer trust than the two dimensions of reputation. If a bank crisis occurs, the lacking feeling of security will affect consumer trust far more than the loss of reputation. In another situation, where a bank has no real reputation (the bank is new and unknown), but its customers feel very secure, the customers may have strong feelings of trust. Therefore, the following hypothesis is deduced:

H13: ***Bank security has a stronger effect than reputation on a) affective, b) cognitive, and c) conative consumer trust.***

3.9.2. Operationalization of Security

Since no suitable security construct that covers all the important facets of security was available, a new security conceptualization had to be developed. For the conceptualization of a causal model (Task 1, see Figure 23), all constructs found in previous empirical trust studies connected to security were listed to evaluate the theoretical coherence between the construct of interest (security) and content-wise, closely related antecedent constructs (opportunism, intention, discretion, and protection) already measured in the literature (see section 3.9.1).

The specification type of indicators for the antecedents constructs (opportunism, intention, discretion, and protection) are collected and evaluated (Task 2, see Figure 23). The expert interviews were used to supplement the collected and purified indicators from the literature (Task 3, see Figure 23). Each operationalization was analyzed and tested for the correct specification and content validity. With the help of the decision rules by JARVIS ET AL. (2003), the used indicators were theoretically tested to ascertain whether they belong to a reflective or formative measurement. Possible misspecifications were uncovered.

The construct "perception of **opportunism**" by MARTIN/CAMARERO (2005) has originally five items:

1. I need to monitor the company so that it fulfills its promises
2. I fear that the company seeks only its interests
3. I suspect that the company may be hiding relevant information
4. I think that the company will would try to avoid doing its duty if it could
5. I think that the company could shirk if undetected

The first item "I need to monitor the organization so that it fulfils its promises" does not fit the reflective measurement. The other items cover aspects of opportunistic behavior of the company, while the first item is a behavior which belongs to the person. Monitoring behavior is a consequence of perceived opportunistic behavior of the company. It does not belong to the definition and thus, construct of opportunistic behavior (decision rule seven – nomogical net of the construct indicators – by JARVIS ET AL. 2003). Furthermore, a change of the other four items does not automatically lead to a change of the first item (decision rules six – covariation between the indicators – by JARVIS ET AL. 2003), because an increased monitoring behavior is depend on the person. Therefore, this item had to be omitted. The last indicator was deleted, because of the Cronbach´s alpha in the pre-study. Three indicators for the construct opportunism remained for the main study.

Furthermore, every antecedent construct was evaluated concerning overlapping content. If indicators with the same content appeared in more than one construct, the one that was best suited to the construct content remained, whereas the others were omitted. This guarantees a clear separation of the antecedents. If the content of two or more items was too similar within a single construct, the indicator was deleted to avoid inappropriate indicators (ROSSITER 2002). There are, for example, items from the construct "perception of privacy detection" by SUH/HAN (2003) and the construct "security" by CHO (2006) that have overlapping contents.

The indicators from the construct "perception of privacy detection" (labeled "**discretion**" in the current work) by SUH/HAN (2003) originally are:

1. This company will not use my personal information for any purpose unless I authorize it to do so
2. This company never sells my personal information in their computer database to other companies
3. This company devotes time and effort to preventing unauthorized access to my personal information
4. Databases that contain my personal information are protected from unauthorized access
5. This company will really remove my personal information when I request it to do so

One item of the construct "perception of privacy detection" by SUH/HAN (2003) is similar to another item in the same construct. The item "this company will not use my personal information for any purpose unless I authorize it to do so" is very similar to "this company never sells my personal information in their computer database to other companies." Using personal data for any purpose or selling personal information does not cover different contents. Therefore, it was omitted, to consider ROSSITER´s (2002) statement of not only adding highly correlated, but unnecessary and conceptually inappropriate indicators to gain high Cronbach´s alpha.

Furthermore, the indicators "this company devotes time and effort to preventing unauthorized access to my personal information" and "databases that contain my personal information are protected from unauthorized access" were deleted from the "perception of privacy discretion" construct because this construct content should only cover the organization's releasing of information (discretion) and not rejection of active protection.

Protecting activities are covered through the indicators of the construct "security" (labeled "**protection**" in the current work) by CHO (2006):

1. This company offers secure web transactions
2. This company ensures the security of my information
3. This company makes an offer to increase security from an unlawful intruder to retrieve my information

The omitted indicators "this company devotes time and effort to preventing unauthorized access to my personal information" and "databases that contain my personal information are protected from unauthorized access" are very similar to the indicators "this company ensures the security of my information" and "this company makes an offer to increase security from an unlawful intruder to retrieve my information". There are therefore covered through the protection construct.

The construct "intention and values" (labeled "**intention**" in the current work) by MARTIN/CAMARERO (2005) has originally six indicators:

1. I trust in the company's good intentions
2. I believe that the company's behavior is ethical
3. I believe that the company fulfills its promises
4. The company makes an effort to give personal attention
5. The company gives detailed information to its customers without being request
6. The company's service and working style are the ones I like

The indicator "I believe that the company fulfills its promises" has a very similar content to the indicator "the company seems to be a reliable partner for customers" of the quality construct. The same goes with "the company's service and working style are the ones I like" which is very similar to the indicator "the services my house bank offers are good" of the quality construct. Therefore, both indicators of the "intention" construct are omitted. The indicator "the company makes an effort to give personal attention" does not fit in the reflective measurement, because good intentions of a company are not necessarily shown by personal attention. If the company acts less ethical, this does not automatically lead to lower personal attention. Thus, a change of the first indicator can not necessarily associated with changes of the other indicators. The decision rule six – covariation between the indicators - by JARVIS ET AL. (2003) is not fulfilled for a reflective measurement. Therefore, this indicator was omitted.

Further indicators gained through the expert interviews (see appendix), which fit in the global content "security" were added to the indicators above:

1. My house bank offers impositions of sanctions
2. My house bank offers me the possibility to talk to a personal financial adviser

3. The house bank does not take careless risks for the whole company (e.g., high-risk investments)
4. The house bank is reachable at customer-friendly hours
5. I feel safe and in good hands with my house bank
6. My house bank offers ratings, certificates about the company's performance etc.
7. My house bank monitors the customers´ creditworthiness
8. Relevant information for bank customers are easy accessible

A quantitative pre-study (see section 4.1.2) is done with the goal to ideally get an empirical reproduction of the existing measurement approaches of antecedent constructs (Task 4, see Figure 23). An explorative factor analysis helped to assign all the indicators, including the ones from the expert interviews to one of the constructs (opportunism, intention, discretion, and protection). The factor analysis showed that the item from the expert interview "I feel safe and in good hands" was the only item of all that could not clearly assigned to one factor, because it loaded strongly above the extracted factors protection, discretion, and opportunism (Task 5, see Figure 23)[29]. Thus, this item was taken to measure the over construct "security" with a single-item measurement.

As a result, a reflective first order and a formative second order construct, is developed. The four upstream constructs (drivers) of security were analyzed and optimized by means of Cronbach's alpha and based on the pre-study data.

"**Opportunism**" was specified reflectively and, according to MARTIN/CAMARERO (2005), the operationalization has three indicators. In the pre-study, Cronbach's alpha was 0.789. The constructs mirror the bank's perceived opportunistic behaviors (as perceived by the consumer).

"**Intention**" was specified reflectively, and, according to MARTIN/CAMARERO (2005), the operationalization has two indicators. In the pre-study, Cronbach's alpha was 0.803. The constructs mirror the bank's (adviser's) perceived ethical intentions (as perceived by the consumer).

"**Discretion**" was specified reflectively, and, according to SUH/HAN (2003), the operationalization has two indicators. In the pre-study, Cronbach´s alpha was 0.780. The constructs mirror the caution of the bank (adviser) (as perceived by the consumer).

"**Protection**" was specified reflectively, and, according to CHO (2006), the operationalization has three indicators. In the pre-study, Cronbach's alpha was 0.872. The construct mirrors the bank's safeguarding activity.

---

29 The results from the factor analysis gained through the main study can be seen in the appendix.

The following figure summarizes the steps taken to develop the security construct's measurement approach in detail.

	Description	Objective	Result
Task 1: Literature overview	Evaluate theoretical coherence between construct of interest and content-wise, closely related antecedent constructs that have already been measured	Internal content validation (CHURCHILL 1979; NUNNALLY 1967)	Causal model of relevant antecedent construct (e.g., opportunism) and focal construct (security)
Task 2: Evaluation specification type	Collect items and evaluate specification type of indicators for antecedent constructs (intention, opportunism, discretion, and protection): Reflective or formative items? Focus on reflective items as goal is a parsimonious formative measurement of construct of interest (security) (assumption: each antecedent construct can be measured reflectively). Avoid synonymous items.	Initial item selection (BERGVIST/ ROSSITER 2007; JARVIS ET AL. 2003; ROSSITER 2002; DIAMANTO-POULOS 2005)	Literature-based reflective measurement model for antecedent constructs. Reflective first order and formative second order construct
Task 3: Qualitative pre study	Expert interviews to uncover unconsidered facets of security construct of interest: Include new items in existing measurement model	External content validation (CHURCHILL 1979)	Selection of additional "new" items and inclusion in measurement model
Task 4: Quantitative pre study	Factor analysis: Check for coherence of items and antecedent constructs	Empirical validation of existing measurement models (BAGOZZI/YI 1988)	Ideally, empirical reproduction of existing measurement approaches of antecedent constructs (intention, opportunism, discretion, and protection)
Task 5: Operationali-zation	Items that load on all antecedent constructs can cause multicollinearity problems and should be regarded as a global, reflective measurement of a focal construct (security)	Identifying reflective items for focal construct (security)	Identification of one indicator for focal the construct security
Task 6: Main study			Representative validation of the new measurement approach to security (single-item measurement with four up-streamed constructs: intention, opportunism, discretion, and protection)

Figure 23: Summarized steps for the development of the new security measurement

The main study validates (Task 6) the new measurement approach to security (see also section 4.3). The quality criteria of the operationalization of the constructs are summarized in the following table.

Scales	Item loading	Item weights	Coefficient alpha of main study (and pre study in parantheses)	Author	Specification
Security (1. I totally disagree - 7. I totally agree) 1. I feel safe and in good hands with my house bank*	1.00	1.00	1.00 (1.00)	Expert interview	reflective
Intention (1. I totally disagree - 7. I totally agree) 1. I trust in my house bank's good intentions towards customers 2. I believe that my house bank behaves ethically* Deleted items after pre study: - The house bank does not take careless risks for the whole company (e.g., high-risk investments) - The house bank is reachable at customer-friendly hours* - The house bank informs customers without being explicitly asked (open communication)*	0.923 0.902	0.580 0.515	0.800 (0.803)	according to MARTIN/CAMARERO (2005) (* indicator also named in expert interviews: see appendix)	reflective
Opportunism (1. I totally disagree - 7. I totally agree) 1. I fear that my house bank only seeks its own interests* (recoded) 2. I suspect that my house bank may be hiding relevant information (e.g., about products) or that the relevant information is only written in the small print* (recoded) 3. I think that my house bank would try to avoid doing its duty if it could (recoded) Deleted item after pre study: - I think that my house bank would shirk if undetected - Relevant information for bank customers are easy accessible*	0.812 0.829 0.742	0.463 0.453 0.335	0.712 (0.789)	according to MARTIN/CAMARERO (2005) (* indicator also named in expert interviews: see appendix)	reflective
Discretion (1. I totally disagree - 7. I totally agree) 1. My house bank respects privacy protection and does not sell my personal information to other companies* 2. My house bank would remove my personal information if I requested it to do so Deleted items after pre study: - My house bank offers impositions of sanctions - My house bank offers me the possibility to talk to a personal financial adviser*	0.816 0.867	0.549 0.637	0.590 (0.780)	according to SUH/HAN (2003) (* indicator also named in expert interviews: see appendix)	reflective
Protection (1. I totally disagree - 7. I totally agree) 1. My house bank offers secure transactions (money transactions, standing orders) 2. My house bank ensures the security of my information* 3. My house bank offers to safeguard my information from illegal retrieval (e.g., newest technologies, confirmed limits for money transfers)* Deleted items after pre study: - My house bank offers ratings, certificats about the companies performance etc.* - My house bank monitors the customers´ creditworthiness	0.791 0.795 0.745	0.518 0.415 0.349	0.680 (0.872)	according to CHO (2006) (* indicator also named in expert interviews: see appendix)	reflective

Table 10: Operationalization results and specification of the security construct

Summarizing the previous two sections, reputation and security are the two main trust antecedents that banks can influence. Thus, trust-building measures should focus on these two main trust antecedents. However, how strongly can banks influence consumer trust? To analyze this question, the personal characteristics of consumers are introduced as moderating variables.

3.10. Measurement of Personal Characteristics of Consumers and their Moderating Role

Do personal characteristics influence the perception or organizations and their trust building measures? To give an answer to this question, new moderators in trust research are defined. Therefore, the identified clusters "person," and "satisfaction," as well as "trust propensity" are defined as **moderators** in the theoretical model. The cluster "person" includes the key variables "socio-demographics" and "involvement" (see section 3.3.2), but only the variable "involvement" will be taken into account in respect of the theoretical model as this publication assumes that social demographics have an impact on trust via perceived risk or security, as women and elderly people tend to have a generally higher risk and lower security perception than men or younger people. Since perceived security is a construct in the theoretical model, social demographics will not be included. The cluster "satisfaction" is expressed by the variable "satisfaction." "Trust propensity" will be taken into account due to its impact on specific trust, as explained earlier in section 2.2.1. Consequently, the three constructs "satisfaction," involvement"," and "trust propensity" are defined as moderators in the banking industry and in the B2C trust model.

3.10.1. Satisfaction as a Moderator

Satisfaction is one of the very interesting and important variables in marketing research. The difficulty with satisfaction is that it has a relationship with nearly every construct/variable in marketing research. Four of the most citied articles show the ambiguous character of satisfaction as a consequence and an antecedent of trust. GARBARINO/JOHNSON (1999) analyzes in their study with consistent subscribers of theatre against occasional subscriber, satisfaction as an antecedent of future intentions. To the same results come CROSBY ET AL. (1990). They analyze that the quality of the relationship (i.e., satisfaction and trust) between salespersons and the customer determines future sales opportunities. Therefore, satisfaction can be regarded as an antecedent of consumer trust, which can be influenced by the organization (banks).
In contrast, MOHR/SPEKMAN (1994) examine primary characteristics of partnership success (satisfaction and sales volume) as a consequence of partnership attributes like commitment, coordination, trust, communication quality, participation, and the conflict resolution technique of joint problem solving. Also, ANDERSON/NARUS (1990) define satisfaction as a consequence

of trust in working partnerships between distribution and manufacturer firms. Satisfaction is a consequence of all perceived organizational characteristics.
Consequently, satisfaction leads to trust and trust leads to satisfaction. This positive feedback loop will be expressed through a moderating effect. The grade of satisfaction moderates the perception of trust building measures. A highly satisfied customer might perceive the same trust building measures differently than a dissatisfied customer.
Summarized, the new approach is the definition of **satisfaction as a moderator**. Furthermore, satisfaction expresses more or less the level of consumer expectations. Consumer expectations are personal characteristics. The same organizational services (e.g., bank opening hours) satisfy some consumers, while others are not satisfied, because they have higher expectations of what a bank should provide. A business person who is permanently away on business and works until late would like to have 24-hour service, while the nine-to-five employee would be satisfied with business opening hours. This study therefore defines satisfaction as a personal characteristic and as a moderator.

The **conceptualization** of "satisfaction" either covers consumer satisfaction with different individual aspects of a company or the organization as a whole, for example, their products (IACOBUCCI ET AL. 1994), services (JOHNSON/GRAYSON 2005; VERHOEF ET AL. 2002), websites (ANDERSON/SRINIVASAN 2003), or consumers' overall satisfaction with a company (GARBARINO/JOHNSON 1999; BALASUBRAMANIAN ET AL. 2003; HARRIS/GOODE 2004; CHIOU ET AL. 2002). In the same context, instead of satisfaction, "positive past experience" is operationalized (PAVLOU/GEFEN 2004; PAVLOU 2003; SCHOENBACHLER/GORDON 2002; SIRDESHMUKH ET AL. 2002). In the theoretical model, overall satisfaction with the bank is taken into account by means of a one-dimensional measurement.

The following **hypothesis** is deduced:
H14: ***The impact of organizational competence, likeability, and security is moderated by the existing degree of consumer satisfaction: The higher the existing consumer satisfaction, the lower the importance of organizational a) competence, b) likeability, and c) security in respect of consumer trust.***

Satisfaction is one of the most often used constructs measured in the trust literature on P2O trust interaction. There is no agreement on the "right" **operationalization** among researchers, but the American customer satisfaction index (ACSI) by FORNELL ET AL. (1996) is a globally preferred measurement. ACSI is one of the most employed operationalizations of "satisfaction" in general. The measurement enables the comparability of studies using the same indicators. Their operationalization covers aspects of general overall satisfaction with the company, the fulfillment of expectations, and the requirements to be the "ideal bank" and was therefore used. Especially the question regarding how close the own bank is to an "ideal bank" is a good indicator that mirrors consumers' expectations.

In the measurement, all indicators used aspects of the evaluation of past experience. Thus, the satisfaction items mirror consequences, because they depend on the experience of aspects from a company as perceived by the consumer in the past. Consequently, the reflective specification was used. In the pre-study, Cronbach's alpha was 0.791.

Scales	Item loading	Item weights	Coefficient alpha of main study (and pre study in parantheses)	Author	Specification
Satisfaction (1. I totally disagree - 7. I totally agree) 1. My house bank fulfills my expectations 2. In general, I am satisfied with my house bank* 3. My house bank is very close to an "ideal bank"	0.923 0.943 0.897	0.357 0.363 0.366	0.911 (0.791)	FORNELL ET AL. (1996) (* indicator also named in expert interviews: see appendix)	reflective

Table 11: Operationalization results and specification of the construct satisfaction

3.10.2. Involvement as a Moderator

Involvement can be defined through a person's motivation to process or learn something about a company, product or person (HAWKINS ET AL. 2004, p. 400). A highly involved person is motivated to get a great amount of information of the interested object and show strong attention focused on central, product-related features and factual information. In contrast, a low involved person is not interested in getting actively information and has limited attention focused on peripheral, nonproduct features and feelings (elaboration likelihood model, see HAWKINS ET AL. 2004, p. 400). **Involvement** is strongly dependent on the person, situation, product, medium, and message (TROMMSDORFF 2004, p. 58). A similar differentiation gives FELSER (2001, p. 59) including a time aspect. Personal and product involvement is independent from time, while situational involvement exists only in a special period of time. The focus of the work lies on general time independent perceiving of trust building measures. Consequently, situational involvement will not be taken into account in the empirical study. Personal involvement belongs to the constructs or influencing factors of trust that cannot be (or hardly) influenced by the company. This point is important, as in this case, the company has no levers to steer this antecedent. The empirical results in the next chapter will demonstrate the extent to which involvement actually influences consumer trust. Is involvement, beside trust propensity and satisfaction, an important factor? Is it essential that companies cope with it?

One of the most common **conceptualizations** of the construct "involvement" was developed by LAURENT/KAPFERER (1985). Although this conceptualization was done many decades ago, its multidimensional measurement approach, which includes aspects of importance, risk probability, pleasure, and sign mean that it is still valid. This conceptualization is the most diagnostic of them all, which fits perfectly when an empirical study is focused on involvement, which this work does not, of course, do. Involvement, defined as a moderator, plays a role, but to analyze its impact, only the "importance" dimension will be taken into account, because of multicollinearity, which was analyzed in the pre-study (one path coefficient had a value above 1.0).

This reducing might lead to the fact, that involvement is not covered in all its facets. On the other hand **content overlapping** could be avoided. The dimension "risk probability" is measured by many previous studies (PAVLOU/GEFEN 2004; PAVLOU 2003; SCHOENBACHLER/ GORDON 2002; SCHLOSSER ET AL. 2006). "Risk probability" is very strong connected to security feelings and thus covered to some extend in the study through the construct security. The "pleasure" dimension has content overlaps with the reputation approach by SCHWAIGER (2004). The indicator in SCHWAIGER´s approach "I regard my house bank as a likeability company" of the construct likeability is nearly equal to the indicator "I can not say that I particular like the bank" of the construct pleasure. It is therefore covered to some extend through the construct likeability. The last two LAURENT/KAPFERER dimensions "importance" and "risk importance" are aggregated into one "importance" dimension. In consequence, "involvement" is defined by "importance" (e.g., choosing the "right" bank). The other dimensions of "involvement" are expected to be covered through the constructs security and likeability.

The following **hypothesis** is deduced:

H15: ***The impact of competence, likeability, and security is moderated by the degree of consumer involvement: The greater the consumer involvement, the greater the importance of organizational a) competence, b) likeability, and c) security in respect of consumer trust.***

In the **operationalization** of involvement by LAURENT/KAPFERER (1985), the construct has a originally, more than ten indicators. To reduce the scale, only three main indicators were taken in the pre-study. Even with this reduced measurement, multicollinearity was observed and led to involvement being measured as a single item ("My choice of bank is important for me"). The strong reduction of the measurement approach leads to the fact that important parts of the constructs might be left out. Looking at other studies, which have operationalized involvement, "importance" is by far the most-used item for assessing of involvement in psychology and consumer behavior research (OLSEN 2007, p. 328). Therefore, this indicator should at least be a major indicator measuring involvement.

Scales	Item loading	Item weights	Coefficient alpha of main study (and pre study in parantheses)	Author	Specification
Involvement (1. I totally disagree - 7. I totally agree) 1. My choice of bank is important for me Deleted items after pre study: - I am concerned about which bank I choose - You can really tell about a person by the bank she/he picks out	1.00	1.00	1.00 (1.00)	according to LAURENT/KAPFERER (1985)	reflective

Table 12: Operationalization and specification of the construct involvement

3.10.3. Trust Propensity as a Moderator

Trust propensity, defined as "general trust," is a personal characteristic that is stable over time (see section 2.2.1). Trust propensity is a third moderator variable in the theoretical model.

This statement is deduced, since consumers who have a very low general trust will perceive and evaluate organizations (e.g., bank competence) as untrustworthy. They will not trust the organization and will refrain, for example, from soliciting more information due to the strong impact of their low trust propensity.
One of the top ten cited articles[30] by MAYER ET AL. (1995) introduce - beside the differentiation of perceived trustworthiness and trust - trustor's propensity for the first time as a moderator and not as an antecedent of consumer trust.
Consequently, trust propensity plays a moderating role in respect of the variables "trustworthiness" and "consumer trust."

The one-dimensional **general trust conceptualization** by ROTTER (1967), which is also one of the oldest, became accepted in subsequent trust research (e.g., MCKNIGHT ET AL. 2002, p. 350; GEFEN 2000, p. 732). Therefore, the one-dimensional conceptualization is taken into account in this work (see section 2.2.1).

The following **hypothesis** is deduced:
H16: ***The impact of competence, likeability, and security is moderated by the degree of consumer trust propensity: The higher the consumer trust propensity, the lower the importance of organizational a) competence, b) likeability, and c) security in respect of consumer trust.***

---

30 This information is gained by the meta-analysis in section 3.3.

The **operationalization** of "trust propensity" by HAMPTON-SOSA/KOUFARIS (2005) was used, but adjusted slightly for the main study. It covers three aspects: The general tendency to trust, trust based on a little knowledge, as well as the willingness to trust. In the pre-study, the recommended indicators for the construct "trust propensity" were required to analyze the differences between "trust propensity with respect to persons," the "trust propensity with respect to organizations," and "the trust propensity with respect to banks" three times.

In the pre-study, the values of the Cronbach's alphas were 0.830 ("trust propensity with respect to persons"), 0.810 ("trust propensity with respect to organizations"), and 0.789 ("the trust propensity with respect to banks"). The pre-study revealed that "trust propensity with respect to persons" was the best "trust propensity" measurement, as it had the greatest influence on specific trust. Furthermore, consumers tend to have the highest trust propensity with respect to persons, followed by banks and, finally, trust with respect to organizations.

Consequently, the construct "trust propensity with respect to persons" was the only one to be transferred to the main study. Owing to the high content overlap between trust tendency and trust willingness, one of the three items was omitted. The construct was specified reflectively with two indicators.

Scales	Item loading	Item weights	Coefficient alpha of main study (and pre study in parantheses)	Author	Specification
Trust propensity (1. I totally disagree - 7. I totally agree) 1. It is easy for me to trust people* 2. I tend to trust people even though I know little of them Deleted items after pre study: - My tendency to trust a company is high - It is easy for me to trust companies - I tend to trust companies even though I know little of them - My tendency to trust a bank is high - It is easy for me to trust banks - I tend to trust banks even though I know little of them	0.990 0.563	0.920 0.159	0.610 (0.830)	according to HAPTON-SOSA/KOUFARIS (2005) (* indicator also named in expert interviews: see appendix)	reflective

Table 13: Operationalization results and specification of the construct trust propensity

3.11. A Structural Equation Model for Analyzing Trust Building Measures in the Banking Industry

One important step before the statistical analysis of the SEM is undertaken is the definition of relationships between constructs as based on logical assumptions. Therefore, the SEM has a confirmatory character, which means that it verifies deduced hypotheses. The direction of causal relationships between constructs must, however, be theoretically provided. The SEM

will test whether the empirically surveyed data are consistent with the deduced hypotheses. The direction of the causal relationships between the constructs of the trust building model have been theoretically deduced in the form of hypotheses and are discussed in detail in Chapters 2 and 3 of this publication.
The following table summarizes all developed hypotheses.

H1	*Affective consumer trust is positively related to customers' cognitive trust in an organization*
H2	*Affective consumer trust is positively related to consumer trust behavior (or intention) (conative trust)*
H3	*Consumer trust beliefs (cognitive trust) are positively related to trust behavior (conative trust)*
H4	*Consumer a) affective, b) cognitive, and c) conative trust is positively related to consumer loyalty*
H5	*Bank likeability is positively related to a) affective, b) cognitive, and c) conative consumer trust*
H6	*Bank competence of a bank is positively related to a) affective, b) cognitive, and c) conative consumer trust*
H7	*Bank likeability has a stronger effect than competence on a) affective, b) cognitive, and c) conative consumer trust*
H8	*Bank security is positively related to a) affective, b) cognitive, and c) conative consumer trust*
H9	*Bank intention is positively related to security*
H10	*Bank opportunism is negatively related to security*
H11	*Bank discretion is positively related to security*
H12	*Bank protection is positively related to security*
H13	*Bank security has a stronger effect than reputation on a) affective, b) cognitive, and c) conative consumer trust*
H14	*The impact of organizational competence, likeability, and security is moderated by the existing degree of consumer satisfaction: The higher the existing consumer satisfaction, the lower the importance of organizational a) competence, b) likeability, and c) security in respect of consumer trust*
H15	*The impact of competence, likeability, and security is moderated by the degree of consumer involvement: The greater the consumer involvement, the greater the importance of organizational a) competence, b) likeability, and c) security in respect of consumer trust*
H16	*The impact of competence, likeability, and security is moderated by the degree of consumer trust propensity: The higher the consumer trust propensity, the lower the importance of organizational a) competence, b) likeability, and c) security in respect of consumer trust*

Table 14: Deduced hypotheses

All the developed hypotheses will be analyzed with SEM in a next step. Consequently, no other analysis method will be needed. The identified relevant clusters for B2C relationships, especially in the banking industry, and their mutual relationships are demonstrated in structural equation models in the following figure. All variables used for the theoretical model (including organizational trust antecedents, moderators, consumer trust dimensions, and trust consequence) are unobservable and are therefore constructs. In the SEM graphical user interface, constructs are displayed as circles. The explanation and choice of trust building measures are provided in Chapter 3. For visual clarity, the moderating effects of trust propensity, satisfaction, and involvement only point to H8/H13c, but are measured in respect of all hypotheses up to H5/H7a.

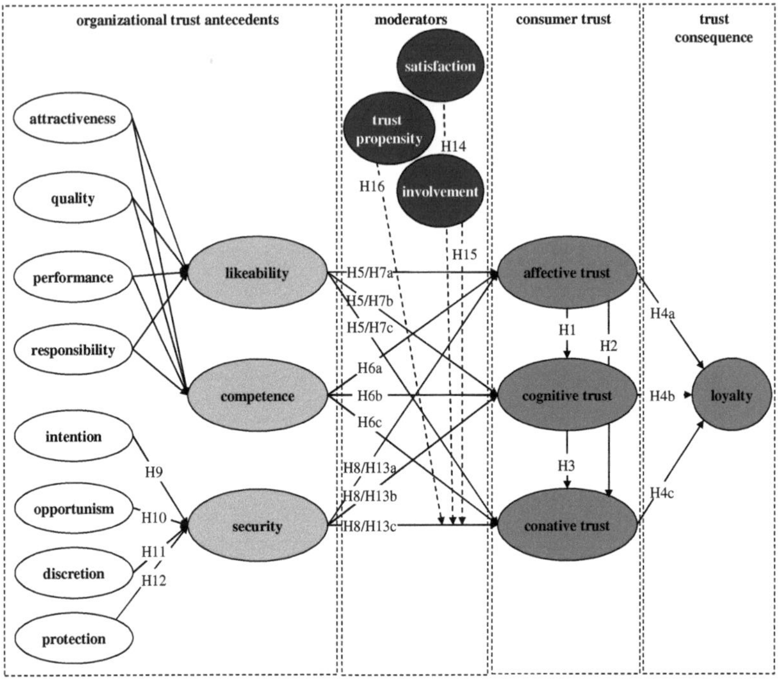

Figure 24: Structural equation model for analyzing trust building measures in the banking industry

The provided SEM of trust building measures includes 18 constructs. The three constructs likeability, competence, and security are direct organizational trust antecedents, while the three constructs trust propensity, satisfaction, and involvement are personal characteristics and defined as moderators. Loyalty is recognized in the analysis as it is a main trust consequence. This developed theoretical model is the basis of the further analysis and verification of the deduced hypotheses.

Summary of Chapter 3:

Chapter 3 developed a structural equation model to analyze trust building measures in the banking industry. It started with an overview of recent trust models. Contrary to existing models, which focus only on partial aspects, this chapter aggregated all of them into one single, new, and enhanced model. In order to achieve this goal, a meta-analysis was undertaken of all highly ranked trust articles during the last 60 years. From this meta-analysis, the main variables leading to eight main clusters, which are important in trust research, were identified, discussed, and conceptualized. Clusters were defined as antecedents, moderators, mediators, or consequences of trust in order to fit into a structural equation model. The use of smartPLS as the analysis method of the SEM is explained and the quality criteria for the SEM were described. Furthermore, a description was provided of the theoretical background of reflective and formative specification, as well as their validation. The operationalization of 18 relevant constructs for the trust model was discussed against the background of the literature and enhanced for the banking industry. The content overlap between constructs was specifically minimized and described. At last the provided trust model with its deduced hypotheses is presented.

4 Research Design and Results

This chapter will provide **data about consumer trust in banks**. Therefore, open response expert interviews, an online mail/web survey, and a Computer-Assisted Telephone Interviewing (CATI) are done to answer the research question and to test the hypotheses. The results gained through the main survey (400 completed interviews) will be presented and discussed. The results from the five expert interviews and the pre-study (74 completed questionnaires) were used to supplement the main study, but will not be described in this chapter. The discussion of the results is divided into four sections, data collection and sample, descriptive results of the main study, evaluation of the goodness of the model, and the testing of the hypotheses as well as trust building measures. The results were analyzed in respect of a German representative population survey.

4.1. Data Collection and Sample

To analyze trust building measures, three **types of surveys** were done: Expert interviews, an online questionnaire, and CATI. The following sections describe the pre and main studies' chosen research designs.

4.1.1. The Unstructured Expert Interviews

The results of the expert interviews are especially important for the formative measurement to guarantee full operationalization, as well as to provide further important measures and antecedents of consumer trust that have not as yet been analyzed in trust research.

The survey was conducted in an **unstructured**, **face-to-face interview** with five experts including a bank employee and bank customers. The advantage of the nondirective interview is that, within the bounds of the topics of interest, the respondent is given maximum freedom to respond (MALHOTRA/BIRKS 2007, p. 381). Maximum freedom is required to acquire all the relevant trust building measures. In contrast, a semi-structured questionnaire might have guided the interviewee in a specific direction. Thus, the survey was an open response interview focusing on the (preliminary) question: What trust building measures does the banking industry utilize and what leads to mistrust?

4.1.2. The Pre-Study: Online Questionnaire

The indicators needed for the operationalization of the constructs were collected from the empirical studies and the expert interviews. The purpose of this pre-study was to pre-test the collected indicators and to enhance the developed theoretical model. Specifically, the research objectives were to: a) Optimize the research design, i.e. the questionnaire, in respect of its wording, understanding, and further aspects for the main study; and, b) Optimize the operationalization of the constructs in order to shorten the main study questionnaire.

The design of the questionnaire includes the following **components**: An introduction, identification of the respondents' trust propensity regarding banks, an open question in which the respondents have to provide the name of a bank of trust and one with no trust. Furthermore, the respondents had to evaluate the degree of agreement with the various attributes of the bank concerning reputation, security, specific trust, customer satisfaction, loyalty, involvement, and demographics. The rating was done on a seven-point Likert scale[31], because in literature a seven-point rating scale is recommended as an optimum (UNTERREITMEIER 2004, p. 102).

The survey was conducted by mailing an invitation to participate in an online questionnaire to approximately 150 bank customers at the beginning of August 2007. The sample **procedure** employed to select the interviewees was a mixture of convenience and snowball sampling technique, which is a nonprobability sampling technique (LEHMANN ET AL. 1998, p. 305). This technique is normally used in the exploratory stages of a research project or for the pre-testing of a questionnaire (AAKER ET AL. 2007, p. 393). The lack of e-mail addresses and the technique's low costs also made it a suitable choice. The processing time required for the survey was about 30 minutes. The questions were also randomized to minimize effects due to the order of items (BÜHNER 2006, p. 63).

74 online questionnaires (approx. 50%) of the pre-study were fully completed.

---

[31] Likert scales require the interviewee to indicate a degree of agreement or disagreement with a variety of statements related to the attitude or object (BEREKOVEN ET AL. 2004, p. 81).

The following table summarizes the information on the participants.

Gender	
Male	55.41%
Female	44.59%
Age	
18-29	56.7%
30-39	36.5%
40-49	5.4%
Over 50	1.4%
Education	
High school diploma	9.5%
University education	74.3%
PhD	16.2%
Work	
Employee	78.4%
In education/ freelancing/ retiree	21.6%
Place of residence	
Big city (over 100,000 habitants)	83.6%
Smaller city	10.9%
Town	5.5%

Table 15: Information on the respondents of the pre-study (n=74)

Online questionnaires are often criticized for not having a systematic probability sample and for the participants being confined to Internet users, but in respect of the initial stage of societally representative surveys the online questionnaire is sufficient to enhance the questionnaire and the operationalization of the constructs for the main study (AAKER ET AL. 2007, p. 393).

4.1.3. The Main Study: CATI Interviews

Using the insights gained from the pre-study, the main study was conducted to verify the deduced hypotheses. The CATI interviews for the **main survey** were done by the Dialog-Factory call center in Augsburg through the population representative Computer-Assisted Telephone Interviewing (CATI interviews) of 400 bank customers.

Telephone interviewing processes such as CATI are very similar to personal interviewing methods. CATI is better than personal interview techniques regarding speed (more interviews can be conducted in a given period), the lack of administrative problems, and cost per completed interview (it is easy to obtain a representative sample through a suitable random digit sample). With the exception of the inability to employ visual aids or execute complex tasks, the potential for sample bias, and the respondents' ability to hang up when they become bored, telephone interviews are relatively problem-free. Furthermore, CATI is a technique that is used to control the administration and sequence of questions (randomization of questions is possible) asked by an interviewer. Thus, interviewing errors such as choosing the wrong respondents and respondents failing to answer questions can be reduced to a minimum (AAKER ET AL. 2007, p. 263). The questions were kept quite simple and the questionnaire was limited to a minimum of questions to discourage abortions.

To minimize **survey errors,** the following conditions (AAKER ET AL. 2007, p. 229) were carefully monitored: a) The pre-study tested the understanding of the questions; b) the selected respondents had agreed to cooperate; c) the population had been correctly identified as bank customers; d) no specific know-how was required to answer the questions; and e) the interviewers had been trained prior to the survey, so that their understanding and recording of the questions were correct.
The interviewing time was about 20 minutes. The list of all questions can be seen in the appendix. Questions were randomized for every interview.

The following figures summarize the information on the respondents.

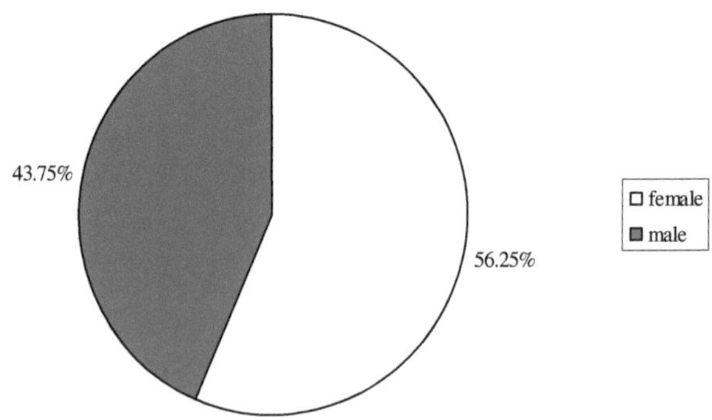

Figure 25: Percentage of male and female respondents (n=400)

43.75% of the respondents were male, 56.25% were female.

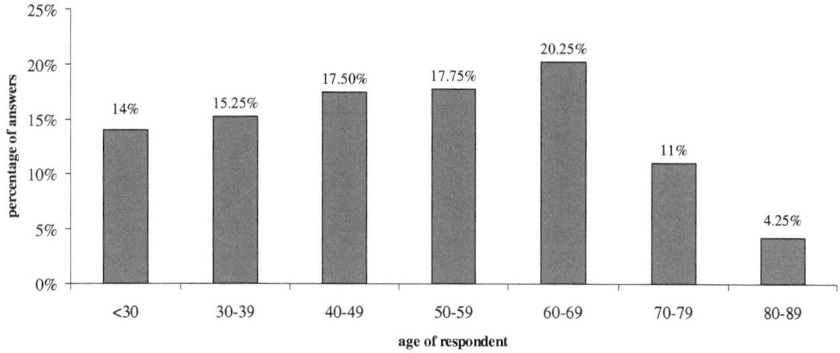

Figure 26: Age of respondents in percentage (n=400)

The age of the respondents ranges from 18 to 90.

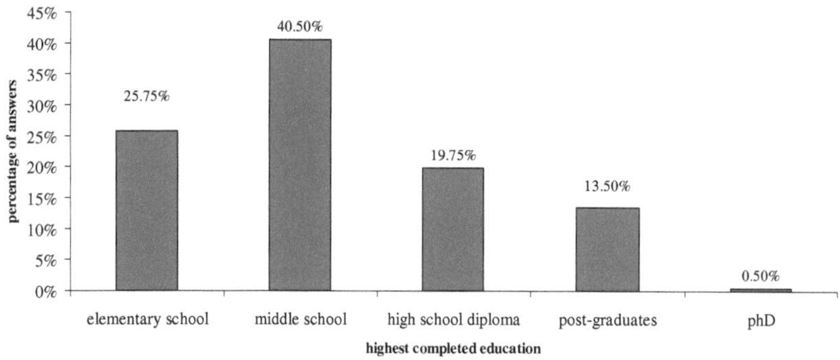

Figure 27: Highest completed education (n=400)

The highest completed education of the respondents ranges from elementary school to PhD.

4.2. Descriptive Results of the Main Study

An optional question was asked in the main German representative survey to ascertain whether some banks in Germany are especially trustworthy and others are not. The following figure shows the banks of trust (BT) in Germany.

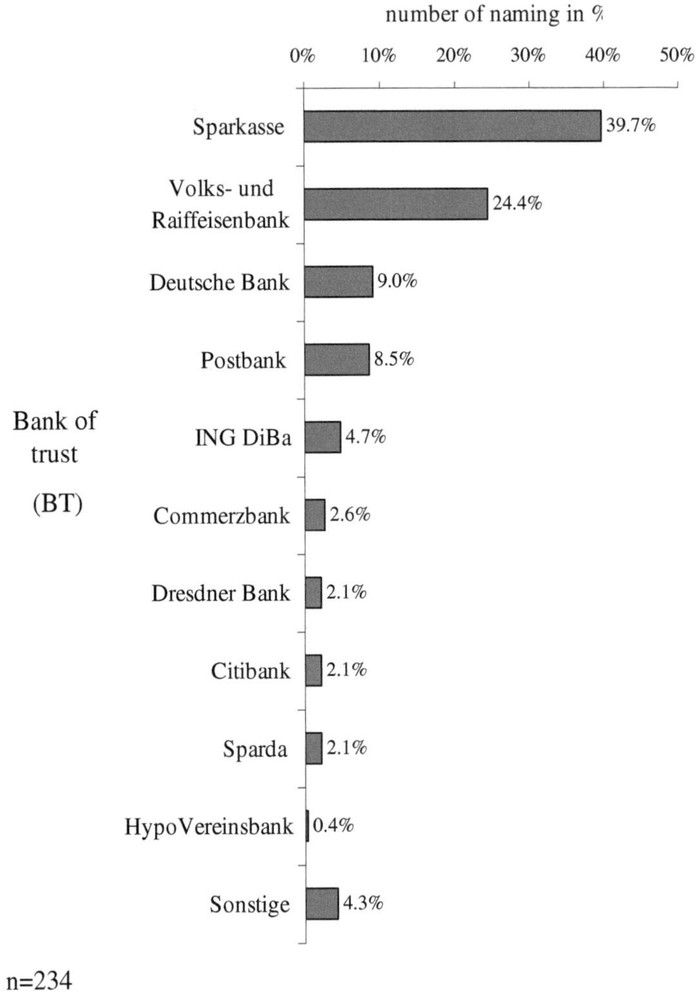

Figure 28: Banks of trust (BT) in Germany

In over 64% of the answers (n=234), the respondents mentioned "Sparkasse" (39.7%) and "Volks- und Raiffeisenbank" (24.4%) as their bank of trust (BT); both these banks belong to the group of banks regulated by public law. The same question (optional) was asked in respect of the bank of no trust (BNT), which leads to the following result:

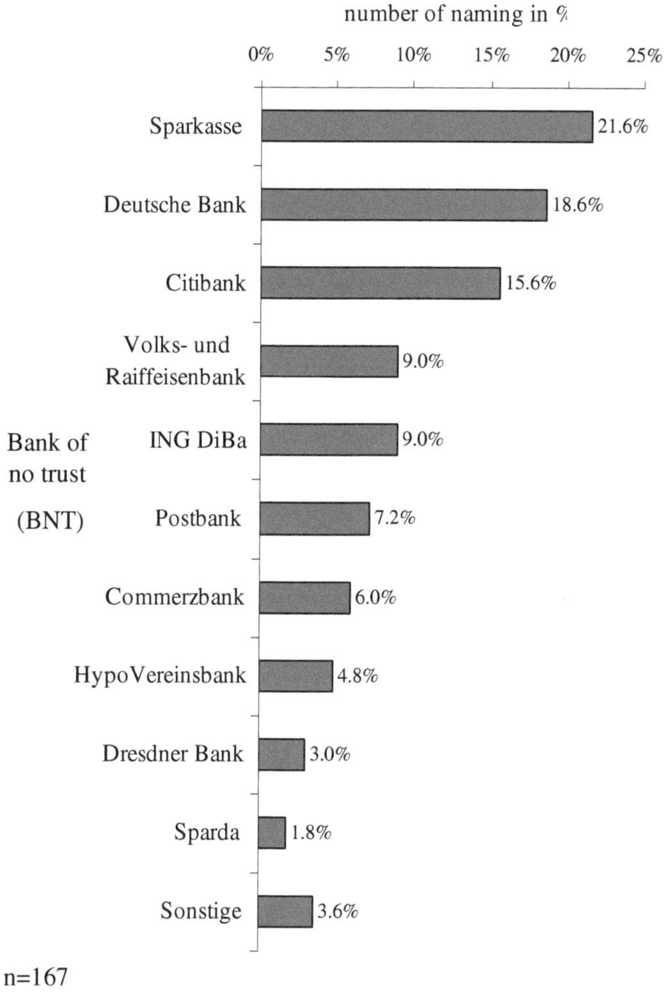

Figure 29: Banks of no trust (BNT) in Germany

The top two banks of no trust are "Sparkasse" (21.6% of a total n=167) and "Deutsche Bank" (18.6%). This result is surprising, because the banks "Sparkasse" and "Deutsche Bank" are evaluated as both the top BT and also the top BNT. The question arises: How and why do German respondents differ between a BT and BNT?

In 86.8% of the answers, the BT belongs to one of the seven largest German banks – five private German banks (cash group) (22.4% of answers) and two regulated by public law ("Sparkasse" and "Volks- und Raiffeisenbank") (64.1%). In 70% of the answers, the BNT also belong to the seven biggest banks, either to one of the private banks (39.5%) or to the banks regulated by public law (30.5%). Therefore, the suggestion that less familiar banks are more likely to be rated as the "bank of no trust" could not be confirmed. This may simply be due to customers not knowing less familiar banks, or customers not really remembering the names of unfamiliar banks. Therefore, consumers might simply mention a famous bank that they are least likely to patronize.

Two banks beside the top seven banks in Germany are noticeable in the studies. "DiBa" was often mentioned beside the top seven banks as a BT bank (4.7%) and a BNT (9.0%). It is a direct bank without any branch offices. Communication with the bank is only possible via e-mail, letters, telephone, or mobile phone/PDA and no eye-to-eye dialog is possible. Also noteworthy is the "Citibank", which ranks between the top seven banks. 2.1% of the participants mentioned it as a BT, but 15.6% as a BNT. The "Citibank" is a part of the global finance service provider Citigroup, which is the biggest banking organization in the world for private customers.

The majority of the Germans (57%) have one bank. 41% of the German population has more than one bank.

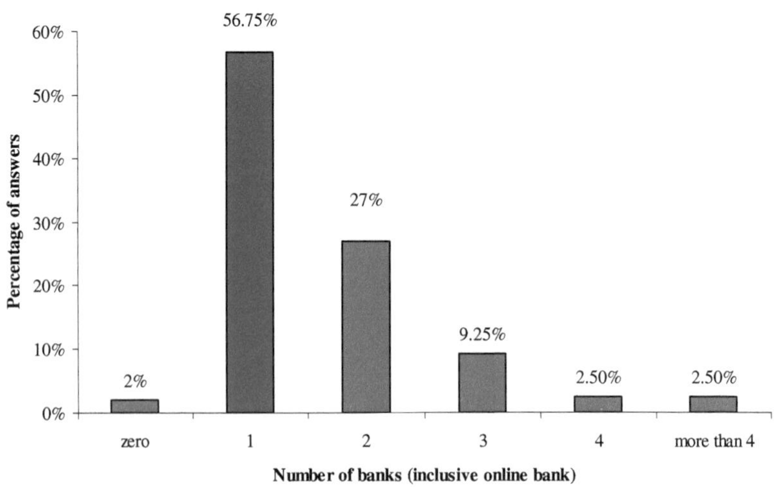

Figure 30: Number of banks (inclusive online banks) (n=400)

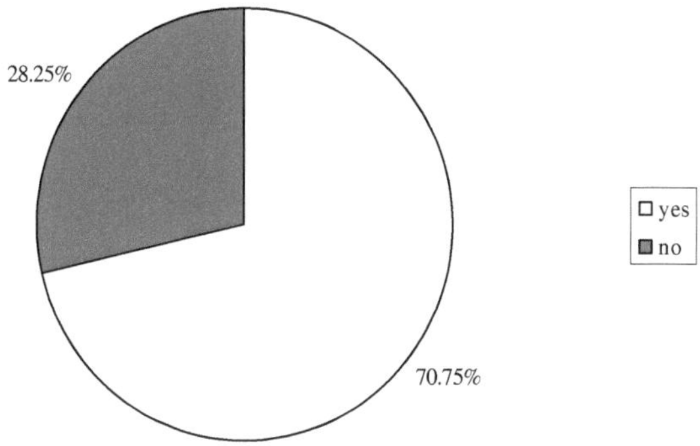

Figure 31: At least one family member is a customer of the same house bank (n=396)

70.75% of the Germans state that a least one family member is a customer of the same house bank.

The following statements given after the bar charts mostly use the sum of the percentage values of scale values 1 and 2 or scale values 6 and 7.

The descriptive results for the construct **trust propensity** are shown in the following figures.

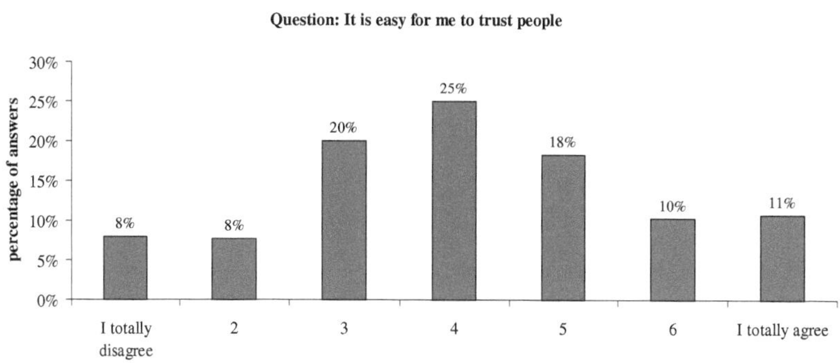

Figure 32: Result for trust propensity in Germany (1)

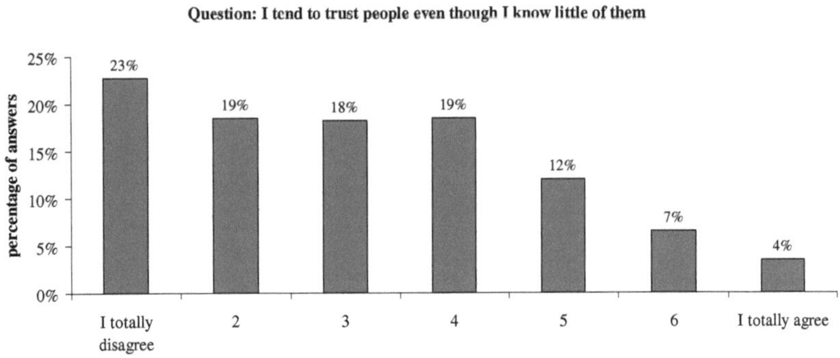

Figure 33: Result for trust propensity in Germany (2)

For 21% of the Germans it is very easy to trust people in general, on contrast for 16% of the German population it is very hard (mean = 4.12). Especially, in situations with little knowledge of the counterpart even more – 44% of the Germans – tend not to trust people (mean = 3.12).

The descriptive results for the construct **attractiveness** are shown in the following figures.

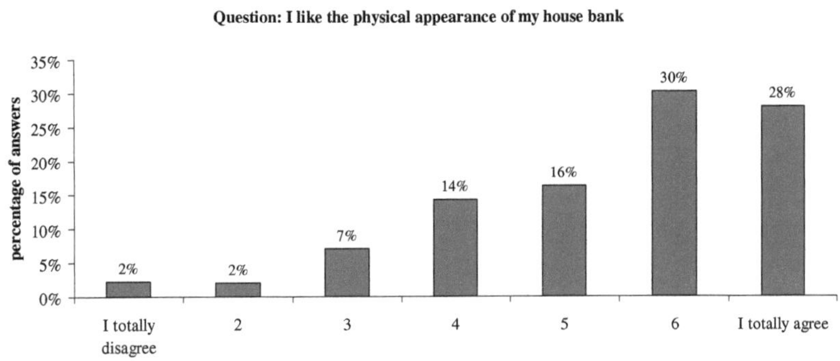

Figure 34: Result for German house bank's attractiveness (1)

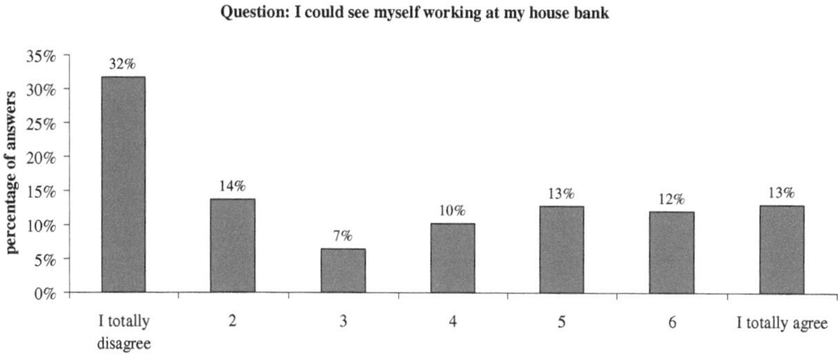

Figure 35: Result for German house bank's attractiveness (2)

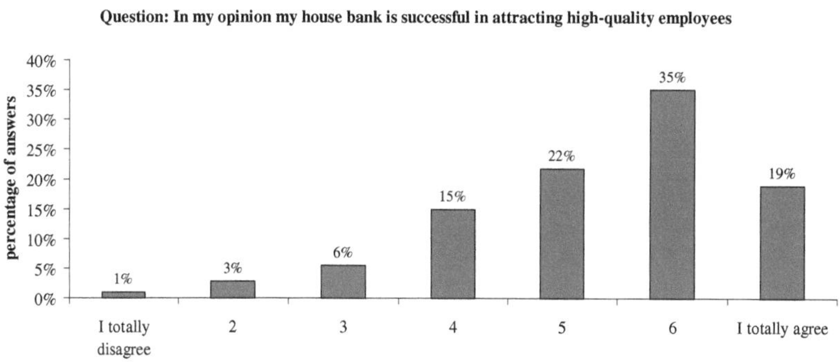

Figure 36: Result for German house bank's attractiveness (3)

58% of the Germans like the physical appearance of their house bank (mean = 5.43). Although 54% of the Germans expect that their house bank attracts high quality employees (mean = 5.35), only 25% could imagine working there (mean = 3.47). Consequently, the half of the Germans perceive their house bank as an attractive bank.

The descriptive results for the construct **quality** are shown in the following figures

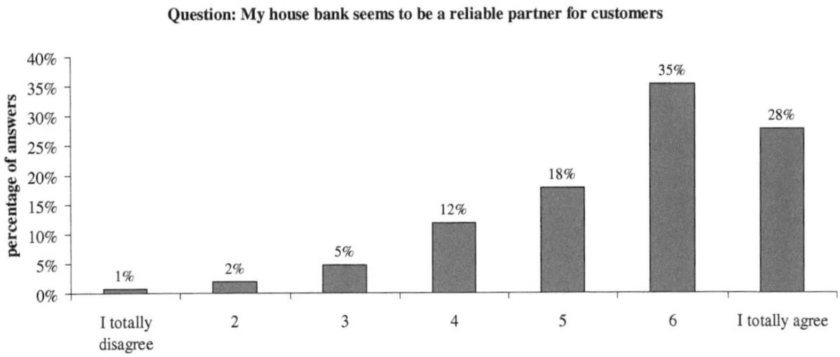

Figure 37: Result for German house bank's quality (1)

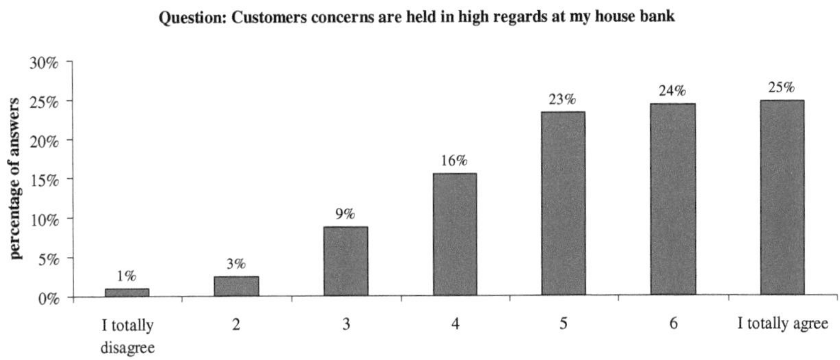

Figure 38: Result for German house bank's quality (2)

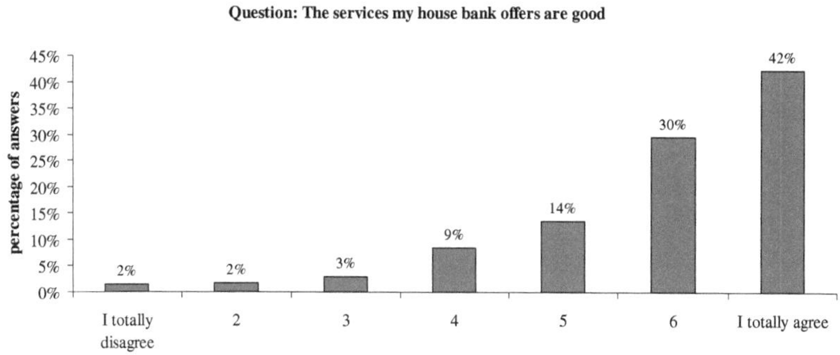

Figure 39: Result for German house bank's quality (3)

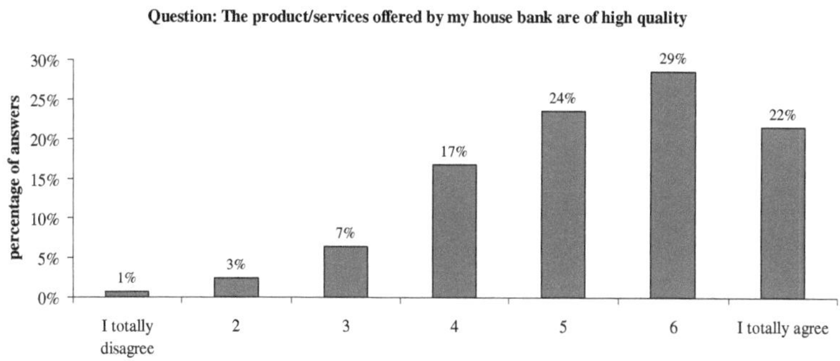

Figure 40: Result for German house bank's quality (4)

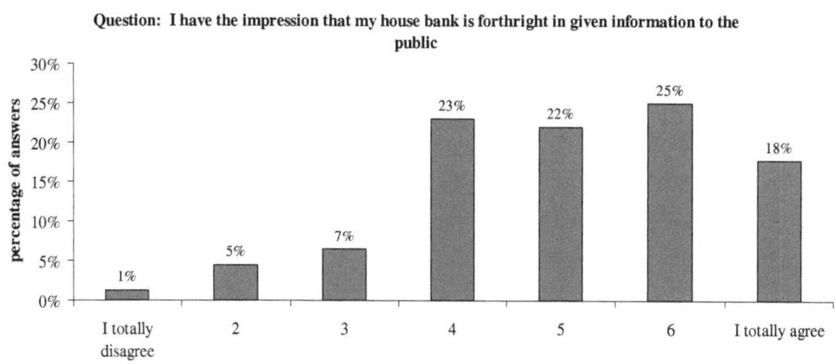

Figure 41: Result for German house bank's quality (5)

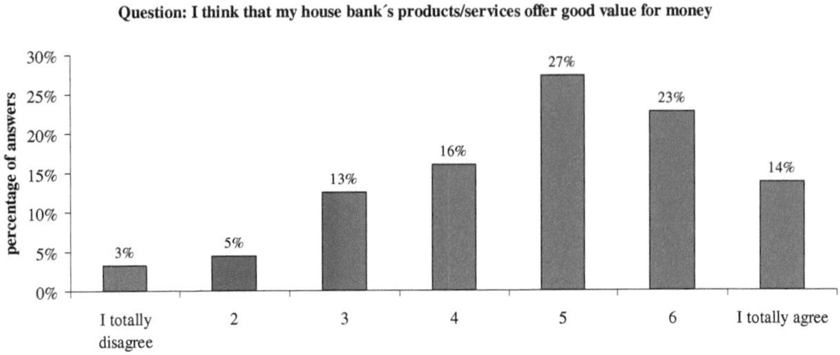

Figure 42: Result for German house bank's quality (6)

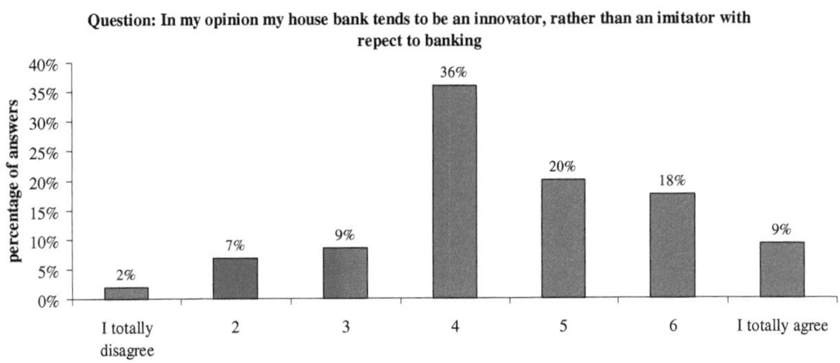

Figure 43: Result for German house bank's quality (7)

63% of the Germans perceive their house bank as a reliable partner (mean = 5.61). 49% of the Germans say that their concerns are held in high regards (mean = 5.29). And even 72% perceived the offered services as good (mean = 5.88). In contrast, only 51% perceive the quality of the product/service highly (mean = 5.31). 43% of the Germans think that their house bank is forthright in given information to the public (mean = 5.06). But still 23% indicate that they are not sure (value 4) if their house bank tells everything which is relevant to the customers. The value for products/services is perceived good for 37% of the Germans (mean = 4.83). 8% of the Germans think the value is not good. 27% of the Germans think that their bank tends to be an innovator, rather than an imitator in respect to banking (mean = 4.55). But still 36% do not have a clear opinion concerning this question. Only 9% perceive their house bank rather as an imitator. Consequently, half of the Germans seem to be quite satisfied with the quality and newness of the products and services of their house bank.

The descriptive results for the construct **performance** are shown in the following figures.

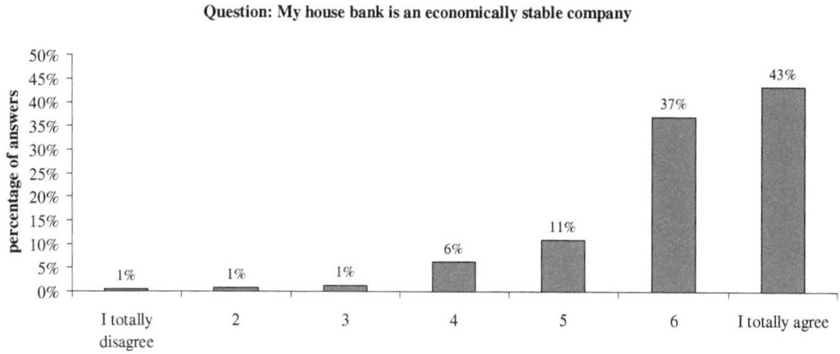

Figure 44: Result for German house bank's performance (1)

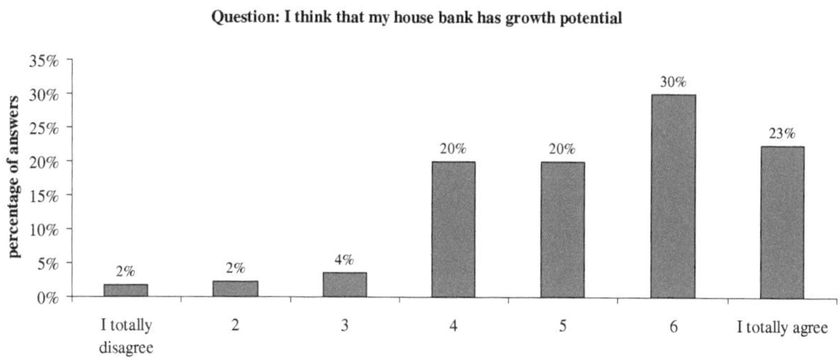

Figure 45: Result for German house bank's performance (2)

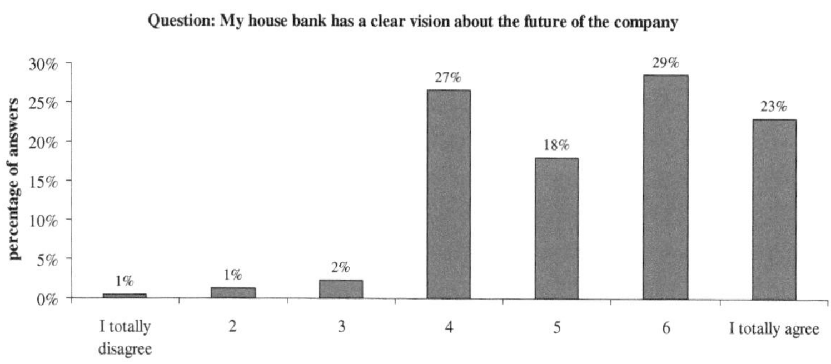

Figure 46: Result for German house bank's performance (3)

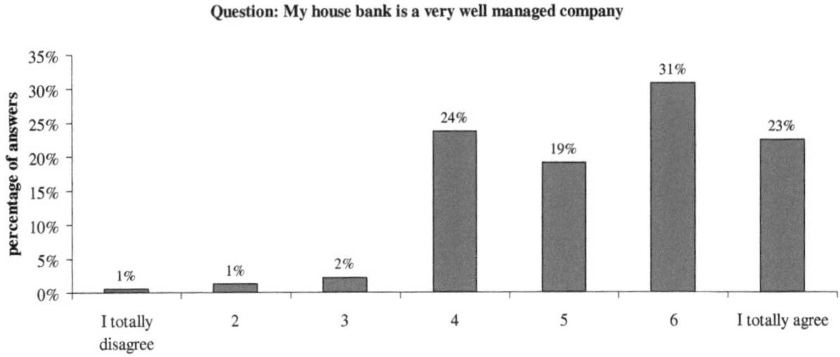

Figure 47: Result for German house bank's performance (4)

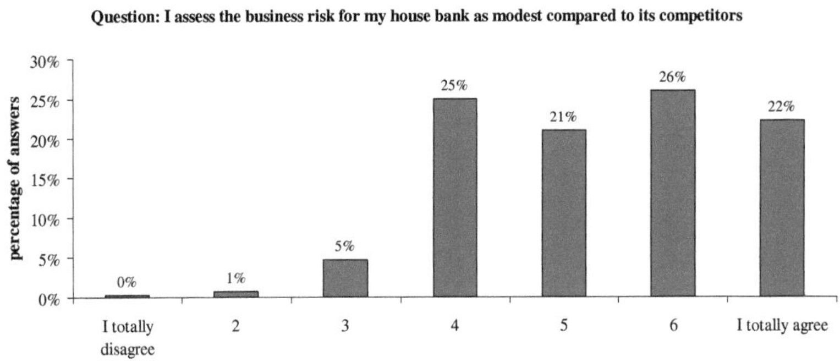

Figure 48: Result for German house bank's performance (5)

80% of the Germans perceive their house bank as an economically stable company (mean = 6.11). Only 2% disagree with this statement. 53% of the Germans think that their house bank has growth potential (mean = 5.34). 52% of the Germans state, that their house bank has a clear vision about the future of the company (mean = 5.38). Still 27% are not sure, if their house banks really do. 54% of the Germans perceive their house bank as well managed (mean = 5.42). Only 2% perceive it as bad managed. 48% of the Germans perceive the business risk for their house bank as modest compared to its competitors (mean = 5.33). Only 1% have a totally different opinion in perceiving a high risk compared to the competitors.

Consequently, the majority of the Germans perceive a high performance of their house banks.

The descriptive results for the construct **responsibility** are shown in the following figures.

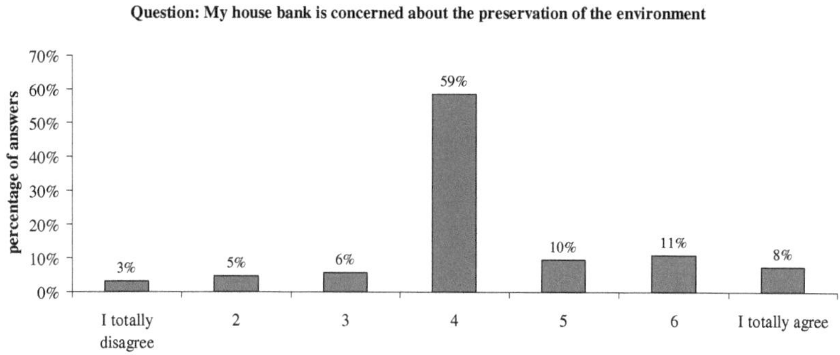

Figure 49: Result for German house bank's responsibility (1)

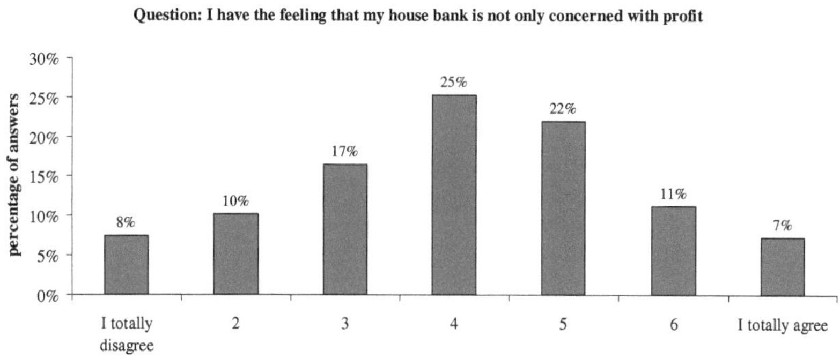

Figure 50: Result for German house bank's responsibility (2)

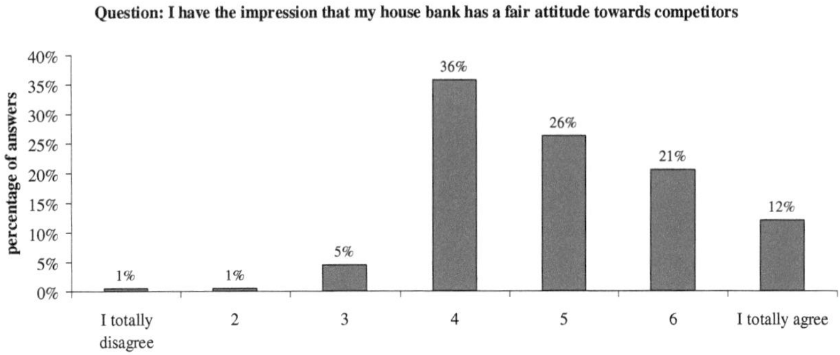

Figure 51: Result for German house bank's responsibility (3)

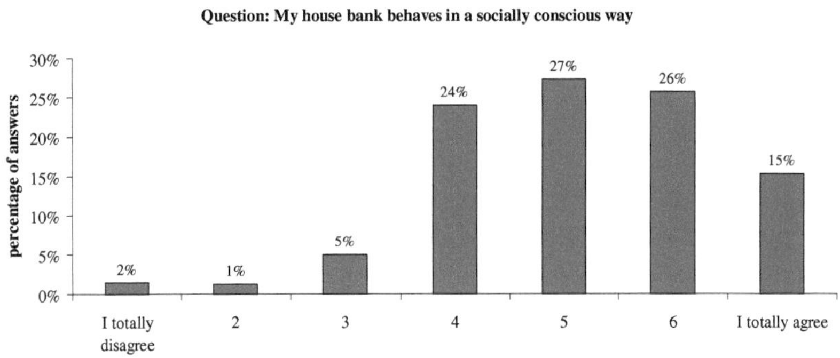

Figure 52: Result for German house bank's responsibility (4)

The result that 59% of the Germans indicate value 4 for the perceived concern about the environment of their house bank seems to mirror, that the majority is not sure, if their house bank really does or does not act for environment (mean = 4.29). In addition, 18% of the Germans expect that their house bank is only concerned with profit (mean = 4.07). Fairness towards competitors of their house bank is expected from 33% of Germans (mean = 4.96). Still 36% have indicated the value 4, which mirrors a medium expected fairness attitude. 24% (value 4) think that their house bank behaves more likely in a socially conscious way (mean = 5.13).

Consequently, a quarter up to a third of the Germans perceive the responsibility of the house banks rather at a medium level.

The descriptive results for the construct **competence** are shown in the following figures.

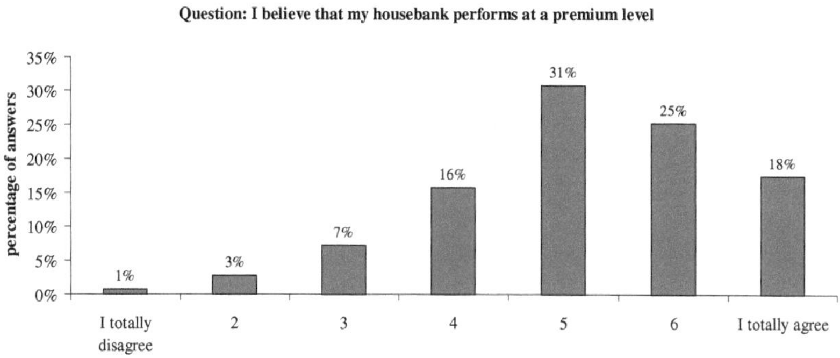

Figure 53: Result for German house bank's competence (1)

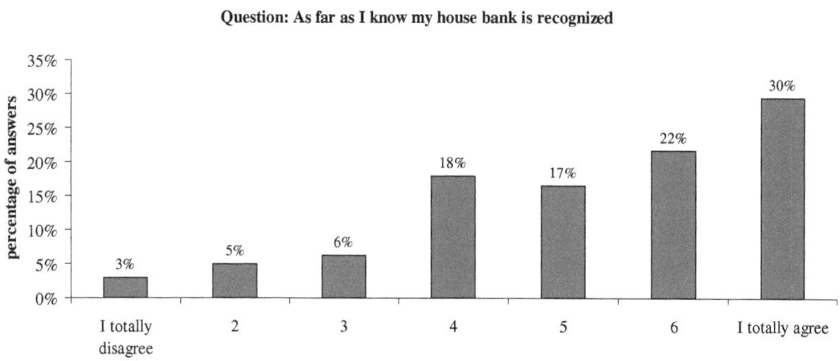

Figure 54: Result for German house bank's competence (2)

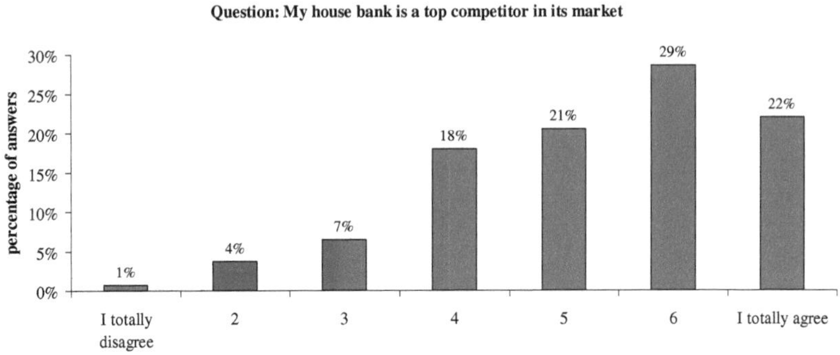

Figure 55: Result for German house bank's competence (3)

43% of the Germans totally agree with a premium level performance of their house bank (mean = 5.19). 52% of the Germans totally agree with the recognition of their house bank (mean = 5.23). 53% state that their house bank is a top competitor in the banking market (mean = 5.27).

Consequently, the competence of the house banks is perceived high for more than half of the Germans.

The descriptive results for the construct **likeability** are shown in the following figures.

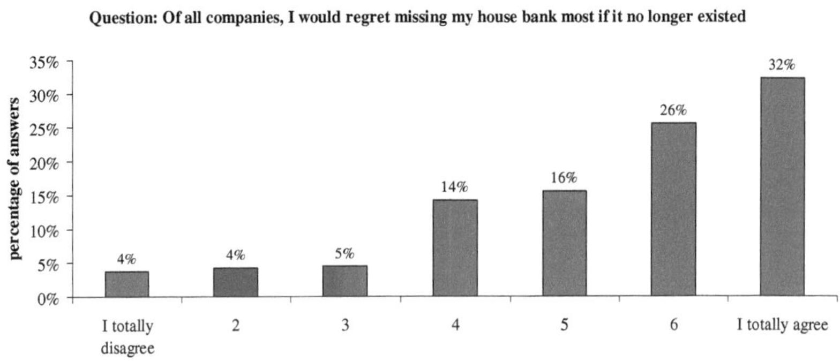

Figure 56: Result for German house bank's likeability (1)

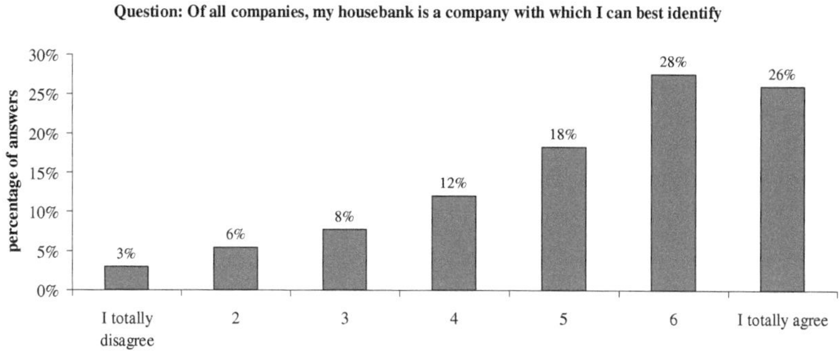

Figure 57: Result for German house bank's likeability (2)

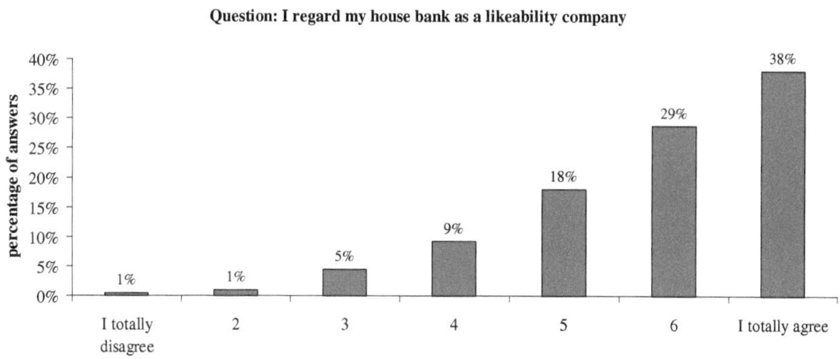

Figure 58: Result for German house bank's likeability (3)

58% of the Germans would regret missing their house bank (mean = 5.39). Even 54% state that their house bank is a company with which they can best identify (mean = 5.24). Only 3% totally disagree with this statement. Therefore, it is not surprisingly, that 67% of the Germans perceive their house bank as a likeability company (mean = 5.82).

The descriptive results for the construct **affective trust** are shown in the following figures.

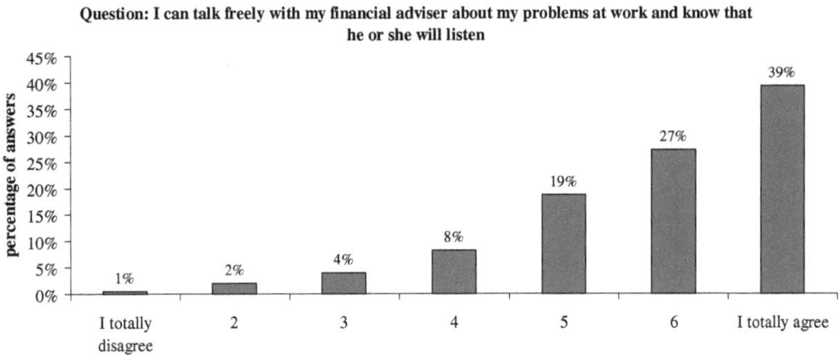

Figure 59: Result for German house bank's affective trust (1)

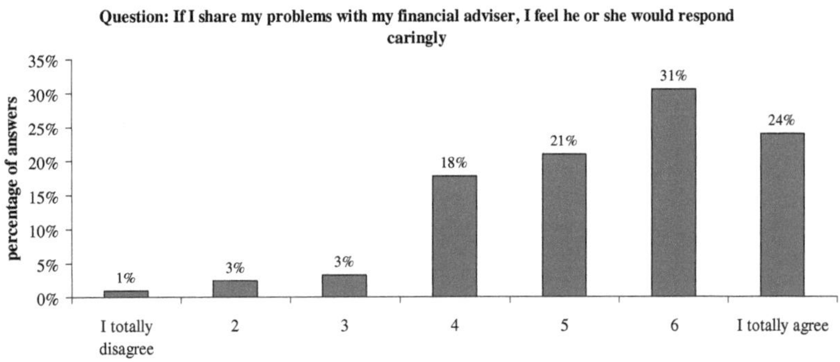

Figure 60: Result for German house bank's affective trust (2)

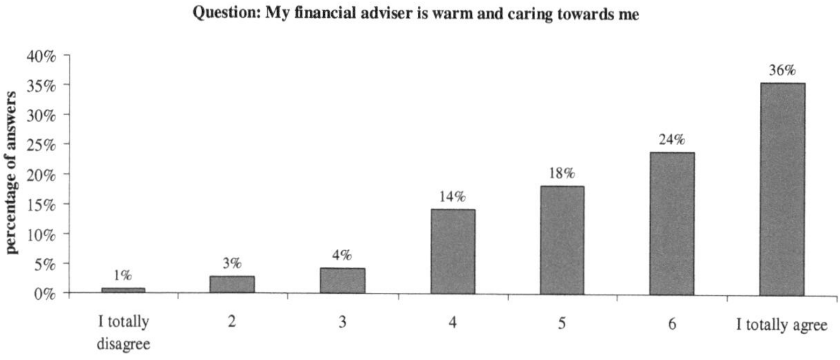

Figure 61: Result for German house bank's affective trust (3)

66% of the Germans state that they can talk freely with their financial adviser about problems and expect that their financial adviser will listen (mean = 5.82). Only 3% of the Germans totally disagree with that statement. A caringly respond with their problems is only, but still, expected from 55% of the Germans (mean = 5.43). But 60% perceive their financial adviser as warm and caring (mean = 5.62).

Consequently, two-thirds of Germans have a high affective trust in their financial advisers, and thus in their house banks.

The descriptive results for the construct **cognitive trust** are shown in the following figures.

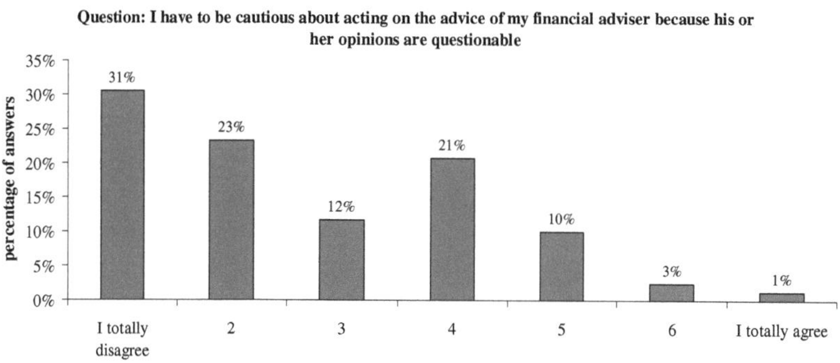

Figure 62: Result for German house bank's cognitive trust (1)

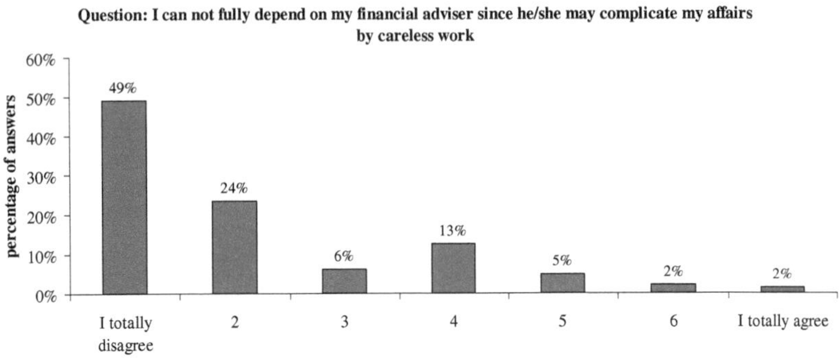

Figure 63: Result for German house bank's cognitive trust (2)

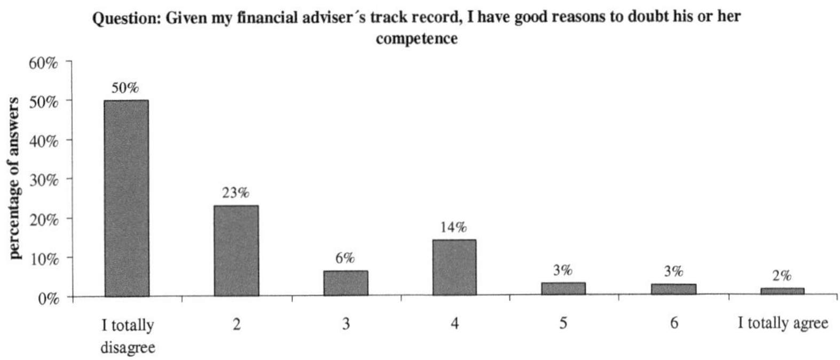

Figure 64: Result for German house bank's cognitive trust (3)

54% of the Germans have trust in their financial adviser's acting. Only 4% have the feeling of being cautions about the acting on the advice of the financial adviser, because of questionable opinions (mean = 2.69). Still 21% (value 4) of the Germans do perceive medium risk acting on the advice. This perceived remaining risk does not seem to develop through careless work of the bank's employee, because 73% of the Germans state that their can depend on the financial advisers work (mean = 2.14). In addition 73% of the Germans trust in the competence of the financial adviser through their made experience (mean = 2.11).

Consequently, three-fourths of Germans do have cognitive trust on their financial adviser of the bank, who mirrors the cognitive trust in their house bank.

The descriptive results for the construct **conative trust** are shown in the following figures.

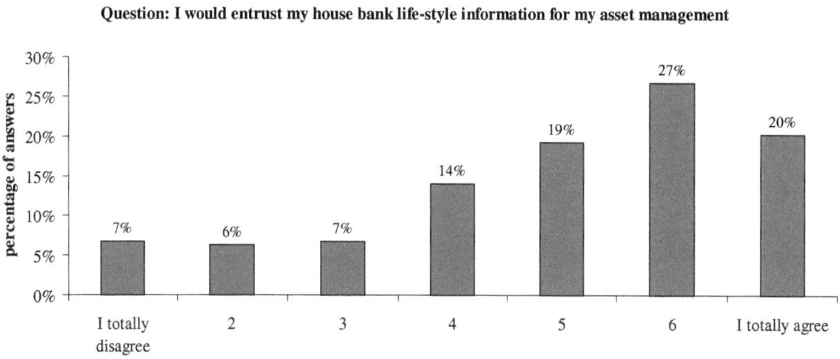

Figure 65: Result for German house bank's conative trust (1)

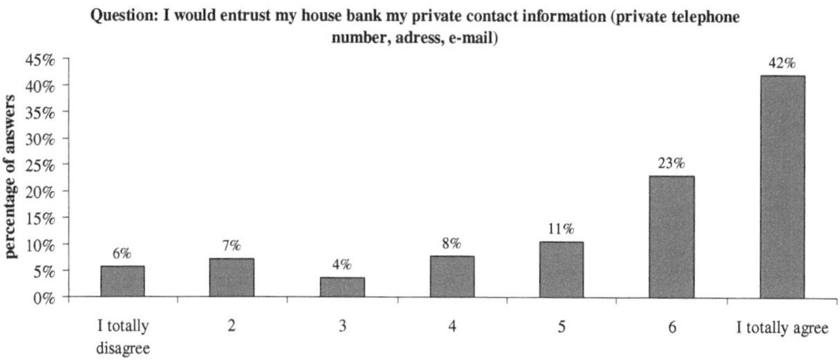

Figure 66: Result for German house bank's conative trust (2)

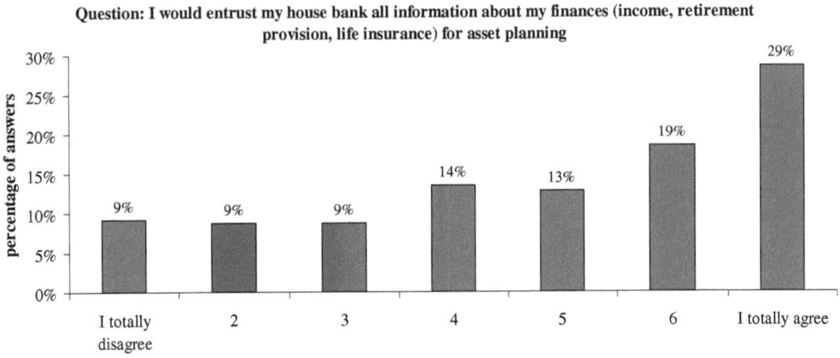

Figure 67: Result for German house bank's conative trust (3)

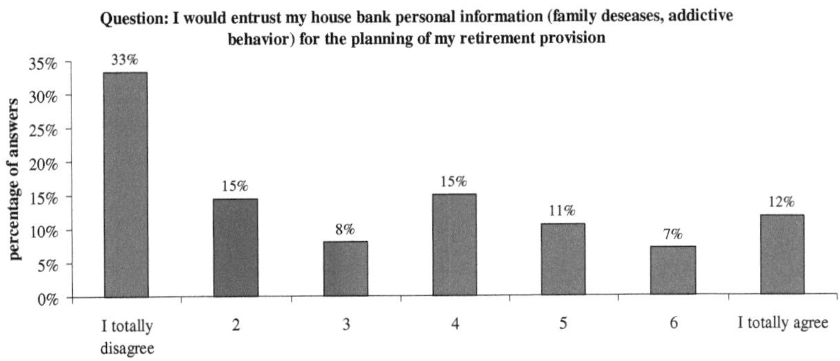

Figure 68: Result for German house bank's conative trust (4)

47% of the Germans would entrust life-style information for a detailed asset management. But 13% state that they would not do that at all (mean = 4.94). 65% of the Germans would entrust all kinds of private contact information to their financial adviser. Still 13% of the German population would not provide all private contact data (mean = 5.47). 48% of the Germans would entrust their finance information for a detailed asset planning. In contrast, 18% of the Germans would not do that (mean = 4.81). Only 19% of the Germans would entrust one of the most private information, for example family diseases. Nearly half of the Germans with 48% would not give this kind of information to their financial adviser (mean = 3.23).

Consequently, the majority of Germans do entrust private information like contact information or financial information. In contrast, highly private information will nearly never be given to the bank. The conative trust in the financial adviser, and thus house bank, exists for a lower level of privacy and not a critical theme for the customer.

The descriptive results for the construct **loyalty** are shown in the following figures.

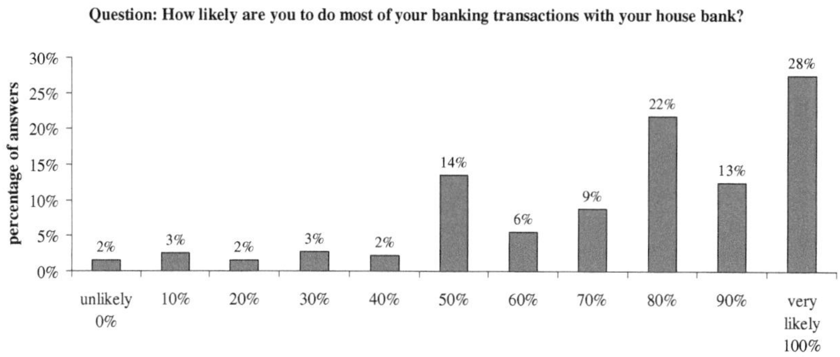

Figure 69: Result for German house bank customer loyalty (1)

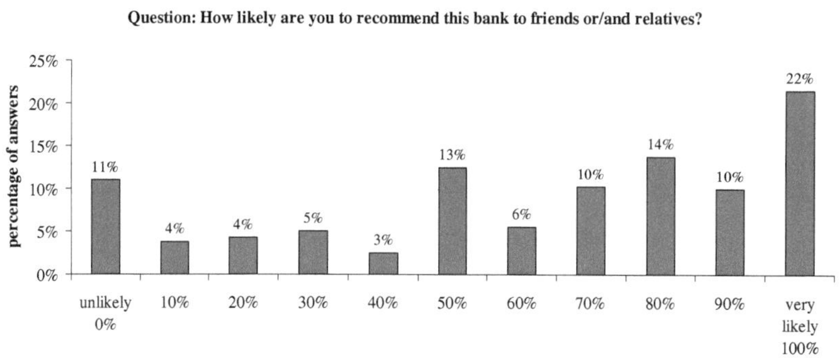

Figure 70: Result for German house bank customer loyalty (2)

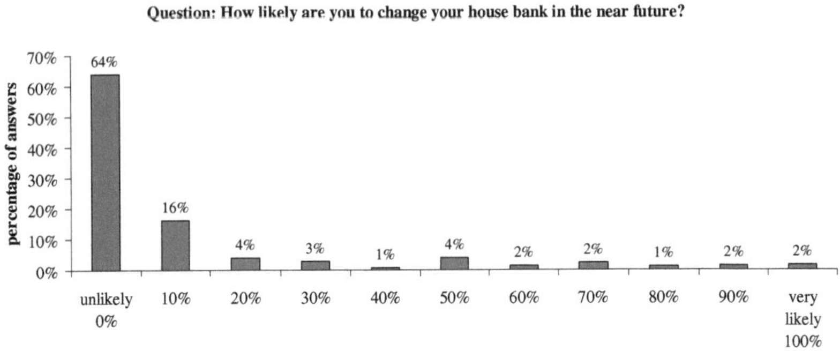

Figure 71: Result for German house bank customer loyalty (3)

Only 28% of the Germans will do most of their banking transactions with their house bank (mean = 8.46). Even if 22% of the Germans would recommend their house bank, 11% of the Germans would very unlikely do so (mean = 7.20). Two-third of the Germans will not change their house bank in the near future (mean = 2.21). Consequently, Germans do not tend to change their house bank in the near future, but they will not strongly recommend their bank or do most of their transaction with their house bank.

The descriptive results for the construct **security** are shown in the following figure.

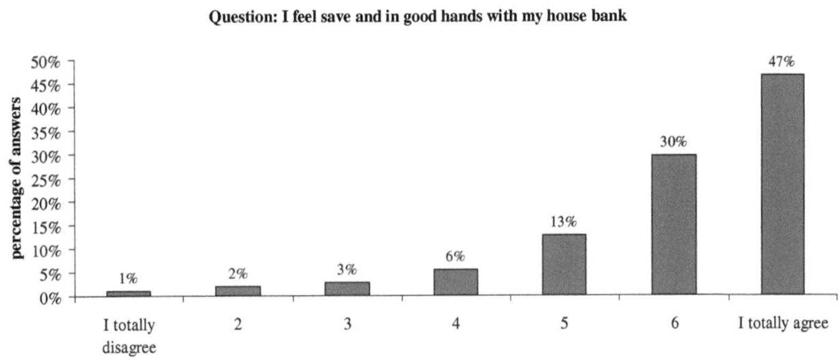

Figure 72: Result for German house bank's security

77% of the Germans feel save and in good hands with their house bank (mean = 6.02).

The descriptive results for the construct **protection** are shown in the following figures.

Figure 73: Result for German house bank's protection (1)

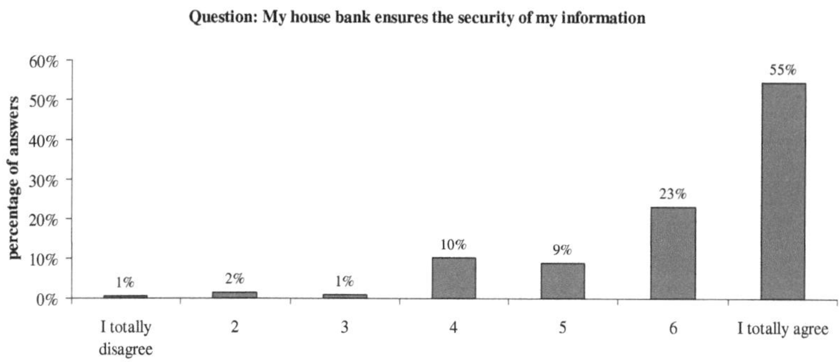

Figure 74: Result for German house bank's protection (2)

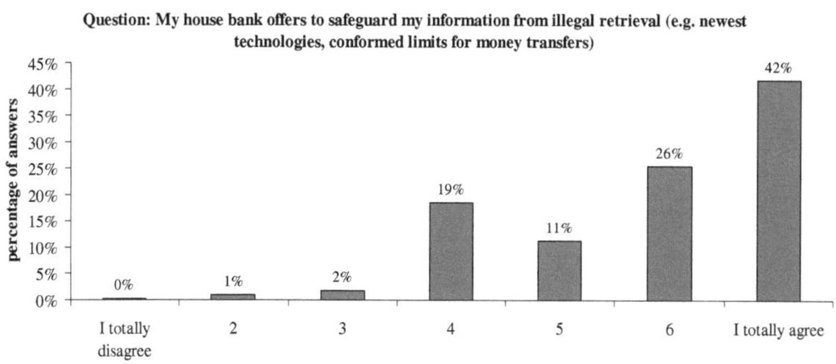

Figure 75: Result for German house bank's protection (3)

86% of the German population perceive that their house bank offer secure transactions (mean = 6.38). In addition 78% of the Germans have the feeling that their house bank ensures their information (mean = 6.14). Also, 68% of the Germans state that their house bank offers to safeguard their information from illegal retrieval (mean = 5.83). Consequently, the majority of Germans feel that the bank protects their information.

The descriptive results for the construct **opportunism** are shown in the following figures.

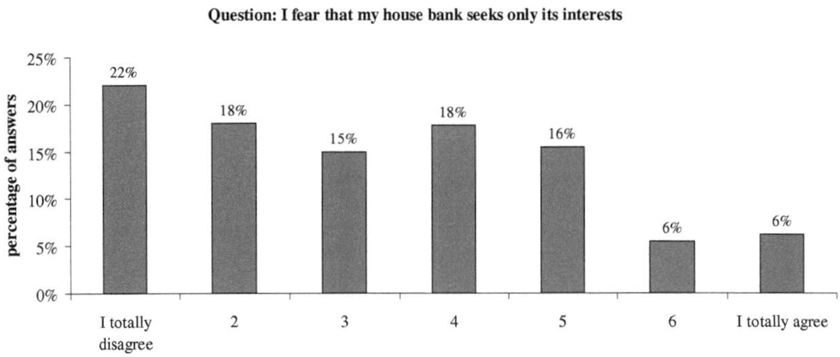

Figure 76: Result for German house bank's opportunism (1)

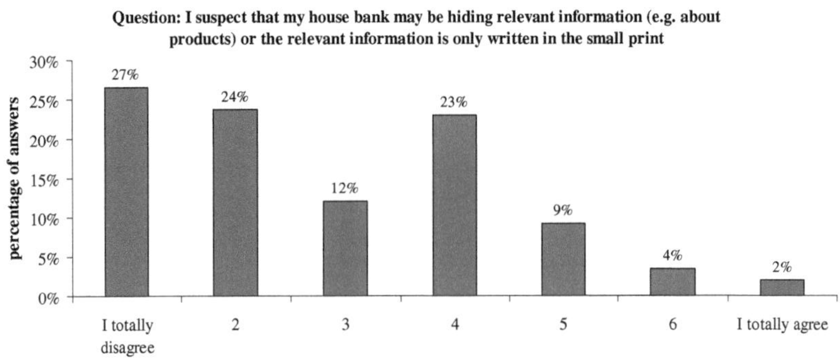

Figure 77: Result for German house bank's opportunism (2)

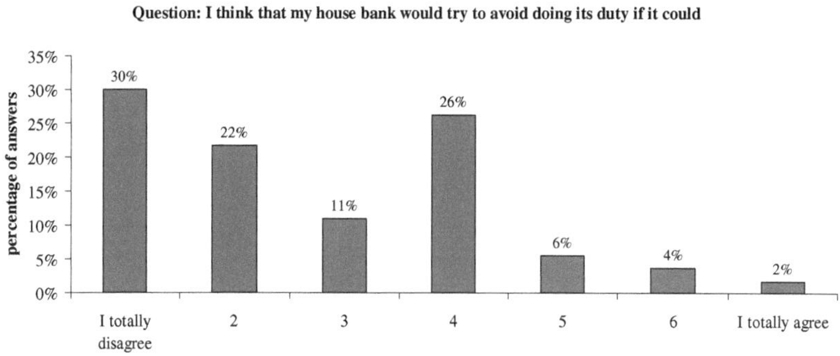

Figure 78: Result for German house bank's opportunism (3)

12% of the Germans belief that their house bank seeks only its interest. In contrast, 40% totally disagree with this statement (mean = 3.28). After all, 6% of the Germans think that their house bank may hide relevant information or the relevant information is only written in the small print. But, 51% of the Germans think they do not (mean = 2.83). 52% of the Germans state that they think that their house bank is doing its duty. Only 6% state that the bank would try to avoid doing its duty if it could (mean = 2.74). Consequently, the perceived opportunistic behavior of the house bank is not very strongly pronounced. Nevertheless, the seeking of bank interests (e.g. profit maximation) is still perceived from approx. 10% of the Germans.

The descriptive results for the construct **intention** are shown in the following figures.

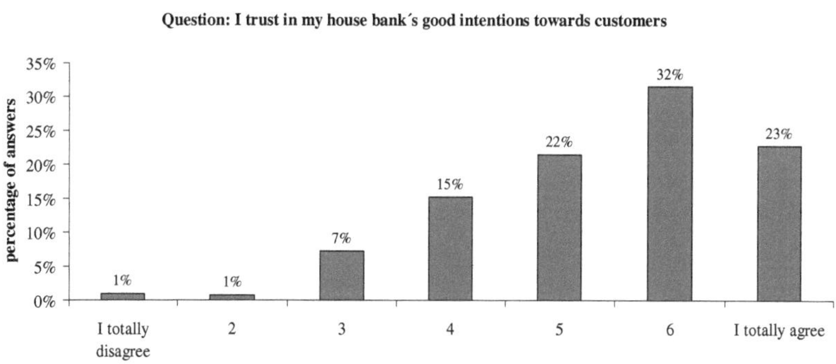

Figure 79: Result for German house bank's intention (1)

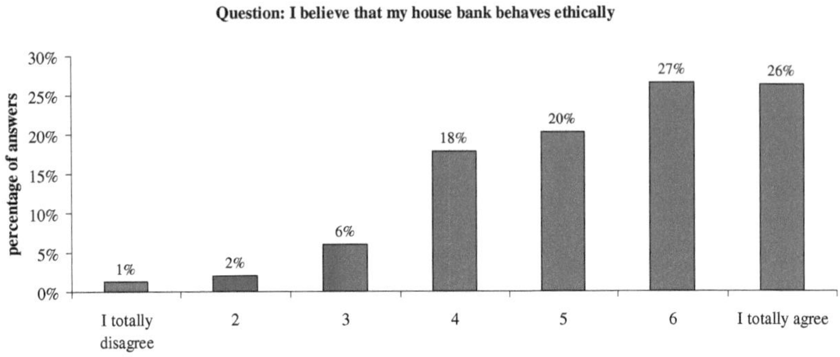

Figure 80: Result for German house bank's intention (2)

55% of the Germans trust in the bank's good intentions towards their customers (mean = 5.41). In addition 52% of the Germans believe in an ethical behavior of their house banks (mean = 5.38). Consequently, half of the Germans do believe in good intentions of their house bank.

The descriptive results for the construct **discretion** are shown in the following figures.

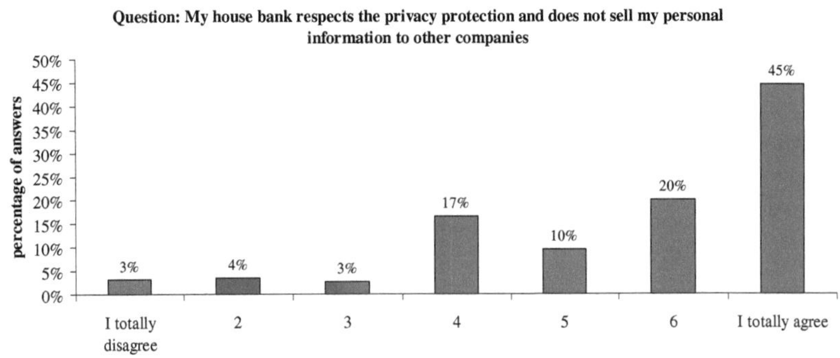

Figure 81: Result for German house bank's discretion (1)

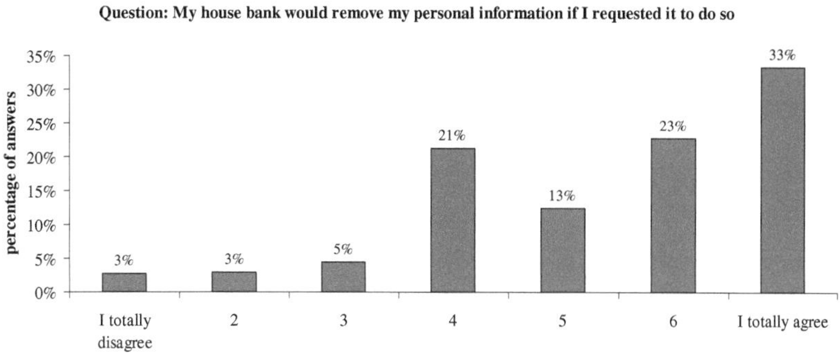

Figure 82: Result for German house bank's discretion (2)

65% state that their house bank respects the privacy protection and does not sell personal information to other companies. But still 7% do think house banks do sell private information (mean = 5.64). 56% of the Germans think that the house bank would remove personal information if they request to do so. In contrast 6% believe house banks would not do it (mean = 5.39). Consequently, two-thirds of the Germans believe that their banks have a discrete behavior, while 6-7% of the Germans think banks use private customer information for further purposes.

The descriptive results for the construct **satisfaction** are shown in the following figures.

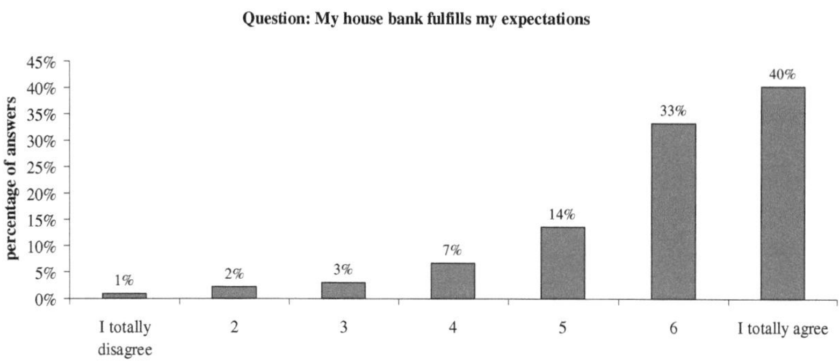

Figure 83: Result for bank customer's satisfaction in Germany (1)

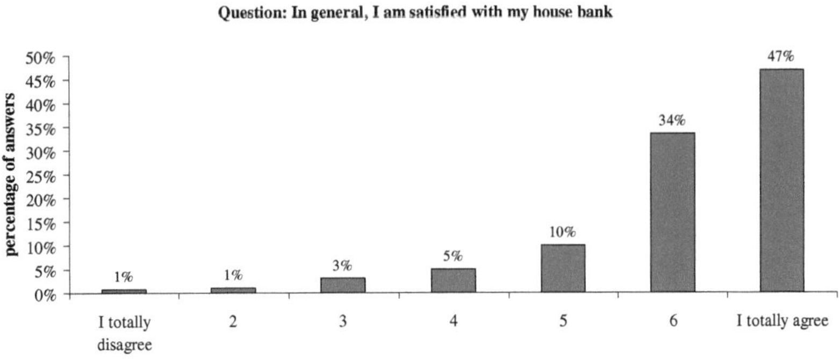

Figure 84: Result for bank customer's satisfaction in Germany (2)

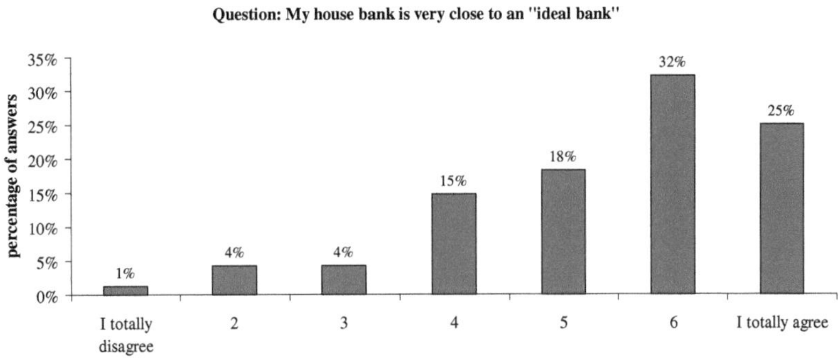

Figure 85: Result for bank customer's satisfaction in Germany (3)

73% of the Germans state that their house bank fulfills their expectations (mean = 5.90). Only 3% totally disagree with this statement. Even 81% are generally satisfied with their house bank. Only 2% of the Germans are not (mean = 6.10). Calling the house bank an "ideal bank" is stated from 57% of the Germans. 5% perceive their house bank far away from perfect (mean = 5.41). Consequently, three-quarters of the Germans are generally satisfied with their house bank.

The descriptive results for the construct **involvement** are shown in the following figures.

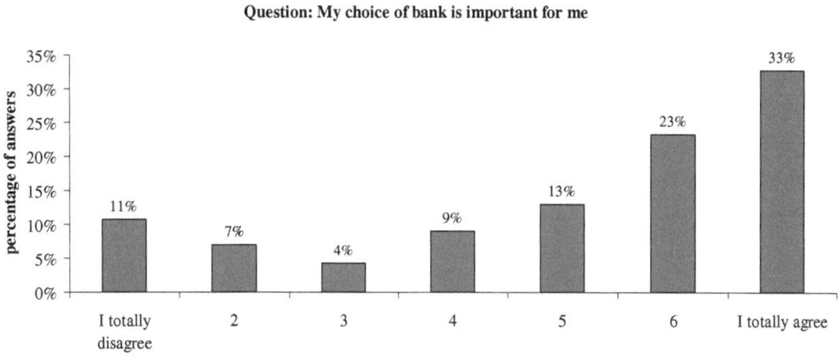

Figure 86: Result for bank customer's involvement in Germany

The choice of the bank is important for 56% of the Germans. In contrast 18% of the Germans do not really care about the choice of their bank (mean = 5.07).

In summary, the descriptive results of the banking industry in Germany show that 87% of the Germans are customers of one of the top seven banks (Sparkasse, Volksbank/Raiffeisenbank, and the cash group) in Germany. The banking industry is perceived in nearly all aspects (trust, likeability, competence, quality, performance, appearance, responsibility, security, intention, opportunism, protection, discretion, satisfaction) above average, because the mean values of the questions are almost all above the medium value "4". One noteworthy aspect is that banks do not seem to be a preferred employer. The means value for the question if the respondent could image working at the house bank was "3.47" and thus, below the medium value "4". Furthermore, questions about security and protection were answered with mean values above "6", which leads to the conclusion, that Germans have very high security and protection feelings towards their house banks. The same goes with the perception of the economic stability of their banks. In general, Germans are highly satisfied with their bank, which is expressed through the mean value "6.1". This empirical survey was done before the bank crash in 2007. Therefore, these positive results might have changed. Security and satisfactions feelings have been significantly negatively affected by the banking crash, which has been analyzed in an experiment for and after the bank crash by RAITHEL/EBERT (2008). Trust building measure help to recapture these high levels.

4.3. Evaluation of the Quality of Measurement and Structural Equation Models

As already mentioned, the validity and reliability of the measurement and the structural equation models can be partly tested by the output of smartPLS. In a first step the evaluation of the latent variables in the structural equation model will be analyzed without the moderator effects. The consideration of moderators in the analysis will lead to higher R^2 values. Thus, to achieve a more stringent evaluation of the goodness of the model, the moderator effects will be analyzed and discussed in a second step.

Since there is no global goodness value like the "Goodness of Fit Index" (GFI) with which to evaluate the structural equation model, RINGLE (2004b, p. 27) recommends an evaluation of the entire model. This evaluation should be undertaken by taking all calculated quality criteria for the measurement models and structural equation models into account. Therefore, the quality criteria calculated by smartPLS for the measurement model (AVE, composite reliability, and Cronbach's alpha), as well as for the structural equation model (R^2 and cross-validated redundancy) in the main survey are shown in the following table.

Construct	Number of Indicators	AVE	Composite Reliability	Cronbach´s Alpha	R^2	Crossvalidated Redundancy (=Q^2)	All values above threshold (yes/no)
Threshold values		≥ 0.5	≥ 0.6	≥ 0.7 (2 to 3 indicators ≥0.4)	≥ 0.2	≥ 0.0	
Affective trust	3	0.783	0.915	0.861	0.556	0.435	yes
Cognitive trust	3	0.689	0.869	0.774	0.296	0.201	yes
Conative trust	4	0.592	0.852	0.769	0.294	0.174	yes
Likeability	3	0.772	0.91	0.853	0.530	0.401	yes
Competence	3	0.654	0.850	0.740	0.468	0.293	yes
Attractiveness	3	-	-	-	-	0.542	yes
Quality	7	-	-	-	-	0.527	yes
Performance	5	-	-	-	-	0.490	yes
Responsibility	4	-	-	-	-	0.535	yes
Security	1	1.00	1.00	1.00	0.382	0.382	yes
Intention	2	0.833	0.909	0.800	-	0.833	yes
Opportunism	3	0.632	0.837	0.712	-	0.632	yes
Discretion	2	0.709	0.829	0.590	-	0.709	yes
Protection	3	0.605	0.821	0.680	-	0.605	yes
Satisfaction	3	0.849	0.944	0.911	-	0.849	yes
Involvement	1	1.00	1.00	1.00	-	1.00	yes
Trust propensity	2	0.648	0.774	0.610	-	0.629	yes
Loyalty	3	0.601	0.818	0.666	0.334	0.200	yes

Table 16: Quality criteria for the measurement and structural equation model calculated by smart PLS (main study)

The table clearly shows that all constructs in the main study[32] fulfill the threshold values of AVE, composite reliability, Cronbach's alpha, R^2, and the cross-validated redundancy (see last column in Table 16).

[32] The calculated quality criteria for the pre-study fulfill the thresholds as well, but are not listed in detail.

The values of the AVE and the composite reliability of the reflective constructs are far above the thresholds. Cronbach's alpha values are above 0.7 for most of the constructs. Just the three constructs discretion, trust propensity, and loyalty are under 0.7, but still above 0.4. These three constructs have less than four indicators, thus their Cronbach's alpha, which is above 0.4, is still adequate. Five of the seven reflectively dependent latent variables have an R^2 above 0.33, which mirrors an average value. Of these, the constructs affective trust (R^2=0.56), likeability (R^2=0.53), and competence (R^2=0.47) have the highest values, which indicates a high proportion of explained variance to total variance (high information). Two of the dependent constructs (cognitive and conative trust) have values under 0.33, but still far above 0.19, which mirrors still an adequate result. The low R^2 of cognitive and conative trust might be due to missing antecedents not recognized in the theoretical model.
As explained, formatively specified constructs cannot be evaluated by these quality criteria. However, the formatively specified constructs have already been evaluated by several empirical studies, e.g. through the tetrad test for banking industry by EBERL (2006, p. 169). Therefore, the accuracy (validity and reliability) of the formatively specified constructs is expected to be good.
The cross-validated redundancy of all reflectively and formatively specified constructs is above "0" and thus adequate. Therefore, the predictive relevance is indicated in respect of the latent variables. Consequently, all calculated quality criteria indicated by smartPLS are above the recommended thresholds.

The analysis of correlations by the Bravais-Pearson coefficients for all pairs of variables are shown in the appendix, where all 55 items are integrated. An explorative factor analysis was done with the principle component analysis on the complete data set revealed 12 factors with an eigenvalue > 1, which explain 62.76% of the original information (see appendix). 12 factors are as a result adequate for such a complex model. 47 items of a total of 55 items could be assigned to the "right" factor, which is a good result for such a complex model.

Summarized, looking at the goodness of the whole model, the existing measurement and structural equation models are evaluated as adequate and suitable for testing the deduced hypotheses in Chapter 2 and 3.

4.4. Examination of Hypothesized Relationships

The section will discuss the testing of the hypotheses, which cover the main effects and moderator effects. The examination of the hypothesized relationships is done by means of the bootstrapping procedure of smartPLS for the path coefficients γ (path between the constructs) and weights λ (path between the indicator and construct) of the reflectively specified constructs with t-values above 1.96. For the formatively specified constructs, weights above 0.1 as recommended by LOHMÖLLER (1989, p. 60) are recognized as relevant trust building measures.

The following table presents the results of the smartPLS calculations in respect of the theoretical model (without moderator effects). The results are based on the data of the main study (n=400). The adjustment of 500 bootstrapping samples is recommended with 400 elements to obtain suitable t values for the estimation of path coefficients. In the following paragraphs, the testing of the hypotheses is described. Each paragraph is introduced by a question that summarizes the relevant hypothesis:

Hypothesis and paths	Proposed path	Coefficient	t Value	Standard Error	Sample Mean	Standard Deviation
H1	Affective trust -> Cognitive trust	0.308***	4.583	0.067	0.315	0.067
H2	Affective trust -> Conative trust	0.165**	2.461	0.071	0.173	0.071
H3	Cognitive trust -> Conative trust	0.034	0.664	0.052	0.033	0.052
H4a	Affective trust -> Loyalty	0.197***	5.853	0.054	0.321	0.054
H4b	Cognitive trust -> Loyalty	0.195***	3.912	0.053	0.201	0.053
H4c	Conative trust -> Loyalty	0.346***	7.093	0.049	0.343	0.049
H6a	Competence -> Affective trust	0.193***	3.886	0.050	0.189	0.050
H6c	Competence -> Cognitive trust	-0.098	0.786	0.049	-0.044	0.049
H6c	Competence -> Conative trust	0.037	1.118	0.061	0.071	0.061
H5/H7a	Likeability -> Affective trust	0.330***	5.447	0.061	0.330	0.061
H5/H7b	Likeability -> Cognitive trust	0.021*	1.807	0.068	0.121	0.068
H5/H7c	Likeability -> Conative trust	0.093	1.395	0.066	0.091	0.066
H8/H13a	Security -> Affective trust	0.132*	1.717	0.077	0.130	0.077
H8/H13b	Security -> Cognitive trust	0.065	1.297	0.082	0.113	0.082
H8/H13c	Security -> Conative trust	0.251***	2.586	0.107	0.255	0.107
H9	Intention -> Security	0.318***	6.379	0.050	0.314	0.050
H10	Opportunism -> Security	-0.148***	3.139	0.0471	-0.149	0.047
H11	Discretion -> Security	0.058	0.979	0.059	0.063	0.059
H12	Protection -> Security	0.275***	4.486	0.061	0.277	0.061
	Attractiveness -> Competence	0.064	1.085	0.059	0.052	0.059
	Attractiveness -> Likeability	0.250***	4.362	0.057	0.236	0.057
	Corporate responsibility -> Competence	0.153***	2.745	0.0558	0.149	0.056
	Corporate responsibility -> Likeability	0.224***	4.817	0.047	0.227	0.047
	Performance -> Competence	0.383***	6.575	0.058	0.384	0.058
	Performance -> Likeability	-0.007	0.142	0.049	0.003	0.049
	Quality -> Competence	0.200***	3.099	0.0645	0.215	0.064
	Quality -> Likeability	0.366***	6.409	0.057	0.374	0.057
	Involvement -> Affective trust	0.022	0.524	0.042	0.024	0.042
	Involvement -> Cognitive trust	0.051	0.965	0.060	0.061	0.060
	Involvement -> Conative trust	0.123***	2.692	0.048	0.130	0.048
	Satisfaction -> Affective trust	0.216***	2.743	0.079	0.220	0.079
	Satisfaction -> Cognitive trust	0.247***	3.496	0.090	0.312	0.090
	Satisfaction -> Conative trust	0.045	0.909	0.101	0.113	0.101
	Trust propensity -> Affective trust	-0.006	0.145	0.044	-0.004	0.043
	Trust propensity -> Cognitive trust	-0.133**	2.465	0.055	-0.124	0.055
	Trust propensity -> Conative trust	0.049	0.854	0.051	0.041	0.051

***.p<0.01; **:p<0.05; *.p<0.10

Table 17: Structural model path results

How do trust dimensions interact with one another (H1 – H3)?

The main study shows a significant impact of affective on cognitive trust (H1: γ_{H1} = 0.308, t = 4.583) and of affective on conative trust (H2: γ_{H2} = 0.165, t = 2.461). The path coefficients γ_{H1} and γ_{H2} are significant, whereby H1 and H2 are verified. There were no significant relationships between conative and cognitive trust (H3: γ_{H3} = 0.034, t = 0.664). H3 was not verified.

Which of the consumer trust attitude dimensions has the most significant impact on loyalty (H4a, b, c)?

All three trust dimensions – affective (H4a: γ_{H4a} = 0.197, t = 5.853), cognitive (H4b: γ_{H4b} = 0.195, t = 3.912), and conative (H4c: γ_{H4c} = 0.346, t = 7.093) – have a strong significant impact on loyalty, whereby H4a, H4b and H4c are verified. Conative trust has the highest path coefficient of all three and therefore best effects consumer loyalty.

What are the most important antecedents (likeability, competence, security) that influence trust in consumers (H5 – H8, H13)?

Affective trust is significantly and strongly influenced by **likeability** (H5a: γ_{H5a} = 0.330, t = 5.447). Likeability has a significant impact on cognitive trust on a 0.10 level (H5b: γ_{H5b}= 0.021, t = 1.807) and no significant impact on conative trust (H5c: γ_{H5c} = 0.093, t = 1.395). Consequently, H5a and H5b are verified, H5c are not verified.

The significant effects of the bank's **competence** on consumer trust could be partly analyzed. Competence has a significant positive impact on affective trust (H6a: γ_{H6a} = 0.193, t = 3.886). No significant impacts could be established in respect of competence on cognitive and conative trust (H6b: γ_{H6b} = -0.098, t = 0.786 and H6c: γ_{H6c} = 0.037, t = 1.118). Consequently, H6a is verified. H6b and H6c are not verified. The competence of a bank therefore leads to higher affective consumer trust.

Security has a significant impact on conative trust (the main driver of loyalty) (H8c: γ_{H8c} = 0.251, t = 2.586). A significant impact of security on affective trust is analyzed on a 0.1 level (H8a: γ_{H8a} = 0.132, t = 1.717). The other path coefficient on cognitive trust is not significant (H8b: γ_{H8b} = 0.065, t = 1.297). Consequently, H8a and H8c are verified, while H8b is not. Customers who have strong feelings of security – to feel safe and in good hands - will be more likely to provide personal information and develop trust feelings.

H7 could only be analyzed in respect of affective trust (H7a: γ_{H7a} = 0.330, t = 5.447 > γ_{H6a} = 0.193, t = 3.886), due to the need for significant path coefficients, which are verified by H5a. The path coefficient of likeability on affective trust is higher, which leads to the verification of H7a. Therefore, a bank's likeability has a stronger impact on affective consumer trust than its competence does.

H13 could only be analyzed for affective trust. The other paths could not be analyzed, due to the lack of significant path coefficients:

- $\gamma_{H5/7a}$ = 0.330, t = 5.447 > γ_{H6a} = 0.193, t = 3.886 > $\gamma_{H8/13a}$ = 0.132, t = 1.717;
- $\gamma_{H8/13b}$ = 0.065, t = 1.297 > $\gamma_{H5/7b}$ = 0.021, t = 1.807 > γ_{H6b} = -0.098, t = 0.786;
- $\gamma_{H8/13c}$ = 0.251, t = 2.586 > γ_{H6c} = 0.037, t = 1.118 > $\gamma_{H5/7c}$ = 0.093, t = 1.395).

The likeability dimensions has the strongest effect on affective trust followed by competence, and lastly security (H13a: $\gamma_{H5/7a}$ = 0.330, t = 5.447 > γ_{H6a} = 0.193, t = 3.886 > $\gamma_{H8/13a}$ = 0.132, t = 1.717).

On examining the direct antecedents of trust, reputation has a significant impact on two of three consumers trust dimensions (affective and cognitive trust). Affective trust is beneficial as the second most important driver of customer loyalty. Security influences affective and conative trust which are the main drivers of consumer loyalty.

What are the most important trust building measures?

The drivers of reputation and security building were explicitly analyzed and thus indirectly in respect of consumer trust. For this step, the impact of attractiveness, quality, performance, and responsibility were analyzed with regard to the two reputation dimensions and also the impact of intention, opportunism, discretion and protection on security (H9 – H12).

Three of the four **security sub-constructs** (intention, opportunism, and protection) have a significant impact on security (H9: γ_{H9} = 0.318, t = 6.379, H10: γ_{H10} = -0.148, t = 3.139, and H12: γ_{H12} = 0.279, t = 4.486). Only discretion reveals no significant impact on security, which leads to a rejection of H11 (γ_{H11} = 0.058, t = 0.979). Good intentions has the strongest influence on security, closely followed by protection, and, finally, by perceived opportunistic behavior. Therefore, H9, H10, and H12 are verified.

No hypotheses were deduced with respect to the four antecedents' impact on reputation, because they have already been verified in previous studies (SCHWAIGER 2004; EBERL 2006), but significant results were provided.

Attractiveness has a significant impact on the likeability of the bank (γ_{AL} = 0.250, t = 4.362) and no impact on the perceived competence (γ_{PL} = 0.064, t = 1.085).

The **quality** of the bank has a significant effect on both the likeability (γ_{QL} = 0.366, t = 6.409) and competence (γ_{QC} = 0.200, t = 3.099) of the bank. Quality influences likeability a bit more than the competence of the bank does. The **performance** of the bank has a significant impact on the competence dimension (γ_{PC} = 0.383, t = 6.575) and no impact on the perceived likeability (γ = -0.007, t = 0.142). The performance of a bank contributes to the perceived competence of the trust bank. Corporate **responsibility** has a significant impact on both reputation dimensions. Corporate responsibility affects the perceived likeability (γ_{RL} = 0.224, t = 4.817) of the bank stronger than the perceived competence of the bank (γ_{RC} = 0.153, t = 2.745) does.

Trust building measures were analyzed through the formative specification of the attractiveness, quality, performance, and responsibility of the bank. All 19 measures have path coefficients λ above 0.1 (as recommended in section 3.5.2), thus all measures have a significant influence.

"Employing qualified employees": λ_{A1} = 0.631 is the strongest measure that causes a bank to be attractive besides an "investments in an attractive physical appearance" λ_{A2} = 0.477 and, less importantly, "being an appealing employer" λ_{A3} = 0.146.

Quality is caused by the measures "providing reliable services and products" with λ_{Q1} = 0.256, "being innovative" with λ_{Q7} = 0.241, "providing good service offers" with λ_{Q3} = 0.240, and "regarding customer concerns" with λ_{Q3} = 0.227. Minor important measures are "offering high value products/services" with λ_{Q6} = 0.156, "high quality products/services" with λ_{Q4} =0.140, and least "information giving e.g., on the growth of funds to consumers" with λ_{Q5} = 0.112.

The strongest measure of five to cause performance is "good management" with λ_{P4} =0.499. Further important measures are "economic stability" with λ_{P1} =0.316 and "modest business risk for the bank" with λ_{P5} =0.203. Minor measures are "clear visions of the future" with λ_{P3} =0.189 and "growth potential of the bank" with λ_{P2} = 0.162.

The perceived social responsibility of the bank is mainly caused by the measures "social conscious behavior" with λ_{R3} = 0.446 and "fairness" λ_{R4} = 0.357. Further important measures are "preservation of the environment" with λ_{R1} =0.294 and "goals besides profit maximation" with λ_{R2} = 0.246.

Consideration of the path coefficients from the measures to consumer trust leads to a following ranking of the measures. For the determination of the rank, the path coefficients (see Table 18) were multiplicated. For example the value for the indicator "reliableness" was calculated by the following formula:

Value path (reliableness) =

$$[x_1 * x_2 * (x_3 * x_5 + x_3 * x_6 * x_7 + x_3 * x_8 * x_9 + x_4 * x_9)] +$$
$$[x_1 * x_{10} * (x_{11} * x_5 + x_{11} * x_6 * x_7 + x_{11} * x_8 * x_9)]$$

Value path (reliableness) =

$$[0.26 * 0.37 * (0.33 * 0.2 + 0.33 * 0.17 * 0.35 + 0.33 * 0.31 * 0.2 + 0.02 * 0.2)] +$$
$$[0.26 * 0.2 * (0.19 * 0.2 + 0.19 * 0.17 * 0.35 + 0.19 * 0.31 * 0.2)] = 0.013$$

x_1 is the path between "reliableness and quality", x_2 is the path between "quality and likeability", x_3 is the path between "likeability and affective trust", x_4 is the path between "likeability and cognitive trust", x_5 is the path between "affective trust", x_6 is the path between "affective trust and conative trust", x_7 is the path between "conative trust and loyalty", x_8 is the path between "affective trust and cognitive trust", x_9 is the path between "cognitive trust and loyalty", x_{10} is the path between "quality and competence", x_{11} is the path between "competence and affective trust".

The highest value of all the calculated values gets on rank one. This procedure can be only done for paths with formative constructs at the start of the paths. The calculation results of each path[33] can be found in the appendix.

Measure	Rank
Qualified employee	1
Social behavior	2
Regarding customer concerns	3
Reliableness of work	4
Attractive appearance	5
Innovativeness	6
Good assortment	7
Fairness	8
Good management	9
Preservation of environment	10
Pursuing not only profit goals	11
Good value for products/services	12
Economic stability	13
Quality of products/services	14
Providing of information	15
Low business risk	16
Clear future vision	17
Appealing employer	18
Good growth potential	19

Table 18: Ranked list of measures

33 Significant path coefficients on a 0.01 level were taken for the calculation.

The top three important measures are qualified employees, social behavior, and considering customers concerns.

Measures, which can be deduced theoretically through the four constructs intention, opportunism, discretion, and protection. Therefore, the path coefficients (item loading), item weight and coefficient alpha of each indicator to its construct are listed below.

Scales	Item loading	Item weights	Coefficient alpha
Intention			
1. I trust in my house bank's good intentions towards customers	0.923	0.580	0.800
2. I believe that my house bank behaves ethically	0.902	0.515	
Opportunism			
1. I fear that my house bank only seeks its own interests (recoded)	0.812	0.463	0.712
2. I suspect that my house bank may be hiding relevant information (e.g., about products) or that the relevant information is only written in the small print (recoded)	0.829	0.453	
3. I think that my house bank would try to avoid doing its duty if it could (recoded)	0.742	0.335	
Discretion			
1. My house bank respects privacy protection and does not sell my personal information to other companies	0.816	0.549	0.590
2. My house bank would remove my personal information if I requested it to do so	0.867	0.637	
Protection			
1. My house bank offers secure transactions	0.791	0.518	0.680
2. My house bank ensures the security of my information	0.795	0.415	
3. My house bank offers to safeguard my information from illegal retrieval	0.745	0.349	

Table 19: Item loading, weights and coefficient alpha of the indicators regarding intention, opportunism, discretion, and protection

How much impact does personal characteristic have a moderating effect between the relationship of likeability, competence, and security on the three trust dimensions?

The direct effects of trust propensity, satisfaction, and involvement as antecedents of consumer trust could be analyzed in respect of some trust dimensions (pictured in Table 17). But do theses variables play a moderating role (H14 – H16)? Strong moderating effects by consumers would lower the influence potential of banks' reputation and security measurements.

The following table summarizes the empirically gained results.

Hypothesis and paths	Proposed path	Coefficient	t Value	Standard Error	Sample Mean	Standard Deviation
H15 a	Competence * Involvement -> Affective trust	-0.018	0.290	0.056	-0.028	0.056
H14 a	Competence * Satisfaction -> Affective trust	0.320*	1.840	0.064	0.127	0.064
H16 a	Competence * Trust propensity -> Affective trust	-0.007	0.492	0.051	-0.014	0.051
H15 b	Security * Involvement -> Affective trust	-0.028	0.993	0.061	-0.059	0.061
H15 c	Security * Involvement -> Conative trust	0.010	0.919	0.012	-0.01	0.012
H14 b	Security * Satisfaction -> Affective trust	0.232***	3.009	0.096	0.262	0.096
H14 c	Security * Satisfaction -> Conative trust	-0.076**	2.119	0.026	0.049	0.0259
H16 b	Security * Trust propensity -> Affective trust	-0.022	0.417	0.066	0.001	0.066
H16 c	Security * Trust propensity -> Conative trust	-0.049	0.378	0.014	0.001	0.013
H15 d	Likeability * Involvement -> Affective trust	0.051	0.64	0.065	0.053	0.065
H15 e	Likeability * Involvement -> Cognitive trust	0.044	0.601	0.02	0.016	0.029
H14 d	Likeability * Satisfaction -> Affective trust	-0.688***	2.759	0.084	-0.225	0.084
H14 e	Likeability * Satisfaction -> Cognitive trust	0.260**	2.211	0.03	-0.067	0.03
H16 d	Likeability * Trust propensity -> Affective trust	0.125	1.005	0.077	0.0298	0.0774
H16 e	Likeability * Trust propensity -> Cognitive trust	-0.049	0.959	0.023	0.01	0.023
	R^2 Affective Trust: 0.58 (higher value, because of moderating effect calculations)					
	R^2 Cognitive Trust: 0.32 (higher value, because of moderating effect calculations)					
	R^2 Conative Trust: 0.34 (higher value, because of moderating effect calculations)					

***.p<0.01; **:p<0.05; *.p<0.10

Table 20: Results for moderating effects of trust propensity, involvement, and satisfaction

Moderating significant effects of satisfaction can be analyzed between "competence and affective trust" (H14a: γ = 0.320 t = 1.840), "security and affective trust" (H14b: γ = 0.232 t = 3.009), "security and conative trust" (H14c: γ = -0.076 t = 2.119), "likeability and affective trust" (H14d: γ = -0.688 t = 2.759), and "likeability and cognitive trust" (H14e: γ = 0.260 t = 2.211). Thus, H14 can be verified in respect to affective, cognitive and conative trust. No moderating significant effects of involvement (H15a: γ = -0.018, t = 0.290; H15b: γ = -0.028, t = 0.993; H15c: γ = 0.010, t = 0.919; H15d: γ = 0.051, t = 0.640; and H15e: γ = 0.044, t = 0.601) and trust propensity (H16a: γ = -0.007, t = 0.492; H16b: γ = -0.022, t = 0.417; H16c: γ = -0.049, t = 0.378; H16d: γ = 0.125, t = 1.005; and H16e: γ = -0.049, t = 0.959) can be analyzed. Nevertheless, trust propensity has a direct significant negative effect on cognitive trust (γ = -0.133, t = 2.465) and involvement has a direct significant positive effect on conative trust (γ = 0.123, t = 2.692). Consequently, moderating effects can be analyzed to respect of the satisfaction of a consumer, which leads to a verification of H14.

Positive moderating effects of satisfaction mean that, if a customer is satisfied, trust building measures are perceived in a stronger way. Their effects have a higher affect on trust building. In contrast, negative moderating effects of satisfaction means that, if a customer is dissatisfied, trust building measures are perceived less. Their effects have a lower affect on trust building. The positive and negative moderating effects of satisfaction on the relationships between likeability, competence, and security on the three trust dimensions are summarized in the following figure with a short description.

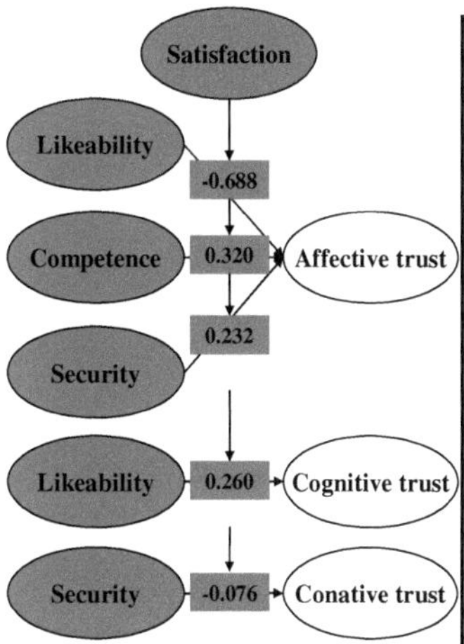

The more satisfied a customer…	The more dissatisfied a customer…
The less emotional (affective) trust can be build up through measures concerning likeability;	The better emotional (affective) trust can be build up through measures concerning likeability;
The better affective trust can be build up through measures concerning competence;	The less affective trust can be build up through measures concerning competence;
The better affective trust can be build up through measures concerning security;	The less affective trust can be build up through measures concerning security;
The better cognitive trust can be build up through measures concerning likeability.	The less cognitive trust can be build up through measures concerning likeability.
The less behavioral (conative) trust can be build up through measures concerning security.	The better behavioral (conative) trust can be build up through measures concerning security.
Implication: Trust building measures concerning: ▪ Competence ▪ Security are recommended*.	**Implication:** Trust building measures concerning: ▪ Likeability are recommended*.

* The recommendation is done regarding the strength of moderating effects, if positive and negative effects (likeability and security) were analyzed.

Figure 87: Moderating effects of satisfaction

Summarized, trust building measures are influenced by the grade of satisfaction of bank customers. The trust antecedents likeability and security are moderating as well positive as negative in their relationship to trust building. Thus, in cases of a satisfied customer, it strengthens the relationship of likeability and cognitive trust, but at the same time lowers the relationship of likeability and affective trust. Since affective trust plays an important role (as it affects significantly cognitive and conative trust) and the path coefficient between likeability and cognitive trust is low (γ = 0.021), the choice of the crucial moderating effect of satisfaction between likeability and affective trust will be taken into account. Consequently, trust building measures concerning likeability of a bank are recommended especially in cases of dissatisfied customers as its negative effect outweighs. The same is true for security, as its positive moderating effect (γ = 0.232) is far above its negative effect (γ = -0.076). Therefore, trust building measures concerning security of a bank are recommended especially in cases of satisfied customers as its positive effect outweighs. Trust building measures concerning competence are especially recommended in cases of satisfied customers. Concluding, it has to be noted, that in both cases (satisfied and dissatisfied customers) all trust building measures through likeability, competence, and security will engender bank customers trust. Only the strength of their effect is affected. The following table summarizes the verified or rejected hypotheses.

Hypotheses		**Significant (yes, partwise, no)**	a) Affective trust	b) Cognitive trust	c) Conative trust
H 1	*Affective consumer trust is positively related to customers´ cognitive trust in an organization*	**yes**	n/a	n/a	n/a
H 2	*Affective consumer trust is positively related to consumer trust behavior (or intention) (conative trust)*	**yes**	n/a	n/a	n/a
H 3	*Consumer trust behavior (conative trust) is positively related to trust beliefs (cognitive trust)*	no	n/a	n/a	n/a
H 4	*Consumer a) affective, b) cognitive, and c) conative trust is positively related to consumer loyalty*	**yes**	**yes**	**yes**	**yes**
H 5	*Bank likeability is positively related to a) affective, b) cognitive, and c) conative consumer trust*	partwise	**yes**	no	no
H 6	*Bank competence of a bank is positively related to a) affective, b) cognitive, and c) conative consumer trust*	partwise	**yes**	**yes**	no
H 7	*Bank likeability has a stronger effect than competence on a) affective, b) cognitive, and c) conative consumer trust*	**yes**	**yes**	n/a	n/a
H 8	*Bank security is positively related to a) affective, b) cognitive, and c) conative consumer trust*	partwise	no	no	**yes**
H 9	*Bank intention is positively related to security*	**yes**	n/a	n/a	n/a
H 10	*Bank opportunism is negatively related to security*	**yes**	n/a	n/a	n/a
H 11	*Bank discretion is positively related to security*	no	n/a	n/a	n/a
H 12	*Bank protection is positively related to security*	**yes**	n/a	n/a	n/a
H 13	*Bank security has a stronger effect than reputation on a) affective, b) cognitive, and c) conative consumer trust*	partwise	**yes** (but opposite direction: reputation has stronger effects than security)	n/a	n/a

Hypotheses		Significant (yes, partwise, no)	a) Affective trust	b) Cognitive trust	c) Conative trust
H 14 (1)	*The impact of organizational competence is moderated by the existing degree of consumer satisfaction: the higher the existing consumer satisfaction, the lower the importance of organizational competence in respect of consumer trust*	**yes**	**yes (but positive moderating effect)**	n/a	n/a
H 14 (2)	*The impact of organizational likeability is moderated by the existing degree of consumer satisfaction: the higher the existing consumer satisfaction, the lower the importance of organizational likeability in respect of consumer trust*	**yes**	**yes**	**yes (but positive moderating effect)**	n/a
H 14 (3)	*The impact of organizational security is moderated by the existing degree of consumer satisfaction: the higher the existing consumer satisfaction, the lower the importance of organizational security in respect of consumer trust*	**yes**	**yes (but positive moderating effect)**	n/a	**yes**
H 15 (1)	*The impact of organizational competence is moderated by the existing degree of consumer involment the higher the existing consumer involvement the greater the importance of organizational competence in respect of consumer trust*	no	no	n/a	n/a
H 15 (2)	*The impact of organizational likeability is moderated by the existing degree of consumer involvement the higher the existing consumer involvement the greater the importance of organizational likeability in respect of consumer trust*	no	no	no	n/a
H 15 (3)	*The impact of organizational security is moderated by the existing degree of consumer involvement the higher the existing consumer involvement the greater the importance of organizational security in respect of consumer trust*	no	no	n/a	no
H 16 (1)	*The impact of organizational competence is moderated by the existing degree of consumer trust propensity the higher the existing consumer trust propensity on, the lower the importance of organizational competence in respect of consumer trust*	no	no	no	n/a
H 16 (2)	*The impact of organizational likeability is moderated by the existing degree of consumer trust propensity the higher the existing consumer trust propensity, the lower the importance of organizational likeability in respect of consumer trust*	no	no	n/a	n/a
H 16 (3)	*The impact of organizational security is moderated by the existing degree of consumer trust propensity: the higher the existing consumer trust propensity the lower the importance of organizational security in respect of consumer trust*	no	no	n/a	no

Table 21: Results of the hypothesized relationships

For reasons of clarity, only significant relationships are summarized in the following figure. Furthermore, formative and reflective indicators which are relevant for making a statement about trust building measures are shown (for a complete overview of all the indicators, please check the Operationalization sections.

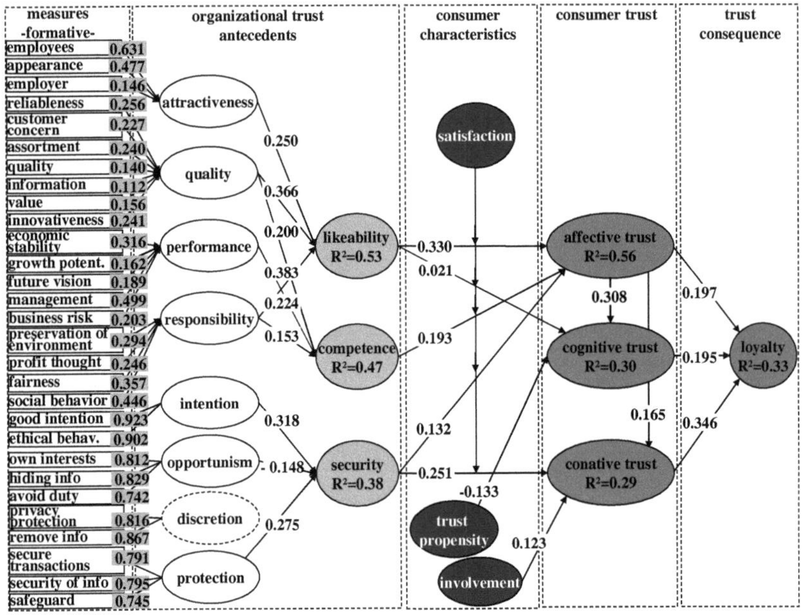

Figure 88: Summary of results

Summary of Chapter 4:

In Chapter 4 an explanation and description were provided of the research design, the data collection through expert interviews as an unstructured interview, the pre-study by means of an online survey, and the main study by means of a CATI. Furthermore, descriptive representative results were shown for the German banking industry. The validity and reliability of the trust model was tested as adequate and suitable for the verification of the hypotheses. The main hypotheses could be verified, which leads to the conclusion that reputation and security lead to significant greater consumer trust, and thus loyalty. Furthermore, trust building measures were identified and the moderating effect of satisfaction was stressed.

5 Discussion, Summary, and Future Prospects

Trust plays an important role in business-to-consumer relationships. Specifically focusing on the banking industry, this work offers a new trust model by means of a meta-analysis, expert interviews, and an empirical study. The latter is a representative study on trust in the German banking system that encompasses the country's main banks. While trust has hitherto been measured only one or two-dimensionally in the banking industry, this work takes in a more detailed three-dimensional approach.

The model measures affective trust with a 56% accuracy level. It combines all previous trust models, simultaneously creating new possibilities to analyze trust measures. By defining the consumer as a moderator, he or she becomes a separate entity who fundamentally influences trust building by banks. The model demonstrates that trust building depends on the degree of customer satisfaction with banks. Nineteen distinct measures that influence trust, and therefore loyalty, in a statistically significant way have been singled out. The model also allows the most influential trust dimension – conative trust, which is engendered by a feeling of security – to be identified. The results point to a combination of factors relating to reputation and security measures that are required in order to enhance trust, and therefore loyalty, towards banks.

The following paragraphs describe **previous trust models**. The interactions between the three **trust dimensions** demonstrate why marketers should choose a combination of measures. The effect of each trust dimension on **loyalty** is given, and important trust dimensions are emphasized. The influence and moderating role of the bank **client's characteristics** on the perception of trust building measures indicate when trust building measures have their strongest effect on trust enhancement. A summary is given of all empirical and quantitative (through reputation) as well as theoretic (through security) **trust building measures**. Lastly, **limitations** of the trust model and ideas for **future research** are given to guide relevant and related research.

Previous research on trust models in the banking industry

The trust model that is introduced in this work encompasses important advantages that have not been addressed in previous trust models for the banking industry. Previous models concentrate on antecedents of trust, but do not empirically and quantitatively analyze concrete measures, which can only be identified through the formative measurement of constructs. They do not consider the hierarchical order of the used constructs: Factors such as quality, performance, and reputation are all measured as direct influences of trust, even if quality and performance are indirect antecedents.

In this publication, a three-dimensional approach is applied, while most previous models used a one-dimensional trust measurement. The influence of trust antecedents on two or three trust dimensions is only analyzed in a limited number of studies. The three-dimensional measurement (affective, cognitive, and conative) of trust supposedly used in some models is more two-dimensional than three-dimensional, as the defined third dimension, e.g., integrity, is more likely an antecedent of the other two trust dimensions. The consumer as a moderator is also not taken into account empirically. These points indicate that the prior models can be enhanced (e.g., by considering more antecedents), diagnostically improved (by using more than one trust dimension), completed (by considering the consumer as a moderator), and augmented (by using a formative measurement of constructs to analyze trust building measures). This work takes all these aspects into account.

The relationship between the trust dimensions

The theoretical model of the three trust dimensions in respect of consumer theories, as well as the principle of consistency, resulted in a three-dimensional model. It is especially suitable for measuring the impact of trust antecedents on the various trust dimensions. Based on the principle of consistency, all three trust dimensions should interact with one another; however, the analyzed survey data does not indicate any statistical significant interaction between cognitive and conative trust. This means that cognitive trust (e.g., competence) does not necessarily lead to personal information being provided. This non-significant effect may occur due to the interpersonal emotional relationship, which is the driving force regarding the disclosure of private information. A competent but unfriendly and unapproachable financial advisor will most likely manage neutral business relationships, but will not be privy to a client's personal data. The latter will always depend on the client's level of trust. If the client shows feelings of trust (affective trust), he or she will be more inclined to provide personal information (conative trust) and will also have more trust in the recommendations of the bank employee (cognitive trust). The significant relationship between the affective and cognitive trust dimensions is congruent to the study by JOHNSON/GRAYSON (2005). The only difference is that these authors assume the opposite effect from cognitive trust to affective trust. In summary, affective (or emotional) trust plays a major role in influencing the other two trust dimensions – cognitive and conative – in the banking industry.

Effects of trust on loyalty

The explicit impact of conative trust on loyalty has never been analyzed. Previous studies have recognized this dimension only as a consequence of affective and cognitive trust, therefore only measuring it implicitly. Surprisingly, conative trust turns out to have the strongest influence on loyalty. If consumers provide personal information, loyalty is increased. Consequently, providing personal information signals readiness to disclose personal information. From a psychological point of view, providing intimate personal data (illness, addictive behavior) leads to a strong bond with the counterpart. Social interaction with the client is therefore not a waste of time, but immediately strengthens loyalty. If consumers provide information on private issues such as familial diseases, lifestyle, and financial incomes, it is a criterion for the measured consumer loyalty in this study. However, trust feelings (affective trust) will also lead to loyal behavior, as well as trust in the form of experience (cognitive trust). These results are congruent to the study by JOHNSON/GRAYSON (2005), who analyzed the positive effects of affective and cognitive trust on the future intention (comparable to loyalty) of bank clients.

In the empirical study, only 29% (R^2=0.29) of conative trust can be explained through the trust model. The value R^2 should preferably be higher than 0.33, or even higher than 0.67. The low value (29%) appears when important antecedents (in this case relating to conative trust) are still missing. Research should therefore focus on further conative trust antecedents besides affective trust, cognitive trust, involvement, and security. Another possibility would be to enhance the measurement of cognitive trust (which also has a low R^2 value of 0.30) and security (which has an average R^2 value of 0.38). AIKEN/BOUSH (2006) obtained a higher R^2 value for cognitive trust (R^2=0.47) and conative trust (R^2=0.66), but their trust measurement included security and privacy aspects, which did not define trust, but security. Both constructs (cognitive and conative trust) seem to have the potential to be measured better through other indicators in respect of the banking industry. The antecedent discretion might specifically have a significant effect in a different industry and should be empirically tested again. The security construct is only measured with a single item, because it loaded above the other driving security constructs in the preliminary study. A single item measurement implies a weak point in the measurement. Further reflective indicators should therefore be identified for the construct security.

The goal of increasing consumer loyalty in the banking industry is possible through affective, cognitive, and conative trust. Private information will only be provided (conative trust) if the consumer feels secure. Reputation and security can enhance affective trust. The measures that banks undertake should therefore be a mixture of the development of reputation and the provision/allocation of security. However, only 33% of loyalty behavior has been explained. As mentioned above, further important loyalty antecedents might be missing. The main antecedent of bank loyalty, identified by LEWIS/SOURELI (2006) – besides consumer trust, satisfaction, and service quality (which can be compared to reputation) – is perceived value. At this point, other constructs could be integrated into the trust model, if one wishes to explain loyalty better.

Influence of consumer satisfaction on the perception of trust building measures by banks

When the **consumer is considered a moderator,** a differentiation can be made between organizational and consumer antecedents of trust. The consumer is then mirrored by "trust propensity," "satisfaction," and "involvement." This approach creates new evidence of the importance of client satisfaction. The character of satisfaction as a moderator must be specifically emphasized. In previous studies (GARBARINO/JOHNSON 1999; CROSBY ET AL. 1990; MOHR/SPEKMAN 1994; ANDERSON/NARUS 1990), satisfaction is regarded as an important trust antecedent or even a trust consequence. It therefore has an ambiguous character. Defining the construct satisfaction as a moderator creates a new understanding of satisfaction itself. Satisfaction influences the perception and effectiveness of organizational measures.

The moderating effects of satisfaction can be explained in two ways. If clients are not satisfied, they do not recognize trust building of organizations, a phenomenon that can be explained as a result of selective perception. Dissatisfied consumers are not interested in perceiving such trust building measures and therefore "ignore" them. Another explanation could be that dissatisfied clients do recognize trust building measures, but interpret them differently than clients who are highly satisfied. In line with the theory of cognitive dissonance, consumers perceive more positive matters in respect of their chosen alternative (bank) when they have decided to be a client of that bank. Similarly, they perceive more negative aspects of the other alternatives (all other banks). Consequently, when clients are dissatisfied they perceive positive trust building measures in a reduced or even negative way. They even interpret the offering of cheap bank products as opportunistic profit maximization.

The results in this work show that the moderator satisfaction has positive as well as negative moderating effects concerning trust building. The more clients are satisfied, the less they perceive trust building measures by means of likeability, but rather through competence and security, and thus build affective trust. Nevertheless, trust building measures that pertain to likeability are perceived better if they pertain to cognitive trust. Owing to the weak relationship between the likeability of a bank and cognitive trust (belief in the recommendations of a financial advisor), this moderating effect is negligible. In the case of a satisfied client, trust building measures through security will be perceived marginally less, and have a marginally lower effect on conative trust. Satisfied bank clients will therefore especially perceive trust building measures concerning competence and security, and build affective trust. The perception of measures concerning likeability is strongly constricted.
The more dissatisfied a bank client, the more affective trust can be built through trust building measures concerning likeability (as consumers perceive them better). Marketers should therefore use trust building measures concerning likeability if clients are dissatisfied.

Summarized it should be noted that even if the perception of trust building measures is moderated by satisfaction, all measures will enhance bank consumers' trust to some extent.

In contrast to the statement of MAYER ET AL. (1995), no significant moderating effect of trust propensity could be shown. This also holds true for clients with different levels of involvement. The perception of trust building measures of banks will not be moderated (and influenced) through the general trust propensity or involvement of bank clients. However, the trust propensity of clients was found to be negatively related as an antecedent to bestowing cognitive trust in banks. This result is in contrast to the study by ANDALEEB/ANWAR (1996), which found a positive relationship, although these authors did not distinguish between various trust dimensions. The involvement of bank clients was found to be positively related to conative trust. Therefore, if bank clients are highly involved in the banking business, they will show a higher level of trusting behavior by providing personal information. These results show that the personal characteristics trust propensity and involvement also determine trust building. The important fact is that the perception of trust building measures by banks is not affected by these two characteristics.

Reputation as a direct trust antecedent in the banking industry

The trust antecedent **reputation** is analyzed by an extensive measurement approach. Reputation is defined by likeability and competence. The results show that likeability and competence (=reputation) are significant predictors of clients' affective trust in banks. JOHNSON/GRAYSON (2005), who measured reputation one-dimensionally, identified a significant influence on affective as well as cognitive trust. The effect of competence on a one-dimensional trust approach was analyzed in several studies (KENNEDY ET AL. 2001; CHO 2005). The effect of likeability on a one-dimensional trust approach was analyzed by ANDALEEB/ANWAR (1996). These results are congruent with previous studies, but provide deeper insights regarding different trust dimensions. Clients who feel a strong self-identification with and liking towards the bank, and who believe in its competence, will have higher trust feelings (affective trust). The liking of a bank also influences cognitive trust – clients who like their bank are more likely to trust the recommendations of their financial advisor. In short, it can be suggested that a bank that lacks likeable and competence qualities may lose clients.

The reputation measurement approach also comprises a formative measurement, which leads to concrete measures. On examining the results closely, 19 measures that influence trust in a statistically significant way have been empirically and quantitatively identified. All of them refer to the reputation measurement approach. To clarify the results, all the empirically gained trust building measures of each of the four constructs (attractiveness, quality, performance, and responsibility) are highlighted and discussed.

Trust building measures referring to the attractiveness of a bank

Attractiveness has significant effects on a bank's likeability (first reputation dimension). No effects could be identified on a bank's competence (second reputation dimension). In the study by EBERL (2006), attractiveness has a significant impact on a bank's likeability as well as on its competence. It seems that when several banks are evaluated (and not only the own house bank), attractiveness is more important through its effect on both reputation dimensions. While focusing on the attractiveness of the own bank of trust (house bank), attractiveness significantly influences likeability, but not competence. Thus, the attractiveness of the house bank does not lead to its competence being perceived more highly. Attractiveness can be built up through the following measures.

Measure 1: High quality employees (ranked 1st)

In respect of the construct attractiveness, the measure "high quality employee," with a path coefficient of $\lambda = 0.631$, has the strongest impact of the first three measures. The significant effect of high quality employees (in the automotive industry) on trust is congruent to the study by KENNEDY ET AL. (2001). Since higher levels of financial expertise can foster greater client trust, it suggests the need for effective recruitment and training of financial advisors. The recruitment process must consider the aptitude and analytical skills of the financial advisors. Product variations, upgrades, and modifications also necessitate the ongoing training of financial advisors. Such training programs must emphasize product knowledge, knowledge of the organization, and knowledge of competitive products, in addition to responsibilities. In addition to this, it is important to train the financial advisors to be bank customers advocates and problem solvers. A highly skilled and trained financial advisor can be crucial in helping bank customers overcome their initial uncertainties. To validate their expertise, financial advisors can direct their clients to other expert sources. The trust generated in clients by the financial advisors' expertise can alleviate product-related concerns, leading to loyalty and potentially long-term relationships (ANDALEEB/ANWAR 1996, p. 46). Although quality employees are considered positive for trust building, most clients do not feel that banks give preference to their clients' interest before their own. Client interest is measured by the construct intention, which, with $\gamma = 0.318$, has the highest path coefficient of the two intention indicators. Banks should therefore communicate the fact that their highly qualified employees use their skills to further client interests, instead of those of the bank, very carefully.

Measure 2: Appearance of bank (ranked 5th)

The bank's whole appearance through its stores, websites, etc. has an impact on attractiveness with a path coefficient of $\lambda = 0.477$. Previous research has found the perception of websites or e-tailors (EVERARD/GALLETTA 2005; GEFEN ET AL. 2003), as well as the appearance of sales personnel (LEE/DUBINSKI 2003) to have a significant impact on consumer trust. These results can be transferred to the general appearance of banks. If banks have a high quality appearance, clients' trust will be built.

Measure 3: Appealing employer (ranked 18th)

Being an appealing employer has an impact on the attractiveness of a bank, with a path coefficient of $\lambda = 0.146$. In respect of the other two measures, it has a minor effect, but should nevertheless be regarded as a trust building measure. If they are rated as top workplaces, banks could put external ratings on their websites. For example, on E.ON's recruiting website, an external rating reads "Great place to work – Best workplaces in Europe 2008" gained from the "Europe institute."

Trust building measures referring to the quality of a bank

The main construct is quality, as it has a strong impact on the two reputation dimensions likeability and competence. This result is congruent to the study by EBERL (2006). The impact of quality on likeability is higher than its impact on competence. Quality can be built by means of the following measures.

Measure 4: Reliability of a bank (ranked 4th)

On examining the construct quality, the "reliability" of the bank, with $\lambda = 0.256$, has the greatest impact. This is no surprise. Client transactions by the bank or by the financial advisor should be undertaken in a reliable way, and should be communicated to them. Bank services should be offered in normal circumstances, as well as in hostile or unexpected circumstances. Banks should be prepared to develop a quick and suitable client-oriented strategy to guarantee the reliability of their services in times of unexpected circumstances (e.g., a bank crisis). Furthermore, clients should be empowered to communicate unreliable bank or financial advisor behavior. Client hotlines can help to find weaknesses in this area.

Measure 5: Focus on client concerns (ranked 3rd)

If clients feel that the bank focuses on their concerns, trust will be enhanced. Its impact on quality is $\lambda = 0.227$. All feedback should be viewed as critical information. What can be done to improve the process? Complaints by clients provide an opportunity to understand that the bank falls short of their expectations. Client concerns could be analyzed by introducing a quick, easy, and prompt system to evaluate banks' consulting services. For example, banks could send a short mobile message shortly after a consultation that gives clients an opportunity to evaluate the service for which they asked (e.g., signing a contract or receiving product information). A negative evaluation could be immediately followed by a call from the bank, thus clarifying specific client needs.

Measure 6: Innovativeness of a bank (ranked 6th)

The second highest measure, "innovativeness", with $\lambda = 0.241$, is far more interesting. Previous research only analyzed the influence of trust climates between people (in organizations or networks) on enhancing the building of innovations (RUPPEL/HARRINGTON 2000). This study has chosen a client's point of view by transferring the theme innovations into a business-to-consumer relationship (instead of an interpersonal trust relationship). A client's trust seems to be built up by a bank's innovative activities, such as new security standards (fingerprint technology) and product developments, rather than traditional values. Technical and product developments could be accelerated through internal divisions that focus on innovations.

Measure 7: Good bank product assortment (ranked 7th)

As a good bank product assortment leads to a higher perceived bank quality with a path coefficient of $\lambda = 0.240$, banks should concentrate on their product assortments. Previous research showed that if clients are uncertain about their preferences, they are more likely to prefer an assortment of bank products whose available options matches their desired purchase quantity (CHERNEV 2008, p. 171). Banks should therefore offer a manageable number of bank products which suit clients.

Measure 8: Quality of products/services (ranked 14th)

High quality and services help to build trust, with the impact on quality being $\lambda = 0.140$. The result of the quality of products on trust is congruent with the study by KENNEDY ET AL. (2001). The standard of the quality of products is almost similar across banks. It is difficult to find information comparing all products, including own products, from competitors. Client service, through a friendly and competent way of providing information, might therefore be more suitable to achieve higher standards than other banks. Banks could consider new ways of giving clients a feeling of comfort (apart from online banking).

Measure 9: Providing information (ranked 15th)

Banks should strive for open communication with their clients. Providing information has an impact of $\lambda = 0.112$ on quality. Even in critical times, such as with a bank crisis, direct and active communication, as well as coping with problems stabilizes clients' trust in their bank. Handling problems constructively, rather than concealing information, is the recommended strategy. The study by SIRDESHMUKH ET AL. (2002) finds that the problem-solving orientation of companies has a positive significant effect on client trust in the context of retail clothing and airline travel.

Measure 10: Good value product/services (ranked 12th)

The value of products and services contributes greatly to the decision in favor of or against a bank, with the impact on quality being $\lambda = 0.156$. It is also a trust building measure, which develops because clients feel the bank is not only interested in maximizing its profit. The perceived good value of services is mirrored by fair bank offers.

Trust building measures related to bank performance

Performance impacts strongly on the competence dimension of reputation. In the study by EBERL (2006), a bank's performance had a positive and significant impact on its competence as well as its likeability. The non-significant path between performance and likeability may be due to the different study designs (mentioned above). The respondents had to evaluate the banks Deutsche Bank, Dresdner Bank, Postbank, and Stadtsparkasse München, not all of which were the house bank. Asking clients about the performance of their house bank does not significantly lead to higher likeability. In contrast, evaluating the performance and likeability of several banks (not only the house bank) leads to significant results. Performance can be built through the measures mentioned below.

Measure 11: Good management of the bank (ranked 9th)

With the highest value of the five measures of the construct performance ($\lambda = 0.499$), the measure "good management" seems a fairly obvious primary requirement. Good management could be interpreted as having a higher probability of good performance and growth of clients' money, which builds trust when it is achieved. Good management also has positive effects on team performance (DIRKS 2000). A more professional atmosphere can thus be created in the bank, which might be perceived by clients and lead to greater trust.

Measure 12: Growth potential (ranked 19th)

Interestingly, the measure with the least influence of these five is "growth potential" ($\lambda = 0.162$), and thus only marginally influences trust. Consequently, banks do not have to concentrate on their growth potential to build consumer trust. Clients seem to prefer the growth of their investments, not that of their bank. This effect might occur because 87% of the evaluated house banks already belonged to the top seven banks in Germany. The expectation that their bank should grow in subsequent years was therefore less important for trust building.

Measure 13: Economic stability (ranked 13th)

Banks should demonstrate their economic stability as a trust building measure. It has an impact of $\lambda = 0.316$ on performance. Growing market value continuously, adjusted by the growth in the industry, could be a suitable sign of economic stability.

Measure 14: Clear future vision (ranked 17th)

Communicating a clear vision of the future is one of the minor trust building measures. A clear future has an impact on performance, with $\lambda = 0.189$. Communicating the bank's goal to clients, supports their perception that the bank concentrates on increasing their money. A clear future vision demonstrates open communication, which helps clients to trust their bank's behavior. Especially in times of uncertainty (such as a bank crisis), a clear future vision will help clients to understand their bank's behavior.

Measure 15: Low business risk (ranked 16th)

If a bank takes lower business risks, it supports clients' feelings that their money is in good hands. Low business risks have an impact on performance, with $\lambda = 0.203$. Banks already try to constrain business risks through equity and liquidity (§ 10 KWG, § 11 KWG). Furthermore, banks should also have adequate equity and a special liquidity ratio when selling credits. These regulations have been revised since the bank crisis in 2007. When new regulations such as these are communicated, consumer trust is stimulated.

Trust building measures related to bank corporate responsibility

Corporate responsibility has a positive effect on the two dimensions likeability and competence in the main study. This could be understood as that banks should have a social conscience, which is regarded as positive (e.g., by not dismissing a large number of employees at any given time). Nevertheless, an ambiguous effect was achieved in the results of EBERL (2006). In this study, corporate responsibility has a significant negative effect (with $\lambda = -0.085$) on competence (EBERL 2006, p. 178). As mentioned, in this study the respondents had to evaluate four German banks, not all of which were the house bank. It seems that respondents evaluate the responsible actions of banks which are not the house bank more negatively than positively. Money spent on social acts by the house bank is more readily accepted by their own clients. Corporate responsibility can be built through the measures mentioned below.

Measure 16: Preservation of the environment (ranked 10th)

Interestingly, consumer trust is positively affected if banks care about the preservation of the environment. It has an impact of $\lambda = 0.294$ on responsibility. This might be the case because clients perceive this as a nonprofit activity which emphasizes that the bank does not only focus on maximizing profit. The expectation that the bank therefore also takes clients' concerns beside their own goals into account might thus be higher. The bank then becomes more trustworthy.

Measure 17: Not only pursuing profit goals (ranked 11th)

As banks do want to maximize their profit, this measure is not easy to communicate. It has an impact of $\lambda = 0.246$ on responsibility. Clients are aware of this goal. In the study by KENNEDY ET AL. (2001), it was found that selling tactics have a significant influence on trust. Nevertheless, banks can try to communicate that in some cases a "win-win" situation might be in place. Clients' money is growing, and, consequently, the performance of the bank improves. Banks should choose the correct combination between fulfilling client concerns and communicating these (e.g., offering products from competitors) and trying to achieve their goal of maximizing profit through high levels of client loyalty.

Measure 18: Fairness (ranked 8th)

Clients perceive bank fairness very positively. It has an impact of $\lambda = 0.357$ on responsibility. This result is congruent to previous studies, considering the fact that these studies found that fairness has a significant effect on trust in interpersonal relationships (DELUGA 1994). Fairness is related to less opportunistic behavior. Fairness towards competitors might be a sign that a bank might also be less opportunistic with its own clients.

Measure 19: Social behavior (ranked 2nd)

Social behavior is closely linked to the construct intention. The distinction between this measure and the following ones is the social consciousness in respect of the population and good intentions towards clients. In both cases, social consciousness plays an important role regarding trust building. It is the second most important measure – after qualified employees – to have been empirically and quantitatively analyzed. It has an impact of $\lambda = 0.446$ on responsibility. Consequently, highly qualified employees who act in a socially conscious way, or in a bank with social consciousness goals will influence trust building. This result is congruent to the study by KENNEDY ET AL. (2001), who found that an organization's ethical concerns have a significant impact on trust. The social behavior of banks can be demonstrated by social sponsoring. The positive effects of sponsoring on a bank's client loyalty were proven by SCHWAIGER/STEINER-KOGRINA (2004). Therefore, banks can build consumer trust through sponsoring activities.

Security as a direct trust antecedent and its deduced measures in the banking industry

Organizations have a good chance of building consumers' affective and conative trust through security. A new comprehensive **security** measurement approach has therefore been developed. Security has four upstream constructs in this publication. However, as no formative measurement has been undertaken, variables that lead to a feeling of security are only specified reflectively. Trust building measures can therefore only be deduced theoretically. In a future study, concrete measures of security should be empirically surveyed through a formative measurement.

As a hygiene factor, organizational security could be defined as a moderator. However, since a clear distinction between the organization and the client is needed to identify the influence of personal characteristics on trust building measures, organizational security is not defined as a moderator in this work. Had security been a moderator and personal characteristics not, it would have the power to influence a dissatisfied consumer. Since dissatisfied consumers will not change their attitude through the construct security, it cannot be defined as a moderator in this model.

Security should nevertheless be regarded as a hygiene factor; without security, it would be impossible to create trust between banks and their clients. Weaknesses in hygiene factors should be eliminated immediately in order to secure the trust relationship. On examining the survey results, it was only possible to make a comparison of the effect of the three antecedents – likeability, competence, and security – on affective trust. The likeability dimension of reputations has the strongest effect on affective trust, followed by competence, and security. Three of the four driving security variables that are statistically significant were identified. To ensure that security is of primary interest to a bank, external institutions should pressure banks to maintain high security standards.

There is a trend towards building internal compliance systems in Germany (FOCKEBROCK ET AL. 2008). Banks have recognized the importance of internal compliance systems in order to demonstrate their good intentions and create an internal security standard. In 2008, Peter Pietsch, media officer of the Commerzbank, stated that a strong compliance division is part of a bank's external presentation (MORTSIEFER/VISSER 2008). Consequently, an external (BaFin) and internal (compliance) security system will be largely in place. Building trust in consumers requires a combination of communication strategies and existing security installations. Not communicating the existence of the current security installations to clients is as bad as communicating non-existent security standards. Since compliance is an internal bank control system that has little to do with the consumer's direct transaction security, it was only marginally included in the survey. However, owing to the media's recent interest in internal control systems to build up trust, these control systems would fit perfectly into a formative measurement approach to security.

Measures for communicating good intentions (strongest antecedent of a bank's perceived security)

Intention is the strongest of the three significant variables which determine security. If banks were to engender a feeling in their clients that their intention is good, trust would increase. The direct relationship of intention on a one-dimensional trust approach was analyzed by KENNEDY ET AL. (2000) in the automotive sector. The results are in line with previous research, but give deeper insights into different trust dimensions. The intentions and ethics of banks significantly contribute towards clients' perceptions of security, and therefore trust. A bank's perceived good intentions, specifically how much it seems to care about its clients, was found to play an important role in creating security and therefore trust in the financial advisor and the bank.

An explanation for this could be that in an increasingly regulated financial services market, clients' perception of the danger of losing their investment through banks' unethical activities is declining. Conversely, financial services products are becoming increasingly sophisticated and clients may attach particular importance to the knowledge base that a financial advisor can use to find the most appropriate investment for them. Given its far-reaching impact, banks should strive to create a caring attitude, and convey this message to their clients. The development of relationships is formed on the basis of honesty and a belief in others' words and actions – something other than legalities and contractual arrangements. Organizations that are interested in building long-term relationships with clients are concerned with more than just obeying the law (BERRY 1995). Measures for showing good intentions might be improved access for clients, detailed guidance relating to bank products, understandable general terms and conditions, and proposing competitive products besides their own products.

Measures against opportunism (negative antecedent of a bank's perceived security)

A sales orientation's negative influence on security, and therefore trust, has been confirmed in this publication. Opportunistic behavior's (e.g. sales orientation's) direct relationship with a one-dimensional consumer trust approach in the financial service sector was revealed by BEJOU ET AL. (1998)and MUKHERJEE/NATH (2003), but also the opposite relationship from trust to perceived opportunism in the automotive industry was analyzed by MARTIN/ CAMARERO (2005). The results were in line with previous research, and were transferred to the general banking industry. These indicate that when a bank's behavior is perceived as opportunistic, clients' security is attenuated. The challenge to international marketers is that this behavior can neither be predicted nor observed. Moreover, a bank that apparently demonstrates good intentions can become opportunistic with a single action. The variability inherent in people's intentions makes it intriguing and challenging to deal with. However, the opportunistic inclinations of banks can be curbed if the rewards from engaging in such behavior are firmly dealt with by imposing penalties. The threat of being fired from a well-paying job can be a strong deterrent to opportunistic inclinations.

It is also important to build other safeguards to control banks' possible opportunistic actions. For example, the disguised client approach can be used occasionally to monitor financial advisors. In addition to external controls, the value and importance of positive intentions could be introduced and reinforced in all financial advisors through seminars and educational programs undertaken by various institutions. Setting sales goals for financial advisors would probably be perceived as a bank demonstrating opportunistic behavior. By providing bank products, there is a strong incentive to sell such products to clients. If financial advisors have a strong focus on sales, this leads to distrust, therefore bank products should only be recommended if they fit the clients' goals.

No further measures to ensure discretion (no significant effects on a bank's perceived security)

Surprisingly, discretion is not a significant variable of security, which means that the disclosure of private information seems to be independent of trust. These results are in contrast with the web survey by SUH/HAN (2003) on the internet banking industry. They found a significant direct relationship between discretion and trust. The reason for the discrepancy might be the difference between online banking and banking in general. Online banking lacks direct personal communication, therefore online banking clients have fewer possibilities to monitor or evaluate other banks. The finding that discretion has no effect in general banking might be due to consumers believing that since banks are bound by the law, they have to be careful with private data anyway.

Measures for communicating protection (antecedent of a bank's perceived security)

SUH/HAN (2003) found that privacy protection has a direct effect on the online banking industry. The results of the study are in the line with previous studies and were transferred to the general banking business. Measures concerning protection could be established through the prevention of losses (pre-protection actions) or minimizing losses (post-protection actions) (MEYER ZU SELHAUSEN 2000, p. 42). The minimization of losses (e.g., banks that cannot repay clients) is already regulated through bank savings, communities or associations (e.g., private banks' fund to ensure the safety of deposits and investments). During bank runs (when a critical number of clients withdraw their savings), the liquidity of the bank will, however, not suffice and its savings will not solve the financial problem (e.g., the Northern Rock crisis of 2007). Bank contracts with insurance companies generally include a 20% cost sharing (SONNTAG, 2001, p. 198). This percentage could possibly be reduced, but never totally avoided, otherwise banks would not have any incentives to avoid financial problems (Contract Theory or Principle Agent Theory, see PICOT ET AL. 2003). Measures regarding post-protection actions therefore seem limited. A more fruitful way is developing trust building measures in the area of pre-protection activities.

Enhancing the risk management of banks can help to avoid financial problems, and resulting bank crises. In the course of Basel II, the analysis of the prospect of banks' credit failure is the responsibility of the BaFin and the German Central Bank. A remaining problem is the time lag between new financial market developments and their regulation. Therefore, banks should voluntarily adhere to regulations and improve their risk management through a prompt and more diagnostic analysis of the probability of credit failure. This could be improved by new financial instruments which measure the fluctuation of market prices more precisely. New and prompt analytical methods and models are therefore needed. Consequently, improving the protection of clients' money leads to increased trust.

Conclusion – Trust building through the right combination of reputation and security measures

One of the interesting and new results of this study is that a combination of reputation (likeability, competence) and security is required in order for trust to influence loyalty. Reputation influences affective and cognitive trust, whereas security positively influences affective and conative trust. On examining reputation closely, it becomes clear that the dimensions likeability and competence both influence affective trust positively. The reason for security not having a significant impact on cognitive trust may be due to cognitive trust (the competence of the financial advisor) being bestowed on the bank's employees and therefore being independent of the bank's security activities. Even when the bank has high security standards, clients do not automatically transfer these abilities to their financial advisor. The advisor is perceived as an independent entity in the bank organization. To have as much effect on trust building, banks should concentrate on their reputation as well as on security aspects. The more satisfied a client is, the more marketers should employ trust building measures related to competence and security. In contrast, the more dissatisfied a client is (e.g., during a bank crisis) the more marketers should employ trust building measures related to likeability.

Limitations of the work and directions for future research

Since no research to date has examined a more comprehensive model of the antecedents and moderators of trust at the consumer level, this research can serve as a guideline for future studies in this area. The findings and implications derived from this research are subject of various limitations, but avenues for future research can nevertheless be suggested that would extend the findings of this study.

Further industries and relationships in the same industry

The study was undertaken in a single industry. While this approach limits the influence of extraneous factors based on industry differences, it may also limit the possibility of generalizing the findings to other branches, particularly those with short-term business-to-consumer (B2C) relationships. The theoretical model in respect of banks could be transferred to the same banking industry, but focus on business-to-business (B2B) relationships, or even internally in the context of trust between bank employees.

Other countries

This work is based on data collected from a single country. The inclusion of other countries was limited by resource constraints, but also different legalities. Comparative analyses could therefore not be presented. Additional data should be obtained from other countries to corroborate the findings. By exploring the concept of trust in different countries, a more global approach to marketing could be incorporated in strategic planning.

Other trust antecedents, consequences and empirically quantified measures

The proposed model of consumer trust in banks was developed to explore the multi-dimensionality of the trust construct and cannot be totally comprehensive. There are several opportunities for further research on the antecedents, especially in respect of cognitive and conative trust, due to their low R^2 values. Additional data on multidimensional measures of consumer trust and variables such as the number of business years, a bank's offline/online presence, and the length of client relationships, would also help to explore more potential antecedents of trust.

One reason for classifying a bank as trustworthy or untrustworthy originates from family members who are already its clients. Is it only the fact that parents are clients of a special bank that is relevant, or are their experiences with their house bank important? Do parents radiate a good feeling towards a bank, thereby influencing their children's decision in their first and subsequent bank choices?

Interesting questions for further research could focus on transaction costs, which were neglected in this work. If trust building becomes too expensive, it loses its attraction for companies. Various authors have taken the first steps to involve transaction costs in trust research (PICOT ET AL. 2007; WANG/CHEN 2006; BENNETT/ROBSON 2004; RIPPERGER 1998).

Enhanced measurement approaches to constructs

As this publication measures security and involvement with a single item, there is a possibility that the construct is not covered in its entirety. Further reflective indicators of security should be found. In addition, further reflective or formative indicators, which do not lead to a multicollinearity problem, should be identified in respect of involvement.

In this work, only reflective indicators of security were used. Formative indicators of security may provide a more comprehensive and richer representation of the construct security.

Dynamic approach to trust building

Another area of investigation could be to conduct a longitudinal study to determine how trust develops over time. The static character of the model (no time variables have been taken into account) is a limitation in this study. Dynamic trust models, including time, would give clear insights into which of the trust building measures shown in this study immediately affect trust enhancement and which of the measures need a longer time period for the full effect on trust levels to become clear. Research could focus specifically on the initial stage of the business-to-consumer relationship. As this was a "snap shot" approach, it would be interesting to evaluate how and why trust levels change over time. For example, how long and in which stage does a financial advisor's experience play a role in trust development? If the quality of the service declines with age, how is trust influenced? How long does it take to rebuild trust when negative situations (e.g., negative news) occur? A potentially fruitful avenue of research is the impact of unsatisfactory events on the different dimensions of trust. LEWIS/WEIGERT (1985) suggest that affective trust is particularly strongly affected when trust is broken. Are unsatisfactory events more likely to influence affective trust than cognitive and conative trust? Are clients with high affective trust levels more likely to voice their dissatisfaction, and as a result experience service recovery, than clients with low levels of affective trust?

High correlations of constructs

Potential interactions between the drivers of trust could be explored. Some of these constructs, such as likeability and satisfaction, are likely to correlate with each other in the empirical study. Researchers should identify whether these strong correlations can always be found. Excluding satisfaction from the trust model would not have led to satisfactory results, as the influence of the person as a moderator would not have been identified.

Other research methods

This research could be extended through behavioral and market experiments by sequentially altering specific trust drivers that were identified in the study. Each identified measure could be tested in an experiment to gain more detailed information about trust building, as in the experiments done by AIKEN/BOUSH (2006) or EBERL (2006). An experiment could, for example, evaluate the types of signals clients use to decide how ethically a bank conducts its business.

The all-in-one trust question

A very extensive approach to consumer trust was chosen for the work. Thus, if one wishes to examine trust by means of a single question, like REICHHELD ET AL. (2000) did with loyalty. This question should consider: The counterpart's perception of a warm attitude towards the client, customer-orientated expertise, and the willingness to provide personal information. An empirical investigation could be undertaken to answer the following theoretically deduced all-in-one question mirroring trust:

"How much (between 0% - 100%) would you reveal about yourself to me/the company?"

Appendix

Expert interviews

1. Offenes, ungestütztes Experteninterview zu

„Vertrauensbildenden Maßnahmen von Banken"

Was führt dazu, dass Sie einer Bank vertrauen?

- Bekannter Name
- Ausstrahlen von Kompetenz
- Sympathisch, aber nicht „zu" freundliche Kundenberater
- Kundenberater, die individuell auf die Bedürfnisse eingehen
- Kundenberater, die zuhören können
- Gute Erfahrungen in der Vergangenheit
- Familienmitglieder bei der gleichen Bank
- Gute Erreichbarkeit (Telefon, Internet)
- Regelmäßige Updates
- Kulanz oder kundenfreundliches Verhalten bei Problemen (Zurückbuchen von Gebühren, Neue Kreditkarte)
- Besonderer Service
- Persönliche Beziehung zur Bank (Bankberater kennt den Kundennamen etc.)

Was führt aus Ihrer Sicht zu Misstrauen in eine Bank?

- Negative Schlagzeilen
- Schlechte Leistungen und schlechter Service

2. Offenes, ungestütztes Experteninterview zu „Vertrauensbildenden Maßnahmen von Banken“

Was führt dazu, dass Sie einer Bank vertrauen?

- Kompetenz der Sachbearbeiter (nicht nur mittlere Reife, Kennen der gesamten Produktpalette und nicht nur die Standard-Produkte)
- Kompetentes Erscheinungsbild der Sachbearbeiter
- Individuelle Beratung
- Grundvertrauen in Banken
- Durch eigene hohe BWL-Kenntnisse, führen Entscheidungen (wie z.B. Entlassungen) nicht zu gemindertem Vertrauen
- Regelmäßiger Zugriff auf Kontostand
- Vorhandensein von Sicherheitsvorkehrungen (z.B. Überweisungslimits)
- Regelmäßige Reports (z.B. monatliche Kontoauszüge)

Was führt aus Ihrer Sicht zu Misstrauen in eine Bank?

- Eigenständige Handlungen von der Bank (z.B. Umbuchungen von Geldern, ohne den Kunden zu informieren)
- Übersehen von Kundendaten (z.B. Dauer der Geschäftsbeziehung und Entwicklung von Kontoständen), keine Kulanz bei Überziehungen
- „nur“ als Privatkunde - und damit unprofitabel für die Bank - und nicht als „Geschäftskunde“ wahrgenommen zu werden
- Keine Möglichkeit die Filiale anzurufen (lediglich das Call-Center), kein privater Ansprechpartner
- Zuviel Ausbildungspersonal

3. Offenes, ungestütztes Experteninterview zu „Vertrauensbildenden Maßnahmen von Banken“

Was führt dazu, dass Sie einer Bank vertrauen?

- Wissen bzw. Informationen im Vorfeld über die Bank (viel gehört, viel gelesen)
- Offene Kommunikation durch die Bank
- Informationszugänglichkeit (z.B. Bedingungen für bestimmte Produkte)
- Persönlicher Ansprechpartner
- Bei größeren Bankgeschäften → positive Erfahrungen und Transaktionen in der Vergangenheit
- Kritische Größe an Kunden und Geschäftsvolumen (→ Risikominimierung, seriöses Angebot)

Was führt aus Ihrer Sicht zu Misstrauen in eine Bank?

- Unterschlagen von Informationen
- Negative Informationen
- Wichtige Informationen im Kleingedruckten
- Öffentliche, große Skandale
- Schlechte Zertifizierungen (Stiftung Warentest Noten schlechter als „3“)
- Negative Erfahrungsberichte von Freunden (WOM)
- Schlechte Betreuung
- Nicht gut aufgehoben fühlen
- Keine optimale persönliche Beratung
- Unterdurchschnittliches Fonds-Wachstum
- Schlechte/Geringe Bekanntheit und Präsenz

4. Offenes, ungestütztes Experteninterview zu „Vertrauensbildenden Maßnahmen von Banken“

Was führt dazu, dass Sie einer Bank vertrauen?

- Vergangene Geschäftsbeziehungen mit positiver Erfahrung
- Familienmitglieder bei der gleichen Bank
- Bei Wechsel: Erfahrungsberichte von Bekannten und Freunde
- Reputation/Ruf
- Öffnungszeiten (z.B. bei Verlust der Kreditkarte)
- Online-Banken: Sicherheitsvorkehrungen (wie z.B. Tan-Nummer)
- Öffentliche Informationen bzw. Medienberichterstattung zu Sicherheit (Phishing-Mails etc.)
- Keine Fehler bei sporadischen Überprüfen der Kontoauszüge (bei Plausibilitätschecks)
- Versorgung von richtigen Infos im Vorfeld bei individuellen Beratungsgesprächen

Was führt aus Ihrer Sicht zu Misstrauen in eine Bank?

- Falsche bzw. schlechte Beratung
- Nicht-Einhalten von Diskretion (z.B. Bankberater erzählt interne Daten von Kunden an Freunde)

5. Offenes, ungestütztes Experteninterview zu „Vertrauensbildenden Maßnahmen von Banken"

Was führt dazu, dass Sie einer Bank vertrauen?

- Grundvertrauen in Banken durch die Überwachung durch die Bundesanstalt für Finanzdienstleistung und Basel II
- Zeit nehmen und Zuhören der Kundenberater
- Image der Bank (Geschäfte der Bank laufen gut, gute Qualität)
- Zuschreiben von Qualität bei großen Banken überträgt sich auf den Kundenberater
- Präsenz der Bank (z.B. auf dem Land)
- Erfahrung mit und Kennen der Bank über einen langen Zeitraum
- Dauer der „Existenz" der Bank
- Kundenberater bzw. Bank „kennen das Geschäft" bzw. haben Erfahrungen und (Fach-)wissen
- Die Nennung und Beschreibung des Bankgeheimnisses in den AGBs

Was führt aus Ihrer Sicht zu Misstrauen in eine Bank?

- Auszubildende bei Kundengesprächen (besonders bei vermögenden Privatkunden), da die Gefahr besteht, dass sie den Job nicht ernst genug nehmen und daher eventuell private Kundeninformationen weiter erzählen oder den Kunden schlecht beraten
- Weitergeben von Lebensplanungs- und Lebensstilinformationen aufgrund von Vertriebsaktivitäten
- Abfragen der Bank von Kundendaten (Kreditwürdigkeit) bei der SCHUFA (und damit die Überprüfung und Kontrolle des Kunden)
- Die Weitergabe von privaten Kundendaten an das Finanzamt

Questionnaire with Descriptive Results (I)

	N	loading	weights	Mean	Std. Error of Mean	Std. Deviation	Variance	Min	Max
Trust propensity (1. I totally disagree - 7. I totally agree) ***Cronbach´s alpha: 0.610***									
d7 It is easy for me to trust a person	400	0.990	0.920	4.12	0.08	1.67	2.78	1	7
d8 I tend to trust a person, even though I have little knowledge of it	400	0.563	0.159	3.12	0.09	1.70	2.90	1	7
Attractiveness (1. I totally disagree - 7. I totally agree) ***Cronbach´s alpha: n/a***									
d17 I like the physical appearance of my house bank	400	0.779	0.477	5.43	0.07	1.49	2.21	1	7
d19 I could see myself working at my house bank	400	0.488	0.146	3.47	0.11	2.23	4.98	1	7
d20 In my opinion my house bank is successful in attracting high-quality employees	400	0.884	0.631	5.35	0.07	1.33	1.77	1	7
Quality (1. I totally disagree - 7. I totally agree) ***Cronbach´s alpha: n/a***									
d21 My house bank seems to be a reliable partner for customers	400	0.811	0.256	5.61	0.07	1.31	1.71	1	7
d22 Customers concerns are held in high regards at my house bank	400	0.797	0.227	5.29	0.07	1.43	2.04	1	7
d23 The service my house bank offers are good	400	0.672	0.240	5.88	0.07	1.35	1.81	1	7
d24 The product/services offered by my house bank are of high quality	400	0.783	0.140	5.31	0.07	1.35	1.82	1	7
d25 I have the impression that my house bank is forthright in given information to the public (incident, growth)	400	0.656	0.112	5.06	0.07	1.43	2.06	1	7
d26 I think that my house bank´s products/services offer good value for money	400	0.664	0.155	4.83	0.08	1.53	2.34	1	7
d27 In my opinion my house bank tends to be an innovator, rather than an imitator with repect to banking	400	0.677	0.241	4.55	0.07	1.40	1.97	1	7
Performance (1. I totally disagree - 7. I totally agree) ***Cronbach´s alpha: n/a***									
d29 My house bank is an economically stable company	400	0.729	0.316	6.11	0.05	1.07	1.14	1	7
d30 I think that my house bank has growth potential	400	0.631	0.162	5.34	0.07	1.38	1.91	1	7
d32 My house bank has a clear vision about the future of the company	400	0.667	0.189	5.38	0.06	1.27	1.61	1	7
d33 My house bank is a very well managed company	400	0.834	0.499	5.42	0.06	1.25	1.56	1	7
d34 I assess the business risk for my house bank as modest compared to its competitors	400	0.616	0.203	5.33	0.06	1.26	1.59	1	7
Responsibility (1. I totally disagree - 7. I totally agree) ***Cronbach´s alpha: n/a***									
d35 My house bank is concerned about the preservation of the environment	400	0.645	0.294	4.29	0.06	1.29	1.66	1	7
d36 I have the feeling that my house bank is not only concerned about the profit	400	0.650	0.246	4.07	0.08	1.60	2.57	1	7
d37 I have the impression that my house bank has a fair attitude towards competitors	400	0.764	0.357	4.96	0.06	1.16	1.35	1	7
d38 My house bank behaves in a socially conscious way	400	0.847	0.446	5.13	0.06	1.28	1.65	1	7

Questionnaire with Descriptive Results (II)

	N	loading	weights	Mean	Std. Error of Mean	Std. Deviation	Variance	Min	Max
Competence (1. I totally disagree - 7. I totally agree) ***Cronbach´s alpha: 0.740***									
d39 I believe that my housebank performs at a premium level	400	0.798	0.493	5.19	0.07	1.32	1.74	1	7
d40 As far as I know my house bank is recognized world-wide	400	0.803	0.357	5.23	0.08	1.65	2.71	1	7
d41 My house bank is a top competitor in its market	400	0.824	0.388	5.27	0.07	1.41	1.99	1	7
Likeability (1. I totally disagree - 7. I totally agree) ***Cronbach´s alpha: 0.853***									
d42 My house bank is a company I would regret more if it didn´t exist any more than I would with other companies	400	0.850	0.328	5.39	0.08	1.64	2.70	1	7
d43 My house bank is a company I can identify with better than with other companies	400	0.902	0.370	5.24	0.08	1.63	2.67	1	7
d44 I regard my house bank as a likeability company	400	0.883	0.439	5.82	0.06	1.26	1.59	1	7
Affective trust (1. I totally disagree - 7. I totally agree) ***Cronbach´s alpha: 0.861***									
d47 I can talk freely with my financial adviser about my problems at work and know that he or she will want to listen	400	0.905	0.390	5.82	0.06	1.30	1.68	1	7
d48 If I share my problems with my financial adviser, I feel he or she would respond caringly	400	0.896	0.372	5.43	0.07	1.33	1.78	1	7
d49 My financial adviser displays a warm and caring attitude towards me	400	0.853	0.367	5.62	0.07	1.41	1.98	1	7
Cognitive trust (1. I totally disagree - 7. I totally agree) ***Cronbach´s alpha: 0.774***									
d50 I have to be cautious about acting on the advice of my financial adviser because of his or her opinions are questionable	400	0.760	0.347	2.69	0.08	1.55	2.39	1	7
d51 I can not confidently depend on my financial adviser since he/she may complicate my affairs by careless work	400	0.859	0.419	2.14	0.07	1.49	2.22	1	7
d52 Given my financial adviser´s track record, I have good reasons to doubt his or her competence	400	0.867	0.434	2.11	0.07	1.47	2.16	1	7
Conative trust (1. I totally disagree - 7. I totally agree) ***Cronbach´s alpha: 0.769***									
d54 I would entrust my house bank life-style informations about my asset management	400	0.787	0.361	4.94	0.09	1.77	3.13	1	7
d55 I would entrust my house bank my private contact information (private telephone number, adress, e-mail)	400	0.650	0.230	5.47	0.09	1.87	3.50	1	7
d56 I would entrust my house bank all informations about my finances (income, retirement provision, life insurance) for asset planning	400	0.881	0.392	4.81	0.10	2.01	4.05	1	7
d57 I would entrust my house bank personal informations(family deseases, addictive behavior) for the planning of my retirement provision	400	0.742	0.297	3.23	0.11	2.12	4.51	1	7
Loyalty (0. unlikely - 11. very likely) ***Cronbach´s alpha: 0.666***									
d58 How likely are you to do most of your banking transactions with your house bank?	400	0.837	0.463	8.46	0.12	2.50	6.24	1	11
d59 How likely are you to recommend this bank to friends or/and relatives?	400	0.769	0.414	7.20	0.17	3.35	11.24	1	11
d60 How likely are you to change your house bank in the near future?	400	0.716	0.412	2.21	0.12	2.38	5.64	1	11

Questionnaire with Descriptive Results (III)

	N	loading	weights	Mean	Std. Error of Mean	Std. Deviation	Variance	Min	Max
Security (1. I totally disagree - 7. I totally agree) ***Cronbach´s alpha: 1.0***									
d63 At my house bank I feel save and in good hands	400	1.00	1.00	6.02	0.06	1.28	1.63	1	7
Protection (1. I totally disagree - 7. I totally agree) ***Cronbach´s alpha: 0.680***									
d64 My house bank offers secure transactions (money transactions, standing orders)	400	0.791	0.518	6.38	0.05	1.00	0.99	1	7
d65 The house bank ensures the security of my information	400	0.795	0.415	6.14	0.06	1.22	1.49	1	7
d66 The house bank makes an offer to garantuee the security from an unlaw intruder to retrieve my information (e.g. newest technologies, conformed limits for money transfers)	400	0.745	0.349	5.83	0.06	1.27	1.63	1	7
Opportunism (1. I totally disagree - 7. I totally agree) ***Cronbach´s alpha: 0.712***									
d68 I fear that my house bank seeks only its interests	400	0.812	0.463	3.28	0.09	1.81	3.28	1	7
d69 I suspect that my house bank may be hiding relevant information (e.g. about products) or the relevant information is only written in the small print	400	0.829	0.453	2.83	0.08	1.58	2.51	1	7
d70 I think that my house bank could shirk if undetected	400	0.742	0.335	2.74	0.08	1.57	2.45	1	7
Intention (1. I totally disagree - 7. I totally agree) ***Cronbach´s alpha: 0.800***									
d71 I trust in my house bank´s good intentions towards customers	400	0.923	0.580	5.41	0.07	1.32	1.73	1	7
d72 I believe that my house bank behavior is ethical	400	0.902	0.515	5.38	0.07	1.40	1.97	1	7
Discretion (1. I totally disagree - 7. I totally agree) ***Cronbach´s alpha: 0.590***									
d73 My house bank respects the privacy protection and does not sell my personal information to other companies	400	0.816	0.549	5.64	0.08	1.64	2.69	1	7
d74 My house bank would remove my personal information when I request it to do so	400	0.867	0.637	5.39	0.08	1.59	2.51	1	7
Satisfaction (1. I totally disagree - 7. I totally agree) ***Cronbach´s alpha: 0.911***									
d75 My expectations about my house bank are fulfilled	400	0.923	0.357	5.90	0.06	1.30	1.68	1	7
d76 In general I am satisfied with my house bank	400	0.943	0.363	6.10	0.06	1.17	1.38	1	7
d77 My house bank is very close to an "ideal bank"	400	0.897	0.366	5.41	0.07	1.43	2.06	1	7
Involvement (1. I totally disagree - 7. I totally agree)									
d79 It is important for me at which bank I am	400	1.00	1.00	5.07	0.10	2.04	4.16	1	7
Other questions									
d83 At how many banks do you have an account (online banks inclusive)?	400			2.61	0.05	0.96	0.92	1	6
d13 Is one of your family members customer of your house bank?	400			2.26	0.49	9.75	94.97	1	99
d87 Gender	400			1.44	0.02	0.50	0.25	1	2
d88 How old are you?	400			50.94	0.86	17.22	296.60	18	89
d89 What is your highest completed education?	400			2.23	0.05	1.00	0.99	1	5
d90 Which bank do you trust most? (optional)	234			-	-	-	-	-	-
d91 Which bank do you trust least? (optional)	167			-	-	-	-	-	-

Correlations I

Item	Trust propensity		Attractiveness			Quality						
	d7	d8	d17	d19	d20	d21	d22	d23	d24	d25	d26	d27
d7 It is easy for me to trust people	1.000											
d8 I tend to trust people even though I know little of them	.439**	1.000										
d17 I like the physical appearance of my house bank	.133**	(.010)	1.000									
d19 I could see myself working at my house bank	(.092)	(.064)	.246**	1.000								
d20 In my opinion, my house bank is successful in attracting high-quality employees	.151**	(.009)	.421**	.357**	1.000							
d21 My house bank seems to be a reliable partner for customers	.154**	(.0112)	.454**	.245**	.593**	1.000						
d22 Customers concerns are held in high regards at my house bank	.190**	(-.033)	.439**	.266**	.456**	.618**	1.000					
d23 The services my house bank offers are good	(.094)	(.003)	.406**	.214**	.398**	.485**	.405**	1.000				
d24 The product/services offered by my house bank are of high quality	.142**	(-.016)	.509**	.222**	.471**	.615**	.624**	.434**	1.000			
d25 I have the impression that my house bank is forthright in given information to the public (incident, growth)	.180**	(.040)	.466**	.243**	.455**	.467**	.463**	.387**	.486**	1.000		
d26 I think that my house bank´s products/services offer good value for money	.153**	(.093)	.288**	.202**	.420**	.451**	.456**	.262**	.513**	.436**	1.000	
d27 In my opinion my house bank tends to be an innovator, rather than an imitator with repect to banking	.183**	(.009)	.303**	.245**	.401**	.372**	.433**	.294**	.438**	.377**	.441**	1.000
d29 My house bank is an economically stable company	(.069)	(-.011)	.360**	.251**	.401**	.432**	.318**	.385**	.335**	.395**	.229**	.235**
d30 I think that my house bank has growth potential	.117*	(-.044)	.226**	.222**	.277**	.246**	.312**	.229**	.243**	.292**	.189**	.371**
d32 My house bank has a clear vision about the future of the company	.130**	(.018)	.298**	.265**	.367**	.276**	.261**	.278**	.257**	.364**	.111*	.215**
d33 My house bank is a very well managed company	.121**	(.051)	.417**	.240**	.395**	.399**	.443**	.378**	.458**	.458**	.354**	.407**
d34 I assess the business risk for my house bank as modest compared to its competitors	(.086)	(.001)	.244**	.230**	.292**	.306**	.238**	.261**	.306**	.288**	.190**	.252**
d35 My house bank is concerned about the preservation of the environment	(.097)	(.024)	.272**	.306**	.338**	.306**	.357**	.242**	.277**	.339**	.200**	.278**
d36 I have the feeling that my house bank is not only concerned with profit	.205**	(.024)	.210**	.204**	.250**	.291**	.355**	.281**	.333**	.310**	.276**	.190**
d37 I have the impression that my house bank has a fair attitude towards competitors	.156**	(.075)	.313**	.253**	.352**	.347**	.404**	.278**	.424**	.406**	.376**	.315**
d38 My house bank behaves in a socially conscious way	.164**	(.087)	.273**	.326**	.412**	.407**	.459**	.296**	.411**	.437**	.381**	.230**
d39 I believe that my housebank performs at a premium level	.130**	(.035)	.374**	.296**	.447**	.443**	.465**	.432**	.446**	.404**	.358**	.422**
d40 As far as I know my house bank is recognized	(.081)	(-.001)	.217**	(.069)	.318**	.271**	.244**	.258**	.284**	.214**	.263**	.330**
d41 My house bank is a top competitor in its market	(.085)	(-.032)	.232**	.224**	.380**	.323**	.241**	.242**	.311**	.235**	.239**	.411**
d42 Of all companies, I would regret missing my house bank most if it no longer existd	(.061)	(.000)	.408**	.222**	.360**	.439**	.423**	.367**	.447**	.334**	.352**	.289**
d43 Of all companies, my housebank is a company with which I can best identify	(.065)	(.006)	.427**	.256**	.452**	.507**	.524**	.350**	.445**	.382**	.403**	.328**
d44 I regard my house bank as a likeability company	(.040)	(-.087)	.524**	.295**	.546**	.552**	.573**	.448**	.521**	.466**	.463**	.370**
d47 I can talk freely with my financial adviser about my problems at work and know that he or she will listen	(.080)	(-.093)	.450**	.202**	.500**	.487**	.466**	.396**	.509**	.461**	.310**	.333**
d48 If I share my problems with my financial adviser, I feel he or she would respond caringly	(.089)	(-.029)	.454**	.207**	.446**	.421**	.461**	.356**	.490**	.425**	.347**	.371**
d49 My financial adviser is warm and caring towards me	(.065)	(-.002)	.437**	.211**	.474**	.463**	.484**	.351**	.471**	.422**	.323**	.318**
d50 I have to be cautious about acting on the advice of my financial adviser because of his or her opinions are questionable	(.080)	(.068)	-.136**	(-.053)	-.227**	-.258**	-.240**	-.144**	-.233**	-.226**	-.178**	-.133**
d51 I can not fully depend on my financial adviser since he or she may complicate my affairs by careless work	(.065)	(.049)	-.187**	(-.080)	-.241**	-.348**	-.267**	-.152**	-.275**	-.244**	-.273**	-.145**
d52 Given my financial adviser´s track record, I have good reasons to doubt his or her competence	(.057)	(.048)	-.254**	-.132**	-.341**	-.357**	-.327**	-.284**	-.291**	-.286**	-.278**	-.262**

** Significant at 1%, * significant at 5%, and ( ) not significant

Correlations II

Item	Trust propensity		Attractiveness			Quality						
	d7	d8	d17	d19	d20	d21	d22	d23	d24	d25	d26	d27
d54 I would entrust my house bank life-style informations about my asset management	.125*	(.034)	.223**	.197**	.322**	.332**	.260**	.164**	.304**	.296**	.304**	.294**
d55 I would entrust my house bank my private contact information (private telephone number, adress, e-mail)	(.041)	(-.046)	.197**	.194**	.220**	.224**	.305**	.122*	.224**	.228**	.194**	.160**
d56 I would entrust my house bank all informations about my finances (income, retirement provision, life insurance) for asset planning	(.042)	(.008)	.225**	.268**	.295**	.332**	.313**	.194**	.332**	.278**	.303**	.274**
d57 I would entrust my house bank personal informations (family deseases, addictive behavior) for the planning of my retirement provision	(.070)	(.052)	.178**	.221**	.268**	.213**	.306**	.101*	.257**	.264**	.271**	.212**
d58 How likely are you to do most of your banking transactions with your house bank?	.104*	(.032)	.190**	.142**	.271**	.261**	.351**	.169**	.341**	.265**	.307**	.287**
d59 How likely are you to recommend this bank to friends or/and relatives?	.102*	(-.003)	.238**	.222**	.265**	.298**	.414**	.206**	.395**	.315**	.382**	.339**
d60 How likely are you to change your house bank in the near future?	(.000)	(.039)	-.242**	(-.082)	-.252**	-.389**	-.371**	-.278**	-.407**	-.207**	-.290**	-.290**
d63 I feel save and in good hands with my house bank	.105*	(.013)	.399**	.239**	.470**	.565**	.540**	.447**	.502**	.422**	.421**	.356**
d64 My house bank offers secure transactions (money transactions, standing orders)	(.029)	(-.018)	.273**	.204**	.317**	.305**	.289**	.289**	.291**	.268**	.237**	.206**
d65 My house bank ensures the security of my information	.101*	(.069)	.249**	.173**	.308**	.298**	.230**	.233**	.346**	.302**	.300**	.245**
d66 My house bank offers to safeguard my information from illegal retrieval (e.g. newest technologies, conformed limits for money transfers)	(.026)	(-.052)	.194**	.222**	.316**	.281**	.305**	.216**	.316**	.336**	.286**	.202**
d68 I fear that my house bank seeks only its interests	(-.077)	(-.039)	-.221**	(-.064)	-.223**	-.264**	-.322**	-.159**	-.264**	-.252**	-.236**	-.192**
d69 I suspect that my house bank may be hiding relevant information (e.g. about products) or the relevant information is only written in the small print	(.041)	(.068)	-.166**	(-.012)	-.167**	-.268**	-.247**	-.138**	-.293**	-.271**	-.269**	-.154**
d70 I think that my house bank would try to avoid doing ist duty if it could	.126*	.117*	-.166**	(-.062)	-.176**	-.227**	-.215**	-.122**	-.247**	-.222**	-.131**	-.154**
d71 I trust in my house bank´s good intentions towards customers	(.089)	(-.044)	.383**	.264**	.425**	.457**	.504**	.327**	.430**	.407**	.339**	.308**
d72 I believe that my house bank behaves ethically	.158**	(.046)	.333**	.221**	.401**	.401**	.488**	.310**	.384**	.392**	.295**	.302**
d73 My house bank respects the privacy protection and does not sell my personal information to other companies	(.072)	(.009)	.185**	.161**	.188**	.254**	.288**	.165**	.236**	.264**	.234**	.215**
d74 My house bank would remove my personal information if I request it to do so	(.059)	(.012)	.264**	.156**	.230**	.286**	.332**	.175**	.305**	.335**	.269**	.175**
d75 My house bank fulfills my expectations	.126*	(-.001)	.358**	.160**	.438**	.576**	.540**	.434**	.522**	.418**	.400**	.391**
d76 In general, I am satisfied with my house bank	.114*	(-.009)	.417**	.216**	.486**	.576**	.559**	.486**	.535**	.406**	.441**	.411**
d77 My house bank is very close to an "ideal bank"	.159**	(.045)	.460**	.267**	.467**	.550**	.585**	.446**	.579**	.451**	.490**	.449**
d79 My choice of the bank is important for me	(-.057)	(-.056)	.241**	.251**	.331**	.331**	.309**	.184**	.353**	.191**	.246**	.314**

** Significant at 1%, * significant at 5%, and ( ) not significant

Correlations III

	Performance					Responsibility				Competence			Likeability		
Item	d29	d30	d32	d33	d34	d35	d36	d37	d38	d39	d40	d41	d42	d43	d44
d7 It is easy for me to trust people															
d8 I tend to trust people even though I know little of them															
d17 I like the physical appearance of my house bank															
d19 I could see myself working at my house bank															
d20 In my opinion, my house bank is successful in attracting high-quality employees															
d21 My house bank seems to be a reliable partner for customers															
d22 Customers concerns are held in high regards at my house bank															
d23 The services my house bank offers are good															
d24 The product/services offered by my house bank are of high quality															
d25 I have the impression that my house bank is forthright in given information to the public (incident, growth)															
d26 I think that my house bank´s products/services offer good value for money															
d27 In my opinion my house bank tends to be an innovator, rather than an imitator with repect to banking															
d29 My house bank is an economically stable company	1.000														
d30 I think that my house bank has growth potential	.391**	1.000													
d32 My house bank has a clear vision about the future of the company	.375**	.437**	1.000												
d33 My house bank is a very well managed company	.397**	.379**	.434**	1.000											
d34 I assess the business risk for my house bank as modest compared to its competitors	.394**	.362**	.352**	.327**	1.000										
d35 My house bank is concerned about the preservation of the environment	.255**	.232**	.237**	.328**	.257**	1.000									
d36 I have the feeling that my house bank is not only concerned with profit	.146**	.219**	.178**	.209**	.204**	.260**	1.000								
d37 I have the impression that my house bank has a fair attitude towards competitors	.326**	.283**	.297**	.341**	.360**	.288**	.403**	1.000							
d38 My house bank behaves in a socially conscious way	.363**	.263**	.338**	.326**	.409**	.413**	.413**	.501**	1.000						
d39 I believe that my housebank performs at a premium level	.370**	.364**	.360**	.455**	.332**	.330**	.371**	.412**	.475**	1.000					
d40 As far as I know my house bank is recognized	.349**	.328**	.320**	.383**	.243**	.250**	.178**	.267**	.244**	.399**	1.000				
d41 My house bank is a top competitor in its market	.353**	.340**	.363**	.409**	.328**	.268**	.170**	.260**	.292**	.418**	.642**	1.000			
d42 Of all companies, I would regret missing my house bank most if it no longer existd	.270**	.166**	.233**	.297**	.267**	.246**	.316**	.359**	.355**	.388**	.218**	.284**	1.000		
d43 Of all companies, my housebank is a company with which I can best identify	.294**	.262**	.299**	.346**	.281**	.280**	.378**	.377**	.465**	.480**	.264**	.358**	.714**	1.000	
d44 I regard my house bank as a likeability company	.401**	.264**	.275**	.428**	.277**	.384**	.351**	.411**	.466**	.562**	.295**	.333**	.588**	.678**	1.000
d47 I can talk freely with my financial adviser about my problems at work and know that he or she will listen	.381**	.230**	.304**	.393**	.254**	.255**	.265**	.321**	.385**	.491**	.324**	.367**	.458**	.521**	.642**
d48 If I share my problems with my financial adviser, I feel he or she would respond caringly	.310**	.210**	.230**	.362**	.211**	.271**	.334**	.326**	.361**	.456**	.318**	.316**	.461**	.507**	.564**
d49 My financial adviser is warm and caring towards me	.334**	.211**	.313**	.409**	.283**	.330**	.250**	.382**	.374**	.429**	.376**	.388**	.403**	.466**	.602**
d50 I have to be cautious about acting on the advice of my financial adviser because of his or her opinions are questionable	-.186**	-.111*	-.110*	(-.082)	-.199**	-.147**	-.162**	-.140**	-.228**	-.207**	(-.070)	-.116**	-.215**	-.212**	-.300**
d51 I can not fully depend on my financial adviser since he or she may complicate my affairs by careless work	-.204**	(-.087)	(-.098)	-.156**	-.217**	-.099**	(-.072)	-.214**	-.200**	-.192**	-.139**	-.134**	-.278**	-.259**	-.356**
d52 Given my financial adviser´s track record, I have good reasons to doubt his or her competence	-.253**	-.128**	-.178**	-.173**	-.206**	-.142**	-.126**	-.202**	-.261**	-.233**	-.178**	-.166**	-.328**	-.294**	-.352**

** Significant at 1%, * significant at 5%, and ( ) not significant

Correlations VI

	Performance					Responsibility				Competence			Likeability		
Item	d29	d30	d32	d33	d34	d35	d36	d37	d38	d39	d40	d41	d42	d43	d44
d54 I would entrust my house bank life-style informations about my asset management	.186**	(.064)	.152**	.272**	.158**	.118***	.148**	.226**	.250**	.265**	.149**	.230**	.244**	.323**	.369**
d55 I would entrust my house bank my private contact information (private telephone number, adress, e-mail)	.182**	(.088)	(.046)	.149**	.154**	(.093)	(.035)	.209**	.107*	.159**	.176**	.148**	.128**	.161**	.265**
d56 I would entrust my house bank all informations about my finances (income, retirement provision, life insurance) for asset planning	.221**	(.067)	.114*	.268**	.161**	.198**	.134**	.270**	.264**	.284**	.211**	.246**	.272**	.317**	.377**
d57 I would entrust my house bank personal informations (family deseases, addictive behavior) for the planning of my retirement provision	.117*	(.083)	.124*	.193**	.109*	.211**	.192**	.235**	.212**	.233**	.165**	.169**	.217**	.323**	.296**
d58 How likely are you to do most of your banking transactions with your house bank?	.152**	.102*	.105*	.334**	.165**	.185**	(.098)	.244**	.223**	.306**	.208**	.249**	.390**	.426**	.384**
d59 How likely are you to recommend this bank to friends or/and relatives?	.199**	.167**	.157**	.376**	.237**	.213**	.235**	.294**	.291**	.340**	.136**	.238**	.411**	.395**	.382**
d60 How likely are you to change your house bank in the near future?	-.203**	(-.089)	(-.065)	-.243**	-.225**	-.197**	-.160**	-.225**	-.201**	-.278**	-.143**	-.191**	-.374**	-.351**	-.397**
d63 I feel save and in good hands with my house bank	.351**	.226**	.236**	.428**	.258**	.306**	.234**	.326**	.371**	.510**	.220**	.278**	.461**	.503**	.642**
d64 My house bank offers secure transactions (money transactions, standing orders)	.292**	.190**	.220**	.276**	.243**	.244**	(.098)	.294**	.280**	.313**	.161**	.307**	.326**	.335**	.372**
d65 My house bank ensures the security of my information	.255**	.170**	.190**	.266**	.232**	.267**	.171**	.317**	.346**	.312**	.254**	.312**	.196**	.231**	.344**
d66 My house bank offers to safeguard my information from illegal retrieval (e.g. newest technologies, conformed limits for money transfers)	.216**	.245**	.221**	.314**	.232**	.249**	.203**	.231**	.356**	.334**	.204**	.257**	.237**	.274**	.308**
d68 I fear that my house bank seeks only its interests	(-.075)	(-.098)	(-.077)	-.185**	-.138**	-.182**	-.255**	-.239**	-.250**	-.265**	-.101*	-.131**	-.297**	-.291**	-.279**
d69 I suspect that my house bank may be hiding relevant information (e.g. about products) or the relevant information is only written in the small print	-.108*	-.121*	-.107*	(-.067)	-.152**	(-.089)	-.164**	-.223**	-.224**	-.208**	-.120*	-.116*	-.262**	-.259**	-.253**
d70 I think that my house bank would try to avoid doing ist duty if it could	-.108*	(-.098)	(-.068)	(-.048)	-.155**	(-.091)	-.160**	-.168**	-.143**	-.219**	(-.098)	(-.091)	-.309**	-.216**	-.221**
d71 I trust in my house bank´s good intentions towards customers	.312**	.241**	.275**	.389**	.301**	.364**	.249**	.387**	.428**	.411**	.222**	.303**	.366**	.483**	.585**
d72 I believe that my house bank behaves ethically	.262**	.238**	.260**	.381**	.283**	.338**	.261**	.381**	.459**	.396**	.228**	.247**	.263**	.413**	.489**
d73 My house bank respects the privacy protection and does not sell my personal information to other companies	.176**	.128**	.162**	.155**	.198**	.162**	.131**	.250**	.244**	.266**	.134**	.188**	.151**	.136**	.240**
d74 My house bank would remove my personal information if I request it to do so	.223**	.114*	.156**	.230**	.165**	.242**	.203**	.303**	.301**	.277**	.176**	.185**	.233**	.234**	.338**
d75 My house bank fulfills my expectations	.409**	.325**	.308**	.505**	.376**	.298**	.243**	.392**	.399**	.540**	.281**	.354**	.471**	.506**	.579**
d76 In general, I am satisfied with my house bank	.395**	.322**	.312**	.464**	.311**	.294**	.273**	.411**	.439**	.540**	.282**	.337**	.522**	.539**	.646**
d77 My house bank is very close to an "ideal bank"	.353**	.308**	.319**	.489**	.367**	.336**	.309**	.423**	.458**	.515**	.304**	.381**	.532**	.566**	.612**
d79 My choice of the bank is important for me	.187**	.160**	.232**	.263**	.154**	.242**	.153**	.217**	.204**	.310**	.232**	.296**	.363**	.427**	.379**

** Significant at 1%, * significant at 5%, and ( ) not significant

Correlations V

	Affective trust			Cognitive trust			Conative trust				Loyalty			Security
Item	d47	d48	d49	d50	d51	d52	d54	d55	d56	d57	d58	d59	d60	d63
d7 It is easy for me to trust people														
d8 I tend to trust people even though I know little of them														
d17 I like the physical appearance of my house bank														
d19 I could see myself working at my house bank														
d20 In my opinion, my house bank is successful in attracting high-quality employees														
d21 My house bank seems to be a reliable partner for customers														
d22 Customers concerns are held in high regards at my house bank														
d23 The services my house bank offers are good														
d24 The product/services offered by my house bank are of high quality														
d25 I have the impression that my house bank is forthright in given information to the public (incident, growth)														
d26 I think that my house bank´s products/services offer good value for money														
d27 In my opinion my house bank tends to be an innovator, rather than an imitator with repect to banking														
d29 My house bank is an economically stable company														
d30 I think that my house bank has growth potential														
d32 My house bank has a clear vision about the future of the company														
d33 My house bank is a very well managed company														
d34 I assess the business risk for my house bank as modest compared to its competitors														
d35 My house bank is concerned about the preservation of the environment														
d36 I have the feeling that my house bank is not only concerned with profit														
d37 I have the impression that my house bank has a fair attitude towards competitors														
d38 My house bank behaves in a socially conscious way														
d39 I believe that my housebank performs at a premium level														
d40 As far as I know my house bank is recognized														
d41 My house bank is a top competitor in its market														
d42 Of all companies, I would regret missing my house bank most if it no longer existd														
d43 Of all companies, my housebank is a company with which I can best identify														
d44 I regard my house bank as a likeability company														
d47 I can talk freely with my financial adviser about my problems at work and know that he or she will listen	1.000													
d48 If I share my problems with my financial adviser, I feel he or she would respond caringly	.748**	1.000												
d49 My financial adviser is warm and caring towards me	.643**	.631**	1.000											
d50 I have to be cautious about acting on the advice of my financial adviser because of his or her opinions are questionable	-.311**	-.291**	-.299**	1.000										
d51 I can not fully depend on my financial adviser since he or she may complicate my affairs by careless work	-.352**	-.333**	-.359**	.481**	1.000									
d52 Given my financial adviser´s track record, I have good reasons to doubt his or her competence	-.418**	-.374**	-.400**	.489**	.629**	1.000								

** Significant at 1%, * significant at 5%, and ( ) not significant

Correlations VI

	Affective trust			Cognitive trust			Conative trust				Loyalty			Security
Item	d47	d48	d49	d50	d51	d52	d54	d55	d56	d57	d58	d59	d60	d63
d54 I would entrust my house bank life-style informations about my asset management	.383**	.311**	.275**	-.161**	-.203**	-.182**	1.000							
d55 I would entrust my house bank my private contact information (private telephone number, adress, e-mail)	.275**	.260**	.247**	-.137**	-.236**	-.176**	.364**	1.000						
d56 I would entrust my house bank all informations about my finances (income, retirement provision, life insurance) for asset planning	.382**	.348**	.328**	-.185**	-.265**	-.209**	.581**	.471**	1.000					
d57 I would entrust my house bank personal informations (family deseases, addictive behavior) for the planning of my retirement provision	.294**	.301**	.255**	-.145**	-.144**	-.157**	.386**	.347**	.575**	1.000				
d58 How likely are you to do most of your banking transactions with your house bank?	.303**	.340**	.322**	-.248**	-.267**	-.231	.365**	.175**	.433**	.295**	1.000			
d59 How likely are you to recommend this bank to friends or/and relatives?	.279**	.314**	.285**	-.231**	-.181**	-.258	.339**	.166**	.327**	.306**	.508**	1.000		
d60 How likely are you to change your house bank in the near future?	-.310**	-.316**	-.315**	.197**	.271**	.281	-.271**	-.194**	-.277**	-.176**	-.414**	-.325**	1.000	
d63 I feel save and in good hands with my house bank	.548**	.492**	.537**	-.280**	-.367**	-.369	.410**	.322**	.433**	.286**	.440**	.474**	-.520**	1.000
d64 My house bank offers secure transactions (money transactions, standing orders)	.270**	.269**	.259**	-.222**	-.199**	-.227	.212**	.194**	.256**	.142**	.193**	.215**	-.308**	.466**
d65 My house bank ensures the security of my information	.318**	.344**	.345**	-.196**	-.178**	-.180	.238**	.225**	.317**	.238**	.247**	.229**	-.189**	.374**
d66 My house bank offers to safeguard my information from illegal retrieval (e.g. newest technologies, conformed limits for money transfers)	.390**	.358**	.335**	-.249**	(-.089)	-.200	.212**	(.090)	.247**	.243**	.171**	.321**	-.117**	.314**
d68 I fear that my house bank seeks only its interests	-.269**	-.267**	-.247**	.317**	.206**	.370	-.189**	-.111*	-.211**	-.227**	-.222**	-.386**	.185**	-.318**
d69 I suspect that my house bank may be hiding relevant information (e.g. about products) or the relevant information is only written in the small print	-.273**	-.220**	-.247**	.326**	.273**	.323	-.173**	-.140**	-.218**	-.165**	-.226**	-.313**	.247**	-.311**
d70 I think that my house bank would try to avoid doing ist duty if it could	-.224**	-.238**	-.160**	.361**	.280**	.347	-.143**	(-.056)	-.209**	-.186**	-.221**	-.289**	.236**	-.230**
d71 I trust in my house bank´s good intentions towards customers	.482**	.453**	.481**	-.233**	-.225**	-.244	.300**	.283**	.402**	.280**	.353**	.297**	-.252**	.510**
d72 I believe that my house bank behaves ethically	.423**	.393**	.461**	-.231**	-.186**	-.219	.278**	.229**	.370**	.279**	.297**	.287**	-.262**	.453**
d73 My house bank respects the privacy protection and does not sell my personal information to other companies	.221**	.168**	.247**	-.225**	-.189**	-.242	.149**	.158**	.144**	.117*	.185**	.233**	-.195**	.275**
d74 My house bank would remove my personal information if I request it to do so	.310**	.255**	.311**	-.164**	-.150**	-.157	.224**	.154**	.345**	.275**	.244**	.278**	0.228**	.319**
d75 My house bank fulfills my expectations	.556**	.527**	.509**	-.245**	-.383**	-.418	.411**	.237**	.350**	.245**	.428**	.440**	-.527**	.722**
d76 In general, I am satisfied with my house bank	.563**	.536**	.514**	-.223**	-.389**	-.452	.379**	.308**	.362**	.243**	.429**	.431**	-.551**	.751**
d77 My house bank is very close to an "ideal bank"	.531**	.572**	.526**	-.295**	-.348**	-.388	.383**	.258**	.404**	.301**	.467**	.509**	-.435**	.669**
d79 My choice of the bank is important for me	.353**	.309**	.295**	-.199**	-.232**	-.221	.246**	(.082)	.303**	.277**	.236**	.269**	-.192**	.295**

** Significant at 1%, * significant at 5%, and ( ) not significant

Correlations VII

	Protection			Opportunism			Intention		Discretion		Satisfaction			Involve-ment
Item	d64	d65	d66	d68	d69	d70	d71	d72	d73	d74	d75	d76	d77	d79
d54 I would entrust my house bank life-style informations about my asset management														
d55 I would entrust my house bank my private contact information (private telephone number, adress, e-mail)														
d56 I would entrust my house bank all informations about my finances (income, retirement provision, life insurance) for asset planning														
d57 I would entrust my house bank personal informations (family deseases, addictive behavior) for the planning of my retirement provision														
d58 How likely are you to do most of your banking transactions with your house bank?														
d59 How likely are you to recommend this bank to friends or/and relatives?														
d60 How likely are you to change your house bank in the near future?														
d63 I feel save and in good hands with my house bank														
d64 My house bank offers secure transactions (money transactions, standing orders)	1.000													
d65 My house bank ensures the security of my information	.374**	1.000												
d66 My house bank offers to safeguard my information from illegal retrieval (e.g. newest technologies, conformed limits for money transfers)	.337**	.534**	1.000											
d68 I fear that my house bank seeks only its interests	-.190**	-.243**	-.296**	1.000										
d69 I suspect that my house bank may be hiding relevant information (e.g. about products) or the relevant information is only written in the small print	-.161**	-.209**	-.246**	.465**	1.000									
d70 I think that my house bank would try to avoid doing ist duty if it could	-.135**	-.169**	-.221**	.409**	.479**	1.000								
d71 I trust in my house bank´s good intentions towards customers	.302**	.400**	.354**	-.232**	-.284**	-.185**	1.000							
d72 I believe that my house bank behaves ethically	.269**	.447**	.386**	-.274**	-.251**	-.241**	.667**	1.000						
d73 My house bank respects the privacy protection and does not sell my personal information to other companies	.234**	.376**	.205**	-.184**	-.175**	-.233**	.298**	.302**	1.000					
d74 My house bank would remove my personal information if I request it to do so	.192**	.342**	.288**	-.234**	-.233**	-.257**	.352**	.347**	.419**	1.000				
d75 My house bank fulfills my expectations	.420**	.363**	.348**	-.326**	-.351**	-.280**	.504**	.482**	.327**	.367**	1.000			
d76 In general, I am satisfied with my house bank	.458**	.402**	.289**	-.319**	-.337**	-.238**	.546**	.491**	.300**	.302**	.843**	1.000		
d77 My house bank is very close to an "ideal bank"	.429**	.395**	.370**	-.369**	-.346**	-.300**	.601**	.584**	.245**	.313**	.713**	.764**	1.000	
d79 My choice of the bank is important for me	.185**	.185**	.200**	-.148**	-.135**	-.203**	.360**	.283**	.227**	.287**	.346**	.350**	.399**	1.000

** Significant at 1%, * significant at 5%, and ( ) not significant

Explorative factor analysis (over all constructs) (I)

Total Variance Explained

Component	Initial Eigenvalues			Extraction Sums of Squared Loadings			Rotation Sums of Squared Loadings		
	Total	% of Variance	Cumulative %	Total	% of Variance	Cumulative %	Total	% of Variance	Cumulative %
1	17.538	31.888	31.888	17.538	31.888	31.888	6.509	11.834	11.834
2	2.743	4.988	36.876	2.743	4.988	36.876	4.489	8.162	19.996
3	2.000	3.637	40.513	2.000	3.637	40.513	3.142	5.712	25.708
4	1.814	3.298	43.811	1.814	3.298	43.811	2.951	5.365	31.073
5	1.711	3.110	46.921	1.711	3.110	46.921	2.572	4.677	35.750
6	1.452	2.640	49.561	1.452	2.640	49.561	2.531	4.601	40.351
7	1.436	2.610	52.172	1.436	2.610	52.172	2.511	4.565	44.916
8	1.368	2.486	54.658	1.368	2.486	54.658	2.410	4.381	49.297
9	1.218	2.215	56.873	1.218	2.215	56.873	2.251	4.092	53.390
10	1.137	2.067	58.939	1.137	2.067	58.939	1.870	3.399	56.789
11	1.089	1.980	60.920	1.089	1.980	60.920	1.647	2.995	59.783
12	1.014	1.844	62.764	1.014	1.844	62.764	1.639	2.981	62.764
13	0.987	1.794	64.558						
14	0.950	1.727	66.285						
15	0.867	1.576	67.861						
16	0.834	1.517	69.378						
17	0.815	1.482	70.860						
18	0.781	1.419	72.279						
19	0.723	1.315	73.594						
20	0.692	1.258	74.851						
21	0.679	1.235	76.086						
22	0.671	1.221	77.307						
23	0.651	1.184	78.491						
24	0.646	1.174	79.665						
25	0.604	1.098	80.763						
26	0.567	1.030	81.793						
27	0.549	0.998	82.792						
28	0.542	0.986	83.777						
29	0.518	0.941	84.719						
30	0.508	0.923	85.642						
31	0.497	0.903	86.545						
32	0.492	0.895	87.440						
33	0.477	0.868	88.308						
34	0.464	0.844	89.151						
35	0.428	0.779	89.930						
36	0.421	0.765	90.696						
37	0.396	0.719	91.415						
38	0.387	0.704	92.119						
39	0.366	0.666	92.785						
40	0.347	0.630	93.415						
41	0.335	0.609	94.024						
42	0.322	0.586	94.610						
43	0.314	0.571	95.181						
44	0.297	0.540	95.721						
45	0.296	0.538	96.259						
46	0.272	0.494	96.752						
47	0.260	0.473	97.225						
48	0.241	0.438	97.664						
49	0.232	0.421	98.084						
50	0.219	0.399	98.483						
51	0.210	0.382	98.865						
52	0.190	0.345	99.211						
53	0.175	0.318	99.529						
54	0.153	0.279	99.807						
55	0.106	0.193	100.000						

Extraction Method: Principal Component Analysis.

Explorative factor analysis (over all constructs) (II)

Item	Factor and assigned constructs											
	Attractiv., Quality, Affective Trust	Likeability, Loyalty, Security, Satisfaction	Perfor-mance	Conative Trust	Cognitive Trust	Respon-sibility	Oppor-tunism	Protection and Intention	Com-petence	Dis-cretion	Trust propensity	Involve-ment
	1	2	3	4	5	6	7	8	9	10	11	12
d7 It is easy for me to trust people											**0.770**	
d8 I tend to trust people even though I know little of them											**0.834**	
d17 I like the physical appearance of my house bank	**0.668**											
d19 I could see myself working at my house bank	0.208		0.375	0.249								**0.567**
d20 In my opinion, my house bank is successful in attracting high-quality employees	**0.561**		0.245									0.254
d21 My house bank seems to be a reliable partner for customers	**0.645**	0.284			0.200							
d22 Customers concerns are held in high regards at my house bank	**0.612**	0.275				0.244				0.221		
d23 The services my house bank offers are good	**0.571**	0.256	0.252									
d24 The product/services offered by my house bank are of high quality	**0.658**	0.256					0.209					
d25 I have the impression that my house bank is forthright in given information to the public (incident, growth)	**0.598**		0.277				0.215					
d26 I think that my house bank´s products/services offer good value for money	**0.480**	0.205					0.251			0.242	0.211	
d27 In my opinion my house bank tends to be an innovator, rather than an imitator with repect to banking	**0.448**		0.202				0.204		0.360			0.214
d29 My house bank is an economically stable company	0.347		**0.566**									
d30 I think that my house bank has growth potential	0.225		**0.634**						0.258			
d32 My house bank has a clear vision about the future of the company	0.222		**0.580**						0.224			
d33 My house bank is a very well managed company	**0.459**	0.251	0.370						0.296			
d34 I assess the business risk for my house bank as modest compared to its competitors			**0.654**			0.222						
d35 My house bank is concerned about the preservation of the environment	0.212		0.263			0.285		0.226				**0.300**
d36 I have the feeling that my house bank is not only concerned with profit	0.252					**0.670**	0.238					
d37 I have the impression that my house bank has a fair attitude towards competitors	0.219		0.361			**0.491**				0.259		
d38 My house bank behaves in a socially conscious way	0.224		0.380			**0.516**						
d39 I believe that my housebank performs at a premium level	**0.365**	0.276	0.305			0.280			0.286			
d40 As far as I know my house bank is recognized			0.264						**0.788**			
d41 My house bank is a top competitor in its market			0.349						**0.700**			
d42 Of all companies, I would regret missing my house bank most if it no longer existed	0.304	**0.473**				0.384						0.319
d43 Of all companies, my housebank is a company with which I can best identify	0.343	0.430				**0.474**						0.337
d44 I regard my house bank as a likeability company	**0.520**	0.390				0.368		0.207				
d47 I can talk freely with my financial adviser about my problems at work and know that he or she will listen	**0.525**			0.218	0.323	0.253		0.334	0.300			
d48 If I share my problems with my financial adviser, I feel he or she would respond caringly	**0.497**	0.201			0.278	0.291		0.308	0.308			
d49 My financial adviser is warm and caring towards me	**0.445**				0.334	0.280		0.312	0.329			

Explorative factor analysis (over all constructs) (III)

Item	Factor and assigned constructs											
	Attractiv., Quality, Affective Trust 1	**Likeability, Loyalty, Security, Satisfaction** 2	**Perfor-mance** 3	**Conative Trust** 4	**Cognitive Trust** 5	**Respon-sibility** 6	**Oppor-tunism** 7	**Protection and Intention** 8	**Com-petence** 9	**Dis-cretion** 10	**Trust propensity** 11	**Involve-ment** 12
d50 I have to be cautious about acting on the advice of my financial adviser because of his or her opinions are questionable					**-0.655**		-0.325					
d51 I can not fully depend on my financial adviser since he or she may complicate my affairs by careless work		-0.220			**-0.777**							
d52 Given my financial adviser´s track record, I have good reasons to doubt his or her competence	-0.259				**-0.741**		-0.242					
d54 I would entrust my house bank life-style information about my asset management		0.263		**0.647**								
d55 I would entrust my house bank my private contact information (private telephone number, adress, e-mail)				**0.709**								-0.223
d56 I would entrust my house bank all information about my finances (income, retirement provision, life insurance) for asset planning		0.211		**0.779**								
d57 I would entrust my house bank personal information (family deseases, addictive behavior) for the planning of my retirement provision				**0.675**								0.228
d58 How likely are you to do most of your banking transactions with your house bank?		**0.549**		0.311			0.226		0.214			0.208
d59 How likely are you to recommend this bank to friends or/and relatives?		0.422		0.222			**0.507**					0.272
d60 How likely are you to change your house bank in the near future?	-0.204	**-0.687**										
d63 I feel save and in good hands with my house bank	0.427	**0.619**		0.226				0.247				
d64 My house bank offers secure transactions (money transactions, standing orders)		**0.435**	0.326					0.411				
d65 My house bank ensures the security of my information								**0.606**		0.375		
d66 My house bank offers to safeguard my information from illegal retrieval (e.g. newest technologies, conformed limits for money transfers)	0.201						0.355	**0.677**				
d68 I fear that my house bank seeks only its interests							**-0.674**	-0.204				
d69 I suspect that my house bank may be hiding relevant information (e.g. about products) or the relevant information is only written in the small print					-0.218		**-0.646**					
d70 I think that my house bank would try to avoid doing ist duty if it could					-0.282		**-0.630**				0.222	
d71 I trust in my house bank´s good intentions towards customers	0.333	0.291		0.233		0.331		**0.388**		0.248		
d72 I believe that my house bank behaves ethically	0.276	0.232				0.319		**0.451**		0.292		
d73 My house bank respects the privacy protection and does not sell my personal information to other companies										**0.744**		
d74 My house bank would remove my personal information if I request it to do so										**0.607**		
d75 My house bank fulfills my expectations	0.375	**0.648**	0.223					0.203				
d76 In general, I am satisfied with my house bank	0.427	**0.672**	0.204									
d77 My house bank is very close to an "ideal bank"	0.417	**0.543**					0.213	0.244				
d79 My choice of the bank is important for me	0.201								0.278	0.222		**0.592**
Variance explained	31.9%	5.0%	3.6%	3.3%	3.1%	2.6%	2.6%	2.5%	2.2%	2.1%	2.0%	1.8%

Database: Complete sample (n=400). Extraction method: Principle component analysis.
Rotation method: Varimax. Loadings < 0,2 suppressed.

Factor analysis (security construct)

Rotated Component Matrix(a)

	Component			
	Intention	**Opportunism**	**Protection**	**Discretion**
d68p (Recode) I fear that my house bank seeks only its interests		**0.74**		
d69p (Recode) I suspect that my house bank may be hiding relevant information (e.g. about products) or the relevant information is only written in the small print		**0.79**		
d70p (Recode) I think that my house bank could shirk if undetected		**0.77**		
d71 I trust in my house banks good intentions towards customers	**0.86**			
d72 I believe that my house bank behavior is ethical	**0.80**			
d73 My house bank respects the privacy protection and does not sell my personal information to other companies				**0.82**
d74 My house bank would remove my personal information when I request it to do so	0.25			**0.74**
d63 At my house bank I feel save and in good hands	**0.60**	**0.24**	**0.41**	**0.06**
d64 My house bank offers secure transactions (money transactions, standing orders)			**0.76**	
d65 The house bank ensures the security of my information			**0.68**	0.39
d66 The house bank makes an offer to garantuee the security from an unlaw intruder to retrieve my information			**0.71**	

Extraction Method: Principal Component Analysis.
Rotation Method: Varimax with Kaiser Normalization.
a Rotation converged in 5 iterations.

Total Variance Explained

	Initial Eigenvalues			**Extraction Sums of Squared Loadings**			**Rotation Sums of Squared Loadings**		
Component	Total	% of Variance	Cumulative %	Total	% of Variance	Cumulative %	Total	% of Variance	Cumulative %
1	4.14	37.65	37.65	4.14	37.65	37.65	1.99	18.11	18.11
2	1.36	12.38	50.03	1.36	12.38	50.03	1.95	17.75	35.86
3	0.98	8.87	58.89	0.98	8.87	58.89	1.88	17.09	52.95
4	0.88	7.99	66.88	0.88	7.99	66.88	1.53	13.93	66.88
5	0.80	7.30	74.18						
6	0.59	5.39	79.57						
7	0.57	5.20	84.78						
8	0.51	4.65	89.43						
9	0.44	3.97	93.40						
10	0.42	3.79	97.18						
11	0.31	2.82	100.00						

Extraction Method: Principal Component Analysis.

Calculation of the rank of the formative indicators/measures

	Measure	Value of whole path
M1	Employee	0.017
M2	Appearance	0.013
M3	Employer	0.004
M4	Reliableness	0.013
M5	Customer concerns	0.014
M6	Assortment	0.012
M7	Quality	0.007
M8	Information	0.006
M9	Value	0.008
M10	innovativeness	0.012
M11	economic stability	0.007
M12	growth potential	0.004
M13	future vision	0.004
M14	Management	0.012
M15	Business risk	0.005
M16	Preservation of environment	0.010
M17	pursuing not only profit goals	0.008
M18	Fairness	0.012
M19	Social behavior	0.015

References

AAKER, David A., V. KUMAR, and George S. DAY (2007), Marketing Research (9 ed.). New Jersey: Wiley.

ADAMSON, Ivana, Kok-Mun CHAN, and Donna HANDFORD (2003), "Relationship Marketing: Customer Commitment and Trust as a Strategy for the Smaller Hong Kong Corporate Banking Sector," International Journal of Bank Marketing, 21 (6/7), 347-58.

AGUSTIN, Clara and Jagdip SINGH (2005), "Curvilinear Effects of Consumer Loyalty Determinants in Relational Exchanges," Journal of Marketing Research, 42 (1), 96-108.

AIKEN, Damon K. and David M. BOUSH (2006), "Trustmarks, Objective-Source Ratings, and Implied Investments in Advertising: Investigating Online Trust and the Context-Specific Nature of Internet Signals," Journal of the Academy of Marketing Science, 34 (3), 308-23.

AMBLER, Tim (1997), "How much of Brand Equity is Explained by Trust?," Management Decision, 35 (4), 283-92.

ANDALEEB, Syed S. and Syed F. ANWAR (1996), "Factors Influencing Customer Trust in Salespersons in a Developing Country," Journal of International Marketing, 4 (4), 35-52.

ANDERSON, James C. and James A. NARUS (1990), "A Model of Distributor Firm and Manufacturer Firm Working Partnerships," Journal of Marketing, 54 (1), 42-58.

ANDERSON, Rolph E. and Srini S. SRINIVASAN (2003), "E-Satisfaction and E-Loyalty: A Contingency Framework," Psychology & Marketing, 20 (2), 123-38.

ARYEE, Samuel and Zhen X. CHEN (2004), "Countering the Trend Towards Careerist Orientation in the Age of Downsizing: Test of a Social Exchange Model," Journal of Business Research, 57 (4), 321-28.

BACKHAUS, Klaus, Bernd ERICHSON, Wulff PLINKE, and Rolf WEIBER (2006), Multivariate Analysemethoden - Eine anwendungsorientierte Einführung (11 ed.). Berlin: Springer Verlag.

BAGOZZI, Richard P. (1984), "Prospectus for Theory Construction in Marketing," Journal of Marketing, 48 (1), 11-29.

BAGOZZI, Richard P. (1994), Advanced Methods of Marketing Research (1 ed.). Cambridge, Massachusetts: Blackwell Business.

BAGOZZI, Richard P. (1994), "Structural Equation Models in Marketing Research: Basic Principles," in Principles in Marketing Research, Richard P. Bagozzi, Ed. Cambridge.

BAGOZZI, Richard P. and Lynn W. PHILLIPS (1982), "Representing and Testing Organizational Theories: A Holistic Construal," Administrative Science Quarterly, 27 (3), 459-89.

BAGOZZI, Richard P. and Youjae YI (1988), "On the Evaluation of Structural Equation Models," Journal of the Academy of Marketing Science, 16 (1), 74-94.

BALASUBRAMANIAN, Sridhar, Prabhudev KONANA, and Nirum M. MENON (2003), "Customer Satisfaction in Virtual Environments: A Study of Online Investing," Management Science, 49 (7), 871-89.

BARON, Reuben M. and David A. KENNY (1986), "The Moderator-Mediator Variable Distinction in Social Psychological Research: Conceptual, Strategic, and Statistical Considerations," Journal of Personality and Social Psychology, 51 (6), 1173-82.

BART, Yakov, Venkatesh SHANKAR, Fareena SULTAN, and Glen L. URBAN (2005), "Are the Drivers and Role of Online Trust the Same for All Web Sites and Consumers? A Large-Scale Exploratory Empirical Study," Journal of Marketing, 69 (4), 133-52.

BAUMGARTNER, Hans and Christian HOMBURG (1996), "Applications of Structural Equation Modeling in Marketing and Consumer Research: A Review," International Journal of Research in Marketing, 13 (2), 139-61.

BEARDEN, William O. and Jesse E. TEEL (1983), "Selected Determinants of Consumer Satisfaction and Complaint Reports," Journal of Marketing Research, 20 (1), 21-28.

BECKETT, Antony, Paul HEWER, and Barry HOWCROFT (2000), "An Exposition of Consumer Behavior in the Financial Services Industry," International Journal of Bank Marketing, 18 (1), 15-26.

BEJOU, David, Christine T. ENNEW, and Adrian PALMER (1998), "Trust, Ethics and Relationship Satisfaction," International Journal of Bank Marketing, 16 (4), 170-75.

BENNETT, Robert J. and Paul J. A. ROBSON (2004), "The Role of Trust and Contract in the Supply of Business Advice," Cambridge Journal of Economics, 28 (a), 471-88.

BEREKOVEN, Ludwig, Werner ECKERT, and Peter ELLENRIEDER (2004), Marktforschung. Methodische Grundlagen und praktische Anwendungen (10 ed.). Wiesbaden: Gabler Verlag.

BERGKVIST, Lars and John R. ROSSITER (2007), "The Predictive Validity of Multiple-Item Versus Single-Item Measures of the Same Constructs," Journal of Marketing Research, 44 (2), 175-84.

BERRY, Leonard L. (1995), "Relationship Marketing of Services - Growing Interest, Energing Perspectives," Journal of the Academy of Marketing Science, 23 (4), 236-45.

BETZIN, Jörg and Jörg HENSELER (2005), "Einführung in die Funktionsweise des PLS-Algorithmus," in Handbuch PLS - Pfadmodellierung. Methoden, Anwendung, Praxis-beispiele, Friedhelm Bliemel and Andreas Eggert and Georg Fassott and Jörg Henseler, Eds. Stuttgart: Schäffer-Poeschel Verlag.

BHATTACHERJEE, Anol (2002), "Individual Trust in Online Firms: Scale Development and Initial Test," Journal of Management Accounting Research, 19 (1), 211-41.

BLALOCK, Hubert M. (1964), Causal Inferences in Nonexperimental Research. Chapel Hill.

BLIEMEL, Friedhelm, Andreas EGGERT, Georg FASSOTT, and Jörg HENSELER (2005), "Die PLS-Pfadmodellierung: Mehr als eine Alternative zur Kovarianzstrukturanalyse," in Handbuch PLS-Pfadmodellierung: Methoden, Anwendung, Praxisbeispiele, Friedhelm Bliemel and Andreas Eggert and Georg Fassott and Jörg Henseler, Eds. Stuttgart: Schäffer-Poeschel.

BOLLEN, Kenneth A. (1989), "A New Incremental Fit Index for General Structural Equation Models," Sociological Methods and Research, 17 (3), 303-16.

BOLLEN, Kenneth A. and Richard LENNOX (1991), "Conventional Wisdom on Measurement: A Structural Equation Perspective," Psychological Bulletin, 110 (2), 305-14.

BOLLEN, Kenneth A. and Kwok-Fai TING (2000), "A Tetrad Test for Causal Indicators," Psychological Methods, 5 (1), 3-22.

BORSBOOM, Denny, Gideon J. MEELENBERGH, and Jaap VAN HEERDEN (2004), "The Concept of Validity," Psychological Review, 111 (4), 1061-71.

BROWNE, James A. and Edgar HOWARTH (1977), "A Comprehensive Factor Analysis of Personality Questionnaire Items: A Test of Twenty Putative Factor Hypotheses," Multivariate Behavioral Research, 12 (4), 339-427.

BÜHNER, Markus (2006), Einführung in die Test- und Fragebogenkonstruktion (2 ed.). München: Pearson Studium.

BUTLER, John K. Jr. (1991), "Toward Understanding and Measuring Conditions of Trust: Evolution of a Conditions of Trust Inventory," Journal of Management 17 (3), 643-63.

CALDWELL, Cam and Stephan E. CLAPHAM (2003), "Organizational Trustworthiness: An International Perspective," Journal of Business Ethics, 47 (4), 349-64.

CASSEL, Claes M., Peter HACKL, and Anders H. WESTLUND (2000), "On Measurement of Intangible Assets: A Study of Robustness of Partial Least Squares," Total Quality Management, 11 (7), 897-909.

CHERNEV, Alexander (2008), "The Role of Purchase Quantity in Assortment Choice: The Quantity-Matching," Journal of Marketing Research, 45 (2), 171-81.

CHIN, Wynne W. (1998), "The Partial Least Squares Approach to Structural Equation Modeling," in Modern Methods for Business Research, George A. Marcoulides, Ed. Mahwah, NJ: Lawrence Erbaum Associates, 295-336.

CHIN, Wynne W. and Peter R. NEWSTED (1999), "Structural Equation Modelling Analysis With Small Samples Using PLS," in Statistical Strategies for Small Sample Research, Rick H. Hoyle, Ed. Thousand Oaks, California: Sage Publications.

CHIOU, Jyh-Shen, Cornelia DROGE, and Sangphet HANVANICH (2002), "Does Customer Knowledge Affect How Loyalty Is Formed?," Journal of Service Research, 5 (2), 113-24.

CHO, Jinsook (2006), "The Mechanism of Trust and Distrust Formation and Their Relational Outcomes," Journal of Retailing, 82 (1), 25-35.

CHURCHILL, Gilbert A. Jr. (1979), "A Paradigm for Developing Better Measures of Marketing Constructs," Journal of Marketing Research, 16 (1), 64-73.

CHURCHILL, Gilbert A. Jr. and Carol SUPRENANT (1982), "An Investigation into the Determinants of Customer Satisfaction," Journal of Marketing Research, 18 (4), 491-504.

COASE, Ronald H. (1937), "The Nature of the Firm," Economica, 4 (16), 386-405.

COCHRAN, William G. (1977), Sampling Techniques (3 ed.). New York: Wiley.

COIFFET, Phillippe and Grigore C. BURDEA (2003), Virtual Reality Technology (2 ed.). Hoboken: Wiley-Interscience.

COHEN, Jacob (1988), Statistical Power and Analysis for Behavioral Sciences (2 ed.). Hillsdale: Lawrence Erlbaum.

CRONBACH, Lee J. and Paul E. MEEHL (1955), "Construct Validity in Psychological Tests," Psychological Bulletin, 52 (4), 281-302.

CROSBY, Lawrence A., Kenneth A. EVANS, and Deborah L. COWLES (1990), "Relationship Quality in Services Selling: An Interpersonal Influence Perspective," Journal of Marketing, 54 (3), 68-81.

CURTIS, Richard F. and Elton F. JACKSON (1962), "Multiple Indicators in Survey Research," American Journal of Sociology, 68 (2), 195-204.

DANAHER, Peter J. and Vanessa HADDRELL (1996), "A Comparison of Question Scales used for Measuring Customer Satisfaction," International Journal of Service Industry Management, 7 (4), 4-26.

DELGADO-BALLESTER, Elena, Jose L. MUNUERA-ALEMÁN, and Marí J. YAGÜE-GUILLÉN (2003), "Development and Validation of a Brand Trust Scale," International Journal of Market Research, 45 (1), 35-53.

DELUGA, Roland J. (1994), "Supervision Trust Building, Leader-Member Exchange and Organizational Citizenship Behaviour," Journal of Occupational & Organizational Psychology, 67 (4), 315-26.

DESPORTES, Yvon (2006), "Trust, Confidence and Reliance: Reflections of a Linguist," Global Economy Journal, 6 (1), 1-15.

DIAMANTOPOULOS, Adamantios (2005), "The C-OAR-SE Procedure for Scale Development in Marketing: A comment," International Journal of Research in Marketing, 22 (1), 1-9.

DIAMANTOPOULOS, Adamantios, Petra RIEFLER, and Katharina P. ROTH (2008), "Advancing Formative Measurement Models," Journal of Business Research, forthcoming.

DIAMANTOPOULOS, Adamantios and Judy A. SIGUAW (2002), "Formative vs. Reflective Indicators in Measure Development: Does the Choice of Indicators Matter?," in Working Paper 05-21-02. Ithaca.

DIAMANTOPOULOS, Adamantios and Heidi M. WINKLHOFER (2001), "Index Construction with Formative Indicators: An Alternative to Scale Development," Journal of Marketing Research (JMR), 38 (2), 269-77.

DIRKS, Kurt T. (2000), "Trust in Leadership and Team Performance: Evidence From NCAA Basketball," Journal of Applied Psychology, 85 (6), 1004-12.

DONEY, Patricia M. and Joseph P. CANNON (1997), "An Examination of the Nature of Trust in Buyer-Seller Relationships," Journal of Marketing, 61 (2), 35-51.

DROLET, Aimee L. and Donlad G. MORRISON (2001), "Do We Really Need Multiple-Item Measures in Service Research?," Journal of Service Research, 3 (3), 196-204.

EARLE, Timothy C. and Michael SIEGRIST (2006), "Morality Information, Performance Information, and the Distinction Between Trust and Confidence," Journal of Applied Social Psychology, 36 (2), 383-416.

EASTLICK, Mary Ann, Sherry L. LOTZ, and Patricia WARRINGTON (2006), "Understanding Online B-to-C Relationships: An Integrated Model of Privacy Concerns, Trust, and Commitment," Journal of Business Research, 59 (8), 877-86.

EBERL, Markus (2004), "Formative und reflektive Indikatoren im Forschungsprozess: Entscheidungsregeln und die Dominanz des reflektiven Modells," in Schriften zur Empirischen Forschung und Quantitativen Unternehmensplanung, Heft 19. München.

EBERL, Markus (2006), Unternehmensreputation und Kaufverhalten: methodische Aspekte komplexer Strukturmodelle. Wiesbaden: Deutscher Universitäts-Verlag.

EBERL, Markus and Markus ZINNBAUER (2004), "Die Überprüfung von Spezifikation und Güte von Strukturgleichungsmodellen: Verfahren und Anwendung," in Schriften zur empirischen Forschung und quantitativen Unternehmensplanung, Heft 21. München.

EBERT, Tara A. E. (2006), "Operationalization of Trust in Business Networks Dealing with Complex Products and Food Products," in Trust and Risk in Business Networks M.; Rickert Fritz, U.; Schiefer, G., Ed. Bonn.

EBERT, Tara A. E. (2007), "Interdisciplinary Trust Meta-Analysis: Analysis of High Rank Trust Articles between 1966 and 2006," in Münchener Wirtschaftswissenschaftliche Beiträge 18, Ludwig-Maximilians-Universität München. München.

EBERT, Tara A. E. (2009), "Facets of Trust in Relationships – A Literature Synthesis of Highly Ranked Trust Articles," in Journal of Business Market Management, 3 (1), 65-84.

EDWARDS, Jeffrey R. and Richard P. BAGOZZI (2000), "On the Nature and Direction of Relationships Between Constructs and Measures," Psychological Methods, 5 (2), 155-74.

EGGERT, Andreas, Georg FASSOTT, and Sabrina HELM (2005), "Identifizierung und Quantifizierung mediierender und moderierender Effekte in komplexen Kausalstrukturen," in Handbuch PLS - Pfadmodellierung. Methoden, Anwendung, Praxisbeispiele, Friedhelm Bliemel and Andreas Eggert and Georg Fassott and Jörg Henseler, Eds. Stuttgart: Schäffer-Poeschel Verlag.

EINWILLER, Sabine, Andreas HERRMANN, and Diana INGENHOFF (2005), "Vertrauen durch Reputation. Grundmodell und empirische Befunde im E-Commerce," Marketing – Zeitschrift für Forschung und Praxis, 2005 (1), 24-40.

EISEND, Martin (2004), "Metaanalyse - Einführung und kritische Diskussion," Diskussionsbeiträge des Fachbereichs Wirtschaftswissenschaften der Freien Universität Berlin, 8.

EISENEGGER, Mark and Kurt IMHOF (2007), "Das Ware, das Gute und das Schöne: Reputations-Management in der Mediengesellschaft," in Fög Discussion Papers, Universität Zürich. Zürich.

EVERARD, Andrea and Dennis F. GALLETTA (2005), "How Presentation Flaws Affect Perceived Site Quality, Trust, and Intentions to Purchase from an Online Store," Journal of Management Information System, 22 (3), 55-95.

FARRIS, George F., Eldon E. SENNER, and Anthony D. BUTTERFIELD (1973), "Trust, Culture, and Organizational Behavior," Industrial Relations, 12 (2), 144-57.

FASSOTT, Georg (2006), "Operationalisierung latenter Variablen in Strukturgleichungs-modellen: Eine Standortbestimmung," Zeitschrift für betriebswirtschaftliche Forschung, 58 (2), 67-88.

FELSER, Georg (1997), Werbe- und Konsumentenpsychologie. Heidelberg: Wiesbaden.

FESTGE, Fabian (2006), Kundenzufriedenheit und Kundenbindung im Industriegüterbereich. Ermittlung zentraler Einflussfaktoren. Wiesbaden: Deutscher Universitäts-Verlag.

FOCKEBROCK, Dieter, Bert FRÖNDHOFF, and Katrin TERPITZ (2008), "Weckruf aus Amerika," Wirtschaftswoche, 26.02.2008.

FORNELL, Claes (1989), "The Blending of Theoretical and Empirical Knowledge in Structural Equations with Unobservables," in Theoretical Empirism - A General Rationale for Scientific Model-Building, Herman Wold, Ed. New York: Paragon House.

FORNELL, Claes and Fred L. BOOKSTEIN (1982), "Two Structural Equation Models: LISREL and PLS Applied to Consumer Exit-Voice Theory," Journal of Marketing Research, 19 (4), 440-52.

FORNELL, Claes, Michael D. JOHNSON, Eugene W. ANDERSON, Jaesung CHA, and Barbara EVERITT (1996), "The American Customer Satisfaction Index: Nature, Purpose, and Findings," Journal of Marketing, 60 (4), 7-18.

FORNELL, Claes D. and David F. LARCKER (1981), "Evaluating Structural Equation Models with Unobservable Variables and Measurement Errors," Journal of Marketing Research, 18 (1), 39-50.

FUKUYAMA, Francias (1995), The Social Virtues and the Creation of Prosperity. London: Free Press.

GABRIEL, Claudia and François SCHALLER (2008), "Navigating Through Turbulent Times," in 7th Private Banking Summit. Zurich: Euroforum.

GÄCHTER, Simon, Benedikt HERRMANN, and Christian THÖNI (2004), "Trust, Voluntary Cooperation, and Socio-Economic Background: Survey and Experimental Evidence," Journal of Economic Behavior & Organization, 55 (4), 505-31.

GANESAN, Shankar (1994), "Determinants of Long-Term Orientation in Buyer-Seller Relationships," Journal of Marketing, 58 (2), 1-19.

GARBARINO, Ellen and Mark S. JOHNSON (1999), "The Different Roles of Satisfaction, Trust, and Commitment in Customer Relationships," Journal of Marketing, 63 (2), 70-87.

GARBARINO, Ellen and Olivia F. LEE (2003), "Dynamic Pricing in Internet Retail: Effects on Consumer Trust," Psychology & Marketing, 20 (6), 495-513.

GEFEN, David (2000), "E-commerce: The Role of Familiarity and Trust," Omega, 28 (6), 725-37.

GEFEN, David, Elena KARAHANNA, and Detmar W. STRAUB (2003), "Trust and TAM in Online Shopping: An Integrated Model," MIS Quarterly, 27 (1), 55-91.

GEFEN, David and Detmar W. STRAUB (2004), "Consumer Trust in B2C E-Commerce and the Importance of Social Presence: Experiments in E-Products and E-Services," Omega, 32 (6), 407-24.

GEISSER, Seymour (1975), "The Predictive Sample Reuse Method with Applications," Journal of the American Statistical Association, 70 (350), 320-28.

GORSUCH, Richard L. and Sam G. MCFARLAND (1972), "Single vs. Multiple-Item Scales for Measuring Religious Values," Journal for the Scientific Study of Religion, 11 (1), 53-64.

GOTSI, Manto and Alan M. WILSON (2001), "Corporate Reputation: Seeking a Definition," Corporate Communications, 6 (1), 24-30.

GÖTZ, Oliver and Kerstin LIEHR-GOBBERS (2004), "Analyse von Strukturgleichungsmodellen mit Hilfe der Partial-Least-Squares (PLS-Methode)," Die Betriebswirtschaft, 64 (6), 714-38.

GRIFFIN, Jill (1995), Customer Loyalty: How to Get It, How to Keep It. San Francisco: Jossey-Bass Press.

HAMPTON-SOSA, William and Marios KOUFARIS (2005), "The Effect of Web Site Perceptions on Initial Trust in the Owner Company," International Journal of Electronic Commerce, 10 (1), 55-81.

HARRIS, Lloyd C. and Mark M. H. GOODE (2004), "The Four Levels of Loyalty and the Pivotal Role of Trust: A Study of Online Service Dynamics," Journal of Retailing, 80 (2), 139-58.

HART, Christopher W. and Michael D. JOHNSON (1999), "Growing the Trust Relationship: Businesses Begin Raising the Bar in Search of 'Total Trust'," Marketing Management, 8 (1), 9-19.

HAUSER, Robert M. (1973), "Disaggregating a Social-Psychological Model of Educational Attainment," in Structural Equation Models in the Social Sciences, Arthur S. Goldberger and Otis D. Duncan, Eds. New York: Seminar Press.

HAWKINS, Del I., Roger J. BEST, and Kenneth A. CONEY (2004), Consumer Behavior: Building Market Strategy (9 ed.). McGraw-Hill: Irwin.

HENNING-THURAU, Thorsten, Gianfranco WALSH, and Ulf SCHRADER (2004), "VHB-Journal: Ein Ranking von betriebswirtschaftlich-relevanten Zeitschriften auf der Grundlage von Expertenurteilen," Zeitschrift für betriebswirtschaftliche Forschung, 56 (9), 520-45.

HERRMANN, Andreas, Frank HUBER, and Frank KRESSMANN (2006), "Varianz- und kovarianzbasierte Strukturgleichungsmodelle - Ein Leitfaden zu deren Spezifikation, Schätzung und Beurteilung," Zeitschrift für betriebswirtschaftliche Forschung, 58 (1), 34-66.

HERZBERG, Frederick, Bernard MAUSNER, and Barbara B. SNYDERMAN (1959), The Motivation to Work (2 ed.). New York: Wiley.

HILDEBRANDT, Lutz (2004), "Strukturgleichungsmodelle für die Konsumentenverhaltensforschung - Methodische Trends und Softwareentwicklungen," in Konsumentenverhaltensforschung im 21. Jahrhundert, Andrea Göppel-Klein, Ed. Wiesbaden: Deutscher Universitäts-Verlag.

HILDEBRANDT, Lutz and Christian HOMBURG (1998), Die Kausalanalyse. Instrument der empirischen betriebswirtschaftlichen Forschung. Stuttgart: Schäffer-Poeschel Verlag.

HÖFLING, Michael and Holger ZSCHÄPITZ (2008), "Kursverluste. Börsianer sind mit ihrem Latein am Ende," Welt Online, 17.03.2008.

HOFSTEDE, Gert (2001), Culture's Consequences - Comparing Values, Behaviors, Institutions and Organizations Across Nations. Thousand Oak, Cali: Sage Publications.

HOGGARTH, Glenn, Ricardo REIS, and Victoria SAPPORTA (2002), "Costs of Banking System Instability: Some Empirical Evidence," Journal of Banking and Finance, 26 (5), 825-55.

HOLLER, Manfred J. and Gerhard ILLING (2003), Einführung in die Spieltheorie (5 ed.). Berlin: Springer Verlag.

HOM, Williard (2002), "Applying Customer Satisfaction Theory fo Community College Planning of Student Services," iJournal, 9.2002.

HOMBURG, Christian and Hans BAUMGARTNER (1995), "Beurteilung von Kausalmodellen - Bestandsaufnahme und Anwendungsempfehlungen," Marketing – Zeitschrift für Forschung und Praxis, 17 (3), 162-76.

HOMBURG, Christian and Annette GIERING (1998), "Konzeptualisierung und Operationalisierung komplexer Konstrukte - Ein Leitfaden für die Marketingforschung," in Die Kausalanalyse. Instrument der Betriebswirtschaftlichen Forschung, Lutz Hildebrandt and Christian Homburg, Eds. Stuttgart: Schäffer-Poeschel Verlag.

HOMBURG, Christian and Bettina RUDOLPH (1997), "Theoretische Perspektiven zur Kundenzufriedenheit," in Kundenzufriedenheit: Konzepte – Methoden - Erfahrungen, Christian Homburg and Simon Herrmann, Eds. (2 ed.) Wiesbaden.

HOYER, Wayne D. and Deborah J. MACINNIS (2001), Consumer Behavior. New York: Houghton Mifflin.

IACOBUCCI, Dawn, Kent GRAYSON, and Amy OSTROM (1994), "Customer Satisfaction Fables," Sloan Management Review, 35 (4), 93-96.

INGENHOFF, Diana (2007), "Integrated Reputation Management System (IReMS). Ein integriertes Analyseinstrument zur Messung und Steuerung von Werttreibern der Reputation," PRmagazin (7), 55-62.

JACOBY, Jacob (1978), "Consumer Research: How Valid and Useful are All Our Customer Bahavior Research Findings? – A State of the Art Review," Journal of Marketing, 42 (2), 87-96.

JARVIS, Cheryl Burke, Scott B. MACKENZIE, and Philip M. PODSAKOFF (2003), "A Critical Review of Construct Indicators and Measurement Model Misspecification in Marketing and Consumer Research," Journal of Consumer Research, 30 (2), 199-218.

JÖRESKOG, Karl G. (1967), "Some Contributions to Maximum Likelihood Factor Analysis," Psychometrika, 32 (4), 443-82.

JÖRESKOG, Karl G. (1969), "A General Approach to Confirmatory Maximum Likelihood Factor Analysis," Psychometrika, 34 (2), 183-202.

JÖRESKOG, Karl G. and Arthur S. GOLDBERGER (1975), "Estimation of a Model with Multiple Indicators and Multiple Causes of a Single Latent Variable," Journal of the American Statistical Association, 70 (351), 631-39.

JÖRESKOG, Karl G. and Dag SÖRBOM (2001), LISREL 8: User's Reference Guide. Lincolnwood: Scientific Software International.

JOHNSON, Devon and Kent GRAYSON (2005), "Cognitive and Affective Trust in Service Relationships," Journal of Business Research, 58 (4), 500-07.

JOHNSON-GEORGE, Cynthia and Walter C. SWAP (1982), "Measurement of Specific Interpersonal Trust: Construction and Validation of Scale to Assess Trust in a Specific Other," Journal of Personality & Social Psychology, 43 (6), 1306-17.

KENNEDY, Mary S., Linda K. FERRELL, and Debbie T. LECLAIR (2001), "Consumers' Trust of Salesperson and Manufacturer: An Empirical Study," Journal of Business Research, 51 (1), 73-86.

KIM, Hee-Woong, Yunjie XU, and Joon KOH (2004), "A Comparison of Online Trust Building Factors between Potential Customers and Repeat Customers," Journal of the Association for Information Systems, 5 (10), 392-420.

KNIGHTS, David, Faith NOBLE, Theo VURDUBAKIS, and Hugh WILLMOTT (2001), "Chasing Shadows: Control, Virtuality and the Production of Trust," Organization Studies, 22 (2), 311-36.

KOOT, Christian (2005), Kundenloyalität, Kundenbindung und Kundenbindungspotential: Modellgenese und empirische Überprüfung im Retail-Banking. München: Verlag Dr. Hut.

KROEBER-RIEL, Werner and Peter WEINBERG (2003), Konsumentenverhalten (8 ed.). München. Verlag Vahlen.

KWON, Hyungil and Galen TRAIL (2005), "The Feasibility of Single-Item Measures in Sport Loyality Research," Sport Management Review, 8 (1), 69-89.

LARSON, Andrea (1992), "Network Dyads in Entrepreneurial Settings: A Study of the Governance of Exchange Relationships," Administrative Science Quarterly, 37 (1), 76-104.

LARZELERE, Robert E. and Ted L. HUSTON (1980), "The Dyadic Trust Scale: Toward Understanding Interpersonal Trust in Close Relationships " Journal of Marriage and the family, 42 (3), 595-604.

LAURENt, Gilles and Jean-Noel KAPFERER (1985), "Measuring Consumer Involvement Profiles," Journal of Marketing Research, 22 (1), 41-53.

LAW, Kenneth S. and Chi-Sum WONG (1999), "Multidimensional Constructs in Structural Equation Analysis: All Illustration Using the Job Perception and Job Satisfaction Constructs," Journal of Management, 25 (2), 143-54.

LEE, Sanghyun and Alan J. DUBINSKY (2003), "Influence of Salesperson Characteristics and Customer Emotion on Retail Dyadic Relationships," The International Review of Retail, Distribution and Consumer Research, 13 (1), 21-36.

LEHMANN, Donald R., Sunil GUPTA, and Joel H. STECKEL (1998), Marketing Research. Reading, Massachusetts: Addison-Wesley.

LEWIS, Barbara R. and Magdalini SOURELI (2006), "The Antecedents of Consumer Loyalty in Retail Banking," Journal of Consumer Behaviour, 5 (1), 15-31.

LEWIS, Jordan D. and Andrew J. WEIGERT (1985), "Trust as a Social Reality " Social Forces, 63 (4), 967-85.

LIANG, Huigang, Yajiong XUE, Kittipong LAOSETHAKUL, and Scott J. LLOYD (2005), "Information Systems and Healthcare-I: Trust, Uncertainty, and Online Perscription Filling," Communications of AIS, 15 (15), 41-60.

LOHMANN, Florian (1997), Loyalität von Bankkunden. Bestimmungsgrößen und Gestaltungsmöglichkeiten. Wiesbaden: Deutscher Universitäts-Verlag.

LOHMÖLLER, Jan-Bernd (1989), Latent Variable Path Modeling with Partial Least Squares. Heidelberg: Springer Verlag.

LUHMANN, Niklas (1979), Trust and Power. New York: John Wiley.

LYONS, Bruce and Judith MEHTA (1997), "Contracts, Opportunism and Trust; Self-Interest and Social Orientation," Cambridge Journal of Economics, 21 (2), 293-57.

MACCALLUM, Robert C. and Michael W. BROWNE (1993), "The Use of Causal Indicators in Covariance Structure Models: Some Practical Issues," Psychological Bulletin, 114 (3), 533-41.

MACKENZIE, Scott B., Philip M. PODSAKOFF, and Cheryl B. JARVIS (2005), "The Problem of Measurement Model Misspecification in Behavioral and Organizational Research and Some Recommended Solutions," Journal of Applied Psychology, 90 (4), 710-30.

MALHOTRA, Naresh K. and David F. BIRKS (2007), Marketing Research. An Applied Approach (3 ed.). London: Prentice Hall.

MARTÍN, Sonia S. and Carmen CAMARERO (2005), "Consumer Reactions to Firm Signals in Asymmetric Relationships," Journal of Service Research, 8 (1), 79-97.

MAYER, Roger C., James H. DAVIS, and David F. SCHOORMAN (1995), "An Integrative Model of Organizational Trust," Academy of Management Review, 20 (3), 709-34.

MCALLISTER, Daniel J. (1995), "Affect- and Cognition-Based Trust as Foundations for Interpersonal Co-Operation in Organizations," Academy of Management Journal, 38 (1), 24-59.

MCKNIGHT, Harrison D., Vivek CHOUDHURY, and Charles KACMAR (2002), "Developing and Validating Trust Measures for E-Commerce: An Integrative Typology," Information Systems Research, 13 (3), 334-59.

MCKNIGHT, Harrison D., Larry L. CUMMINGS, and Norman L. CHERVANY (1998), "Initial Trust Formation in New Organizational Relationships," Academy of Management Review, 23 (3), 473-90.

MEIDAN, Arthur (1996), Marketing Financial Services. Houndmills: MacMillan Press.

MEYER ZU SELHAUSEN, Herrmann (2000), Bank-Informationssysteme. Eine Bankbetriebswirtschaftslehre mit IT-Schwerpunkt. Stuttgart: Schäffer-Poeschel Verlag.

MOHR, Jakki and Robert E. SPEKMAN (1994), "Characteristics of Partnership Success: Partnership Attributes, Communication Behavior, and Conflict Resolution Techniques," Strategic Management Journal, 15 (2), 135-52.

MÖLLERING, Guido (2006), Trust: Reason, Routine, Reflexivity. Oxford: Elsevier.

MOORMAN, Christine, Rohit DESHPANDÉ, and Gerald ZALTMAN (1993), "Factors Affecting Trust in Market Research Relationships," Journal of Marketing, 57 (1), 81-101.

MORGAN, Robert M. and Shelby D. HUNT (1994), "The Commitment-Trust Theory of Relationship Marketing," Journal of Marketing, 58 (3), 20-38.

MORTSIEFER, Henrik and Corinna VISSER (2008), "Weißes Rauschen," Tagesspiegel, 08.06.2008.

MUKHERJEE, Avinandan and Prithwiraj NATH (2003), "A Model of Trust in Online Relationship Banking," International Journal of Bank Marketing, 21 (1), 5-16.

NAGY, Mark S. (2002), "Using a Single-Item Approach to Measure Facet Job Satisfaction," Journal of Occupational and Organizational Psychology, 75 (1), 77-86.

NUNNALLY, Jum C. (1967), Psychometric Theory. New York u. a.: McGraw Hill.

NUNNALLY, Jum C. and Ira H. BERNSTEIN (1994), Psychometric Theory (3 ed.). New York u. a.: McGraw-Hill.

OLIVER, Richard L. (1980), "A Cognitive Model of the Antecedents and Consequences of Satisfaction Decisions," Journal of Marketing Research, 17 (4), 460-69.

OLSEN, Sven O. (2007), "Repurchase Loyalty: The Role of Involvement and Satisfaction," Psychology & Marketing, 24 (4), 315-41.

PAVLOU, Paul A. (2003), "Consumer Acceptance of Electronic Commerce: Integrating Trust and Risk with the Technology Acceptance Model," International Journal of Electronic Commerce, 7 (3), 101-34.

PAVLOU, Paul A. and David GEFEN (2004), "Building Effective Online Marketplaces with Institution-Based Trust," Information Systems Research, 15 (1), 37-59.

PEARCE, John A. and Shaker A. ZAHRA (1991), "The Relative Power of CEOs and Boards of Directors: Associations with Corporate Performance," Strategic Management Journal, 12 (2), 135-53.

PETER, Jean-Paul (1979), "Reliability: A Review of Psychometric Basics and Recent Marketing Practices," Journal of Marketing Research, 16 (1), 6-17.

PETER, Paul J. and Gilbert A. Jr. CHURCHILL (1986), "Relationships among Research Design Choices and Psychometric Properties of Rating Scales: A Meta-Analysis," Journal of Marketing Research, 23 (1), 1-10.

PETER, Sibylle I. (1997), Kundenbindung als Marketingziel: Identifikation und Analyse zentraler Determinanten. Wiesbaden: Gabler Verlag.

PETERSON, Robert A. (1994), "A Meta-Analysis of Cronbach's Coefficient Alpha," Journal of Consumer Research, 21 (2), 381-91.

PICOT, Arnold, Ralf REICHWALD, and Rolf T. WIGAND (2003), Die grenzenlose Unternehmung. Information, Organisation und Management (5 ed.). Wiesbaden: Gabler Verlag.

PICOT, Arnold, Theresia THEURL, Arne DAMMER, and Rahild NEUBURGER (2007), Transparenz in Kreditmärkten. Auskunfteien und Datenschutz vor dem Hintergrund asymmetrischer Information. Frankfurt am Main: Frankfurter Allgemeine Buch.

RAITHEL, Sascha and Tara A. E. EBERT (2008), "Sinkendes Vertrauen der Bankkunden," Banken und Partner. Zeitschrift für Strategie und Management (2), 7.

REICHHELD, Frederik F., Robert G. MARKEY, and Christopher HOPTON (2000), "E-Customer Loyalty - Applying the Traditional Rules of Business for Online Success," European Business Journal, 12, 173-79.

REICHHELD, Frederik F. and Earl W. SASSER (1991), "Zero-Migration: Dienstleister im Sog der Qualitätsrevolution," Harvard Manager, 13 (4), 108-16.

REMPEL, John K., John G. HOLMES, and Mark P. ZANNA (1985), "Trust in Close Relationships," Journal of Personality & Social Psychology, 49 (1), 95-112.

RINGLE, Christian M. (2004a), "Gütemaße für den Partial Least Squares - Ansatz zur Bestimmung von Kausalmodellen " in Industrielles Management, Arbeitspapier Nr. 16, Karl-Werner Hansmann, Ed. Hamburg: Universität Hamburg.

RINGLE, Christian M. (2004b), "Messung von Kausalmodellen: ein Methodenvergleich," in Arbeitspapier Nr. 14, Universität Hamburg: Institut für Industriebetriebslehre und Organisation. Hamburg.

RIPPERGER, Tanja (1998), Ökonomik des Vertrauens. Tübingen: Mohr Siebeck Verlag.

ROSSITER, John R. (2002), "The C-OAR-SE Procedure for Scale Development in Marketing," International Journal of Research in Marketing, 19 (4), 305-35.

ROTH, Martin S. (1994), "Enhancing Consumer Involvement in Health Care: The Dynamics of Control, Empowerment, and Trust," Journal of Public Policy & Marketing, 13 (1), 115-32.

ROTTER, Julian B. (1967), "A New Scale for the Measurement of Interpersonal Trust," Journal of Personality and Social Psychology, 35 (4), 651-66.

RUGMAN, Alan M. and Simon COLLINSON (2006), International Business (4 ed.). New York: Prentice Hall.

RUPPEL, Cynthia P. and Susan J. HARRINGTON (2000), "The Relationship of Communication, Ethical Work Climate, and Trust to Commitment and Innovation," Journal of Business Ethics, 25 (4), 313-28.

RUST, Roland T. and Anthony ZAHORIK (1993), "Customer Satisfaction, Customer Retention, and Market Share," Journal of Retailing, 69 (2), 193-215.

SABATE, Fuerte J. M. and Queredo PUERTE (2003), "Empirical Analysis of the Relationship Between Corporate Reputation and Financial Performance - A Survey of the Literature," Corporate Reputation Review, 6 (2), 161-77.

SAINI, Amit and Jean L. JOHNSON (2005), "Organizational Capabilities in E-Commerce: An Empirical Investigation of E-Brokerage Service Providers," Journal of the Academy of Marketing Science, 33 (3), 360-75.

SALAM, Al F., Lakshimi IYER, Prashant PALVIA, and Rahul SINGH (2005), "Trust in E-Commerce," Communications of the ACM, 48 (2), 73-77.

SALMONES, Ma del Mar García de los, Angel HERRERO GRESPO, and Ignacio RODRÍGUEZ DEL BOSQUE (2005), "Influence of Corporate Social Responsibility on Loyalty and Valuation of Services," Journal of Business Ethics, 61 (4), 369-85.

SARGEANT, Adrian, John B. FORD, and Douglas C. WEST (2005), "Perceptual Determinants of Nonprofit Giving Behavior," Journal of Business Research, 59 (2), 155-65.

SCHEIN, Edgar H. (1985), Organizational Culture and Leadership. London: Jossey-Bass Inc. Publishers.

SCHLOSSER, Ann E., Tiffany B. WHITE, and Susan M. LLOYD (2006), "Converting Web Site Visitors into Buyers: How Web Site Investment Increases Consumer Trusting Beliefs and Online Purchase Intentions," Journal of Marketing, 70 (2), 133-48.

SCHOENBACHLER, Denise D. and Geoffrey L. GORDON (2002), "Trust and Customer Willingness to Provide Information in Database-Driven Relationship Marketing," Journal of Interactive Marketing, 16 (3), 2-16.

SCHOLDERER, Joachim and Ingo BALDERJAHN (2005), "PLS versus LISREL: Ein Methodenvergleich," in Handbuch PLS-Pfadmodellierung. Methode, Anwendung, Praxisbeispiele, Friedhelm Bliemel and Andreas Eggert and Georg Fassott and Jörg Henseler, Eds. Stuttgart: Schäffer-Poeschel Verlag.

SCHWAIGER, Manfred (2000), "Virtual Communities: Der gläserne Kunde wird Realität," in Banking 2000. Perspektiven und Projekte, Marcus Riekeberg and Karin Stenke, Eds. Wiesbaden: Gabler Verlag.

SCHWAIGER, Manfred (2004), "Components and Parameters of Corporate Reputation - an Empirical Study," Schmalenbach Business Review, 56, 46-71.

SCHWAIGER, Manfred and Anastasia STEINER-KOGRINA (2004), "Kultursponsoring bindet Kunden - Ergebnisse einer Studie im Bankenbereich," Marketingjournal, 37 (3), 34-36.

SEAL, W. B. (1998), "Relationship Banking and the Management of Organisational Trust," International Journal of Bank Marketing, 16 (3), 102-07.

SEEMANN, Patricia, David DELONG, Susan STUKEY, and Edward GUTHRIE (2000), "Building Intangible Assets: A Strategic Framework for Investing in Intellectual Capital," in Knowledge Management: Classic and Contemporary Works, Daryl Morey and Mark Maybury and Bhavani Thuraisingham, Eds. Cambridge: MIT Press.

SELLIN, Norbert P. and John P. KEEVES (1994), "Path Analysis With Latent Variables," in The International Encyclopedia of Education, Torsten Husén and Neville T. Postlethwaite, Eds. Vol. 2. Oxford: Pergamon Press.

SERVA, Mark A., Mark A. FULLER, and Roger C. MAYER (2005), "The Reciprocal Nature of Trust: A Longitudinal Study of Interacting Teams," Journal of Organizational Behavior, 26 (6), 625-48.

SHEMWELL, Donald Jr., Joseph J. CRONIN, and William R. BULLARD (1994), "Relational Exchange in Services," International Journal of Service Industry Management, 5 (3), 57-68.

SHEPPARD, Blair H. and Dana M. SHERMAN (1998), "The Grammars of Trust: A Model and General Implications," Academy of Management Review, 23 (3), 422-37.

SIEGRIST, Michael, Heinz GUTSCHER, and Timothy C. EARLE (2005), "Perception of Risk: The Influence of General Trust, and General Confidence," Journal of Risk Research, 8 (2), 145-56.

SINGH, Jagdip and Deepak SIRDESHMUKH (2000), "Agency and Trust Mechanisms in Consumer Satisfaction and Loyalty Judgments," Journal of the Academy of Marketing Science, 28 (1), 150-68.

SIRDESHMUKH, Deepak, Jagdip SINGH, and Barry SABOL (2002), "Consumer Trust, Value, and Loyalty in Relational Exchanges," Journal of Marketing, 66 (1), 15-37.

SLOAN, Jeff A., Neil AARONSON, Joseph C. CAPPELLERI, Diane L. FAIRCLOUGH, and Claudette VARRICCHIO (2002), "Assessiong the Clinical Significance of Single Item Relative to Summated Scores," Mayo Clinic Proceedings, 77 (5), 479-87.

SMITH, Caroline (2005), "Understanding Trust and Confidence: Two Paradigms and their Significance for Health and Social Care," Journal of Applied Philosophy, 22 (3), 299-316.

SOLOMON, Michael, Gary BAMOSSY, Soren ASKEGAARD, and Margaret K. HOGG (2006), Consumer Behavior - A European Perspective. New Jersey: Prentice Hall.

SONNTAG, Alexander (2001), Bewertung von Banken. Ein Discounted Cash Flow-Ansatz für Commercial Banks unter Einbeziehung der Marktzinsmethode. Wiesbaden: Deutscher Universitäts-Verlag.

SPAKE, Deborah F., Sharon E. BEATTY, Beverly K. BROCKMAN, and Tammy N. CRUTCHFIELD (2003), "Consumer Comfort in Service Relationships," Journal of Service Research, 5 (4), 316-32.

SPEKMAN, Robert E. (1988), "Strategic Supplier Selection: Understanding Long-Term Relationships," Business Horizons, 31 (4), 75-81.

STEWART, Katherine J. (2003), "Trust Transfer on the World Wide Web," Organization Science, 14 (1), 5-17.

STONE, Michael (1974), "Cross-Validatory Choice and Assessment of Statistical Predictions," Journal of the Royal Statistical Society, Series B, 36 (2), 111-33.

SUH, Bomil and Ingoo HAN (2003), "The Impact of Customer Trust and Perception of Security Control on the Acceptance of Electronic Commerce," International Journal of Electronic Commerce, 7 (3), 135-61.

SWAN, John E., Michael R. BOWERS, and Lynne D. RICHARDSON (1999), "Customer Trust in the Salesperson: An Integrative Review and Meta-Analysis of the Empirical Literature," Journal of Business Research, 44 (2), 93-107.

TAX, Stephen S., Stephen W. BROWN, and Murali CHANDRASHEKARAN (1998), "Customer Evaluations of Service Complaint Experiences: Implications for Relationship Marketing," Journal of Marketing, 62 (2), 60-76.

TAYLOR, Steven A. (1996), "Consumer Satisfaction with Marketing Education: Extending Services Theory to Academic Practice," Journal of Consumer Satisfaction, Dissatisfaction and Complaining Behavior, 9, 207-20.

THOMSON, Matthew (2006), "Human Brands: Investigating Antecedents to Consumers' Strong Attachments to Celebrities," Journal of Marketing, 70 (3), 104-19.

TONKISS, Fran and Andrew PASSEY (1999), "Trust, Confidence and Voluntary Organisations: Between Values and Institutions," Sociology, 33 (2), 257-74.

TROMMSDORFF, Volker (2004), Konsumentenverhalten. Stuttgart: Kohlhammer.

UNTERREITMEIER, Andreas (2004), Unternehmenskultur bei Mergers & Acquisitions. Ansätze zur Konzeptualisierung und Operationalisierung. Wiesbaden: Deutscher Universitäts-Verlag.

VAN DEN BERG, René J. and Jannine M. VAN LIESHOUT (2001), "Finding Symbolons for Cyberspace: Addressing the Issues of Trust in Electronic Commerce," Production Planning & Control, 12 (5), 514-24.

VERHOEF, Peter C., Philip H. FRANSES, and Janny C. HOEKSTRA (2002), "The Effect of Relational Constructs on Customer Referrals and Number of Services Purchased From a Multiservice Provider: Does Age of Relationship Matter?," Journal of the Academy of Marketing Science, 30 (3), 202-16.

VON STEIN, Johann Heinrich (2000), "Trends im Bankwesen - Wirkungen auf das Bankgeschäft der Zukunft," in Banking 2000. Perspektiven und Projekte, Marcus Riekeberg and Karin Stenke, Eds. Wiesbaden: Gabler Verlag.

WANG, Eric T. G. and Jessica H. F. CHEN (2006), "The Influence of Governance Equilibrium on ERP Project Success," Decision Support Systems, 41 (4), 708-27.

WANG, Sijun, Dwayne D. GREMLER, Sharon E. BEATTY, and William FOXX (2004), "Signaling the Trustworthiness of Small Online Retailers," Journal of Interactive Marketing, 18 (1), 53-69.

WANG, Weiquan and Izak BENBASAT (2005), "Trust in and Adoption of Online Recommendation Agents," Journal of the Association for Information Systems, 6 (3), 72-101.

WANOUS, John P., Arnon E. REICHERS, and Michael J. HUDY (1997), "Overall Job Satisfaction: How Good are Single-Item Measures?," Journal of Applied Psychology, 82 (2), 247-52.

WEBSTER, Jane and Joseph J. MARTOCCHIO (1992), "Microcomputer Playfulness: Development of a Measure with Workplace Implications," MIS Quarterly, 16 (2), 201-26.

WHITE, Tiffany B. (2005), "Consumer Trust and Advice Acceptance:The Moderating Roles of Benevolence, Expertise, and Negative Emotions," Journal of Consumer Psychology, 15 (2), 141-48.

WHITLEY, Richard D. (1991), "The Social Construction of Business Systems in East Asia," Organization Studies, 12 (1), 1-28.

WILLIAMSON, Oliver E. (1975), Markets and Hierarchies. New York: Free Press.

WILLIAMSON, Oliver (1993), "Calculativeness, Trust, and Economic Organizations," Journal of Law & Economics, 36 (1), 453-86.

WOLD, Herman (1966), "Estimation of Principal Components and Related Models by Iterative Least Squares," in Multivariate Analysis: Proceedings if an International Symposium on Multivariate Analysis, Paruchuri R. Krishnaiah (Ed.). Wright State University, Dayton, Ohio.

WOLD, Herman (1980), "Model Construction and Evaluation When Theoretical Knowledge is Scarce," in Evaluation of Economic Models, Jan Kmenta and James B. Ramsey, Eds. New York: Academic.

YI, Youjae (1990), "A Critical Review of Customer Satisfaction," in Review of Marketing, Valerie A. Zeithaml, Ed. Chicago: American Marketing Association.

YOUSAFZAI, Shumaila Y., John. G. PALLISTER, and Gordon R. FOXALL (2005), "Strategies for Building and Communicating Trust in Electronic Banking: A Field Experiment," Psychology & Marketing, 22 (2), 181-201.

ZAND, Dale E. (1972), "Trust and Managerial Problem Solving," Administrative Science Quarterly, 17 (2), 229-40.

ZINNBAUER, Markus, Zoltàn BAKAY, and Manfred SCHWAIGER (2004), "Hohe Reputation stärkt bei Banken und Sparkassen die Kundenbindung," Betriebswirtschaftliche Blätter, 53 (6), 271-74.

ZINS, Andreas H. (2001), "Relative Attitudes and Commitment in Customer Loyalty Models: Some Experiences in the Commercial Airline Industry," International Journal of Service Industry Management, 12 (3), 269-94.

MIX
Papier aus verantwortungsvollen Quellen
Paper from responsible sources
FSC® C105338

If you have any concerns about our products,
you can contact us on
ProductSafety@springernature.com

In case Publisher is established outside the EU,
the EU authorized representative is:
Springer Nature Customer Service Center GmbH
Europaplatz 3, 69115 Heidelberg, Germany

Printed by Libri Plureos GmbH
in Hamburg, Germany